WITHIN HUMAN EXPERIENCE

WITHIN HUMAN EXPERIENCE

The Philosophy of
William Ernest Hocking

LEROY S. ROUNER

Harvard University Press
Cambridge, Massachusetts
1969

For Rita

Who has been to me what Agnes was to Ernest,
"An unfailing source of insight"

PREFACE

THE PURPOSE OF THIS BOOK IS TO GIVE an idea of the scope of Ernest Hocking's philosophy and to point out the central metaphysical principles which integrated his diverse interests. In order to do this I have had to say a good deal about Hocking's life, because his major ideas developed out of his experience. These ideas were something that had happened to him and, therefore, something that he believed. Both the range and method of his philosophy indicate that his subject was not language or logic, but life. He was convinced, however, that there is a core of universality in personal experience—that there is "a human experience" which we all share and which is full of meaning. He also believed that if this experience is carefully analyzed and properly understood it points the way to a human destiny.

In articulating this conviction and relating it to logic, law, psychology, politics, education, religion, and much more, Hocking published seventeen books and 270 essays over a span of sixty-seven years. Some of the shorter papers were brilliantly incisive, but his most characteristic style was ruminative, discursive, dialectical, and poetic. He did not set out to "prove" his ideas, because he understood philosophy as the examination of beliefs garnered from experience. Experience can disprove a false belief by the test of what he called a negative pragmatism—"If it doesn't work, it isn't true"—but a single instance of workability cannot establish the truth of a belief. Because experience is varied, dynamic, and constantly developing, an idea finds authority only by establishing its workability in a number of intellectual disciplines dealing with a wide range of serious human problems. Hocking tends, therefore, to announce and elaborate ideas rather than to construct systematic defenses of them. This style often makes it hard to know exactly what was meant, and the fact that he wrote so much over such a long period adds to the difficulty of giving a clear and comprehensive picture of his philosophy. Some of his views are outdated, and others have undergone major changes in the course of time.

Nevertheless, it has seemed important to me to deal with his philosophy as a whole, since it is the point and purpose of his work to show that a metaphysic is required to give our varied intellectual interests integrity and wholeness. Integrating different areas of human concern is not the only function of philosophy, but a generation which needs integrity in its view of a complex world as badly as does ours cannot afford to dismiss "philosophy in the grand manner" as entirely outdated or irrelevant. Our problems are not so radically new, nor our predecessors so seriously out of touch with them, as we are often tempted to think.

There are, however, a number of disadvantages in my approach to Hocking, not the least of which is an often cruel tendency to condense in order to keep the book from getting too long. Most important, however, is the necessary sacrifice of that sustained critical analysis of Hocking's central philosophical ideas which his system both merits and needs. From time to time I have broken in to emphasize, qualify, or disagree; but my first responsibility has been to present his thought and experience in its own terms. A thorough investigation of his basic categories would require setting aside much of the biographical material and the references to his practical philosophy, and this I have been unwilling to do. On the other hand, a full-scale critical evaluation of his metaphysics is surely the weightiest task for which Hocking scholarship is responsible, and several philosophers are already at work on it. I hope to give them a background for their more specialized work, as well as providing nonspecialists with some idea of who Ernest Hocking was, and what he was about.

It was Wilhelm Pauck, then of Union Theological Seminary in New York, who first interested me in Ernest Hocking's philosophy. No metaphysician himself, Pauck had heard Hocking speak on several occasions during the 1930's, sensed in him—at a time when philosophers were becoming more specialized—a man for all seasons, and noted with some regret that he was no longer widely read and that no full-length study of his work had thus far appeared. At the time I was casting about for a topic for my doctoral thesis at Columbia University. With Pauck's suggestion in mind, I approached John H. Randall, Jr., who noted that Hocking's views on the relationship between Christianity and other world religions were particularly interesting. I adopted his suggestion as a topic, and soon after, M. Searle Bates became the third member of my thesis advisory committee.

One could not have found three more distinguished men in their own fields: Randall, the foremost English-speaking historian of modern Western philosophy; Pauck, Luther scholar without peer and distinguished church historian; and Bates, author of the definitive study of religious liberty and expert on the history of the Christian world mission. The fact that each had an expert interest in one aspect of

Hocking's work was indicative of the breadth of Hocking's interests and the problems involved in integrating them. The essay which they supervised was a technical exercise, and only a very few of its pages have found their way into this book. The book and I, however, owe much to these friends and tutors for the inspiration, knowledge, and advice which they provided.

A good many other friends and colleagues have shared my interest in Hocking and helped the book on its way. J. Edward Dirks of Yale and John B. Carman of Harvard were both in India when I finished the first draft—I was then teaching at the United Theological College in Bangalore—and my conversations with them were immensely helpful as I turned to the business of revision. John C. Bennett of Union Seminary and John E. Smith of Yale also offered careful criticisms which helped me in shaping the final form of the book. Richard Hocking of Emory University gave me his expert counsel on numerous occasions. As Ernest Hocking's son, and a philosopher in his own right, his comments were invaluable.

When my wife and I discovered that Ernest Hocking was our neighbor in the Sandwich range country of New Hampshire he became our good friend, as well as my *guru*. He would not agree with all that I have written about him, but as long as his health lasted he was a tireless source of information about historical facts and elucidation of complex ideas. I am permanently in his debt in a way which is unique in my experience.

No book of this kind is possible without the gracious permission of numerous publishers and copyright owners to use material belonging to them. Details of these quotations are given in the notes.

My wife, Rita, does not type, neither does she proofread.

The dedication of the book to her is not a reward for secretarial services rendered, or even for those numerous occasions when she has held back the domestic surf from pounding at the study door. It is, among many other things, recognition that without her sensitivity to the hidden meanings of the natural world I would not have understood what Ernest Hocking's philosophy was about.

L. S. R.

North Sandwich, New Hampshire
February 1969

CONTENTS

Introduction: *The Formative Years*   1

Part One: *The Metaphysics of Experience*

    I.   The Influence of Royce and James   15
   II. Dialectic   32
  III. Thesis and Antithesis: Natural Fact and
       Personal Will   50
  IV. Monism, Pluralism, and the Absolute   68
   V. Selfhood, Nature, and Other Mind   86
  VI. Our Knowledge of God   103

Part Two: *Man in Society*

  VII. The Human Individual   127
 VIII. Remaking Human Nature   153
  IX. Education   171
   X. Law and Human Rights   187
  XI. The State and Democracy   199

Part Three: *Religion and a World Civilization*

  XII. Art and Destiny   215
 XIII. Religion, Mysticism, and the Prophetic
       Consciousness   235

XIV.   The Christian Ambition   256
XV.   The Coming World Civilization   287

Conclusion: Toward a World Perspective
   in Philosophy   311

Chronology: The Life of William Ernest Hocking   325

Selected Bibliography of Hocking's Works   329

Notes   333

Index   373

WITHIN HUMAN EXPERIENCE

Introduction

THE FORMATIVE YEARS

ERNEST HOCKING LIKED TO REMIND those who thought of him as a Boston Brahmin that he was born and bred in "the briar-bush of the Midwest" where he lived until he went East to study at Harvard. His father was a homeopathic physician in rather modest circumstances; his mother's family claimed an ancestor on the *Mayflower*. Ernest was born in Cleveland in August of 1873, the eldest, and only boy, in what was to be a family of five children.

Hocking's early religious training had a permanent effect on his personal faith and on his philosophy. The most important event of these years was his conversion, at the age of twelve, during a Methodist "Special Meeting."[1] The emphasis of the meeting was on deepening one's religious experience. "Experience" is a key word in Hocking's philosophical vocabulary. He argued that our knowledge of the real, the whole, the absolute substance, is a knowledge-in-experience. Every finite fact casts an "infinite shadow," and every experience of the natural and social world is fraught with the presence of an Other, who is God. So while experience, as he uses the term, has about it the flavor of realism, and especially of the pragmatism of William James, it is also touched with a sense of mystery in matters of aesthetics and religion.

Methodism lays heavy emphasis on personal experience

as the primary source of our knowledge of God. The Methodist Church of Joliet, Illinois—Hocking's home shortly after he was born—held regular Sunday evening special meetings during the years when he was growing up. These were designed to aid the Holy Spirit in the work of conversion, which was conceived as a radical change. True faith required seeking and, Hocking explained,

> . . . if one's search were successful, the result was not more a natural consequence than a boon from life to the seeker. It was both at once, as if growth up to this point had been a subvoluntary occurrence, whereas the last stage of growth had been accomplished with one's own cooperation. In it, something happened to one; and after it had happened, one could never again be just the same.[2]

In such special meetings it was not the particulars of the experience which were definitive. Hocking did not long remember what the evangelist said in his sermon, nor was he very much aware at the time. But there was, he said, "a presence felt, a reality perceived" which was beyond the details of the service and including them. When the call came to "come down and be saved," this boy of twelve— tears streaming down his face—suddenly saw things in "a new light." He saw "the real," in a way which "combined a new resolve with a new insight." He saw himself as part of a "great procession of humanity in which each man had an immortal soul." He had a vision, as he puts it, of "men like souls walking." The effects of this experience—probably his most important "mystical" experience—lasted two or three days. He reports no great excitement, but a tremendous sense of relief and the assurance that he had broken through to a significant new perception. It led to his joining the Methodist Church.

This early conversion is a far cry from the thought and experience of the author of *The Coming World Civilization*. But as one looks for a simple summary of the vision at the heart of that sophisticated book—the hope of a new world community in which men are bound together by their common awareness of God—this vision of "men like souls walking" leaps to mind. And there are other hints of the continuing importance of this early experience. Twenty-seven years later he was asking, with a touch of the evangelist's fervor:

What do you think of hell? The doctrine of hell made religion at one time a matter of first rate importance; getting your soul saved made a difference in your empirical destiny. If your idealism wipes out your fear of hell, and with it all sense of infinite risk in the conduct of life, your idealism has played you false. Truth must be transformed; but the transformation of truth must be marked by a *conservation of power* . . . No religion, then, is a true religion which is not able to make men tingle yes, even to their physical nerve tips, with the sense of an infinite hazard, a wrath to come, a heavenly city to be gained or lost in the process of time and by the use of our freedom. . . .

What, again, do you think of God? The God of orthodoxy is thought of as being so far like man as to have loves, interests, and powers which make themselves temporally felt: this God does things in the world, which, if we like, we may call miracles or, if we like better, deeds of Providence. Upon this differential work of God, as contrasted with his total work, was based much of the urgency of former religious observance, prayer and piety. Pragmatism rightly enquires what becomes of this differential work when God becomes the All-One of idealism . . . In such wise, the pragmatic principle tends to confront idealism, as it has never before been confronted, with the substantial values of orthodoxy; compelling idealism to complete itself by the

standard of these values (I do not say of these propositions)
even if at the cost of its philosophic identity.[3]

For some months the young Hocking was a faithful at-
tender of camp meetings and revivals, where on at least one
occasion, he buttonholed a stranger and inquired whether
he had "the witness." Piety had to keep company with wit,
however, and his faith was shaken by reading Herbert
Spencer—at the age of thirteen. He later recalled:

> Dr. Hocking, my father, was very keen for the scientific
> phase of medicine, as well as for its philosophy. As a good
> Methodist he had a shelf of books for "Sunday Reading."
> One of these books was Drummond (Scottish biologist),
> *Natural Law in the Spiritual World.* I got hold of that book
> as a kid of thirteen; noted the frequent references to a
> stranger called Herbert Spencer; made up my mind that
> Spencer would bear being looked into; got his *First Princi-
> ples* out of the public library and read it with increasing
> fascination until one day, Father, looking over my shoulder,
> indicated that the book was unfit to be read by one of my
> years—would I kindly take it back to the library. As a duti-
> ful son I obeyed. Next day I took it out again, read it by
> stealth in the haymow over the horses' stall—I being in
> charge of the stable. Father's fears were correct: Spencer
> finished me off![4]

Elsewhere he continues:

> I had nothing to oppose his plausible dialectic. Thoroughly
> against my will, and with a sense of unmeasured inner
> tragedy, Spencer convinced me. For years I plodded through
> his volumes. It was an unmixed discipleship, and so far an
> experience of great intellectual joy. Spencer had the truth
> —such modest truth as was to be had. He had written blank
> mystery over the original splendour of the uncharted world.
> His view demanded unqualified resignation to the outlook

of animal death—to me a sweeping desolation; for I had been seized almost violently with a sense of the uniqueness of individual life and I could hardly endure the thought of annihilation. But Spencer's philosophy explained all things, the extra-beliefs of religion among them, only too well.[5]

He had hoped, after graduation from high school, to go to the University of Chicago. His father, however, thought him too young for college (he was only fifteen), and the money for tuition was lacking. Keeping his plan for Chicago in mind and seeking work in line with his interest in engineering, Hocking became a surveyor for the civil engineering department of the Elgin, Joliet, and Eastern Railroad. It was his first job, and he always delighted in the announcement, "I'm a surveyor by trade, you know." It was during this stint that experience provided a crack in the logic of Spencer's philosophy.

The time is 1892, more or less. The scene is the right-of-way of a single-track railroad, between Aurora, Illinois, and Waukegan—the Elgin, Joliet, and Eastern Railroad, then a new belt line around Chicago. It is a summer day. A lone figure carrying a pot of white paint and a brush, stoops every 100 feet to cover a chalk mark on the inside of the rail with a vertical line of paint, and every 500 feet to paint a number. The crew of the civil engineering department are measuring the track of the railway for inventory purposes. The chalk markers, with the steel tape, have moved ahead of the painter, who doesn't mind being alone. He has become interested in the numbers.

He is, at this moment, in a cut. The banks rise on either side of him above his eye level; the breeze is shut off; the heat is oppressive. The only sounds are the humming of insects and the occasional nervous flutter of a disturbed grasshopper's wings. The painter is painting the number 1800. He is amused to note the possibility of putting this number series into one-to-one correspondence with the years of the century. He begins to supply the numbers with events, at first bits of history—Civil War and family background. This imaginary living-through-past-time becomes as real an experience as the rail-painting, and far more exciting! 1865, 1870—suddenly 1873, my birth year: "Hello! Hocking is here!" Every mark, from now on, numbered or not, is entangled with personal history. But very soon, 1892, *the present:* the painter's story and the actual story coincide: I paint the Now! From this point, memory is dismissed; it gives place to anticipation, dream, conjecture—there is something relentless in the onmoving of these numbers, to be filled with something—but with what? 1893—will it be the new Chicago University? 1900—where shall I be? 1950, fairly old, very likely gone. 1973, a hundred years from birth— surely gone: "Good-bye Hocking!" I see myself as dead, the nothingness of non-being sweeps over me. I have been for four years an ardent disciple of Herbert Spencer, unhappily but helplessly convinced that man is as the animals; the race moves on, the individual perishes, the living something has become—nothing; "And not the pillow at your cheek so slumbereth." For the first time I realize, beyond the mere clack of words, the blankness of annihilation. And no doubt, just because of this swift sense of no-sense, the shock was intense as I realized, with the same swiftness, that *it was I, as surviving, who looked upon myself as dead,* that it had to be so, and that, because of this, annihilation can be spoken of, but *never truly imagined.* This was not enough to free me from the spell of Spencer, but it cracked that spell: the rest of the day was spent in lightness of heart, as if I had come upon a truth that was not to leave me.[6]

His plan had been to save enough for college, working evenings on making a map of Will County—a good atlas was much in demand—which he would sell for $15.00 a copy. The Panic of 1893 intervened, however, and the maps brought only $4.00 a copy, enough to pay his bills and no more. He then took himself to Newton, Iowa (where his father had moved the family in the meantime), and had a turn at teaching Latin to the students of the Newton Normal School. In the fall he entered Iowa State College of Agriculture and the Mechanic Arts, at Ames, as a student of engineering.

The most significant event of his days in Ames happened by chance one rainy Sunday afternoon. He set out for the library and asked the librarian whether there was anything new in philosophy. She produced *Principles of Psychology* by William James with the comment that it had been well reviewed. Hocking took it to a side table and spent the rest of the afternoon absorbed in it. It was to be the end of Spencer's hold on him. James spoke of a world which Hocking recognized as his own, and of the kind of experience which Hocking shared. James' view of the world was experimental and lively, not mechanical and dead as Spencer's was. Hocking determined to go to Harvard and study with James, and he left Iowa State College at the end of his second year in order to earn money for this new venture. He had taught school in a little one-room schoolhouse in Grinnell, Iowa, during the summer between his first and second years at Iowa State College; he turned to teaching again, this time as an instructor in business mathematics at Duncan's Business College in Davenport, Iowa. A year later he applied for and received (much to his amazement) a position as Principal of Public School No. 1 in Davenport. He served there for four years until he had earned enough to enter Harvard.[7]

After completing his undergraduate work he spent a year in Germany on a Walker fellowship from Harvard prior to writing his doctoral thesis. The experience is significant for at least two reasons. The first is the grounding it gave him in German philosophy. He was later to comment that the power of American philosophy in that "Golden Age"—which included Dewey, Royce, James, Santayana, and Whitehead, among others—was derived, at least in part, from the fact that these men were conversant with trends in European thought. German philosophy and theology have usually proved too heavy for Americans as a steady diet, and Hocking was later to needle German scholarship as "prolific of the Very True"; but the German mind deserves its reputation for comprehensiveness and thoroughness and Hocking learned much about these virtues from Windelband, the great historian of philosophy whose work is still classic, from Müller in psychology, Abraham in theoretical physics, Max Verworn in problems of body and mind, and perhaps most importantly of all, from Husserl in epistemology.

His work with Husserl made the German experience significant for a second and rather different reason. His contact with the phenomenological approach at this early stage in his career helped him to see the bridge between fact and meaning. But his personal contact with Husserl also gave him a direct experience of "creative suffering." Hocking recalls that "To be with Husserl intimately was to be participant in his own mental agony, his fineness of drawing, his infinite capacity for distinction, to some extent also his worry and intricacy."[8] This striving of Husserl's was not simply that of an isolated individual, "for to him it was the striving of the age, and he must lift not himself alone but the thought of his time into clarity."[9]

Intricacy and mental agony, world-consciousness and world-seriousness are all alien to American experience. The popular culture which is both the bane and the blessing of American democracy regards intricacy as a sign of confusion or pretense. We shun the esoteric. We are impatient with mental agony. Our Puritan heritage has left us with a residue of guilt, but Puritan guilt has been outweighed by Puritan self-confidence. The Protestant ethic's sympathy for the spirit of capitalism has been spelled out by Weber, Tawney, and others. The Puritan's laboring in his calling religiously for the Lord's sake soon gave way to Ben Franklin's burning the midnight oil religiously for the sake of the business. It was clear to the man of affairs that the Lord loved profitable labors. Success indicated stewardship of God's gifts. Poverty became proof that one did not faithfully serve the Lord. And if the theologico-economic rationale was as much an excuse for sharp practice as it was an item of religious faith, the successful could always turn to philanthropy to assuage their consciences. Even today, the greatest compliment one can pay to an American businessman is to tell him that he is working too hard. Few Americans—even the rich ones— have learned how to retire gracefully, unlike the moneyed aristocracy of Catholic Europe who have made retirement a lifelong art. We are happiest when hard at work, and we feel guilty when not working.

The visionary elements of the American Dream and the optimism, self-reliance, and energy of the American self-image were all part of Ernest Hocking. A precocious boy from the rapidly developing American Midwest, he had learned to "think big," and set his sights high on an education at a great Eastern university. He had got himself there by dint of his own unaided efforts, and had made a success of various occupations in the process. And on arrival he discovered himself with new intellectual powers which were rewarded by the opportunity and encouragement of a fellowship for study in Germany.

He remains a distinctively American philosopher, especially in his pioneering attitude toward nature as an area of purposelessness which has been given to man as raw material for his own creative purposes. But his great contribution to American philosophy is his detailing of the new context in which American thought and action must hereafter take place: the context of a world community. Heretofore we have taken characteristic pride in being first among the nations in the world. In a world community, competitiveness must increasingly become cooperation. Nationalism and individualism must be tempered. Optimism and energy are crucial, but along with them must go the patient realization that our major problems will not be solved in a short time or by dramatic means. America's world-involvement is requiring not only political readjustment and financial burden, but a maturing of the American character. We know a great deal about sacrifice, which we equate with hard work. We have only recently begun to learn about "creative suffering," in the sense that Husserl experienced it: not as personal tragedy, but as personal involvement in the universal suffering of man.

Hocking's contact with Husserl did not work any great or immediate change in his own character, but it put him into continuing contact with an experience which was very different from his own, and which he was to draw on in later years. At the end of World War II, he was to return to Germany and later record his reactions in *Experiment in Education*. Here the association with Husserl reached fulfillment, for Hocking's own characteristically American emphasis on man's "will to create" specifically becomes the "will to create *through suffering.*" This new element, introduced into his philosophy of history in *The Coming World Civilization,* was to make possible an appreciation of Existentialism and a more profound sense of those qualities which the growing world community was already requiring of the American character.

Even before World War I, he had caught something of the unease that pervaded Europe, and the sense that something more profound and basic was needed for a recovery of vitality. His experience with Husserl adds point to this passage from the introduction to *The Meaning of God in Human Experience* (1912):

There is, I say, a quiet and canny maturity of conscience abroad which knows surely what it does not want, a new born thing in the world, the source of our new philosophies, —in particular of our pragmatisms, our realisms, our mysticisms,—the doom of the old, the doom also of the new that fail to arrive at reality: the lash at the back of the thinker, and the hope in his soul.

Meanwhile, the general deepening of consciousness, and of conscience, is a deepening of religion itself. . . . This development of religion is still a latent fact, mightier than any yet visible shape or movement, discernible at times only as a cloud dim and vast, strained and full of repressed lightning. The release of these forces is no small human object.[10]

The early and direct association with Husserl was short-lived, however. As holder of the Walker Fellowship, Hocking had reported his doings to the philosophy department at Harvard. Professor Hugo Münsterberg, then Chairman, proved to be more conservative than his young charge and also less prophetic as a judge of prospectively influential philosophers. He wrote a sharp note making it clear that the Department "did not grant Fellowships in order that students might seclude themselves in provincial universities." (Husserl was at Göttingen.) Direct contact between Hocking and Husserl was broken when Hocking left provincial Göttingen for Berlin; but he kept in touch with Husserl by mail during the rest of his time in Berlin and for many years afterward. Later he was to recommend several of his students for study with Husserl, among them Marvin Farber and Dorion Cairns, who helped introduce Phenomenology to the Americas.

Hocking returned to Harvard for doctoral work in the fall of 1903, and plunged immediately into his dissertation. The year had other rewards than academic study, however, for it was then that he met Agnes O'Reilly whom he married two years later and who, for the next fifty years, was an "unfailing source of insight." They were at Andover Seminary from 1904 until 1906, when he was called to the University of California. After two years there, he joined the philosophy department at Yale. There the Hockings spent six of their happiest years. While at Yale Hocking claimed wide attention with the book that remains his *magnum opus, The Meaning of God in Human Experience,* in which he set forth the major outlines of his philosophy. The book elaborates an original thesis about our knowledge of God, but it also indicates the influence of his two great teachers, Josiah Royce and William James.

Part One

THE METAPHYSICS OF EXPERIENCE

Chapter I

THE INFLUENCE OF
ROYCE AND JAMES

WILLIAM JAMES ORIGINALLY ATTRACTED Hocking to Harvard, but when Hocking first arrived there in 1901 James was on leave, delivering his Gifford Lectures in Scotland. Josiah Royce was in Cambridge, however, and under his influence the would-be architect began to develop as a philosopher. Royce was at that time concerned with the sciences and their relation to philosophy—particularly the sciences of mathematics and logic. His lectures were emphasizing the view that:

> Philosophic efforts since Kant have remained incomplete by the lack of the study of the processes of thought embodied in the living sciences, and of such categories as number, quantity, space, time, cause, continuity . . . The mathematician, in so far as he consciously distinguishes significant from trivial problems, and ideal systems, is a philosopher. The philosopher, in so far as he seeks exactness of logical method in his reflection, must meanwhile aim to be within his limits a mathematician.[1]

Hocking had had some previous training in mathematics,[2] and he began a study of its philosophical implications under Royce's direction. The study later became the basis for his doctoral dissertation[3] in which the mathematical idea of a

"group" was used to outline the distinctions betwee[n]
sciences dealing with nature and those dealing with so[c]
Royce's concern was to provide a logical basis for his [m]
physics, especially the concept of the absolute. He had [been]
stimulated by his friend Charles Peirce's work on the [logic]
of the infinite. He saw in Peirce's infinite an ideal logi[c]
model for the formal characteristics of the absolute.[5] Tw[o]
problems faced him, however. For Royce, the absolute was
not only perfect, it was a characteristic of the real world,
and thus perfectly real. But both the perfection and the
reality of the infinite were problematical. Aristotle had
argued that the infinite cannot be real or actual, because
an infinite series cannot be "run through" to its last term.
And Bradley, among others, had argued that since the actual
infinite is unending it is imperfect and therefore irrational.

Peirce, however, had suggested that a real or actual infinite is not irrational, but a perfect order. Following this
lead, Royce adopted the view of the mathematician Dedekind that the infinite is not defined by the fact that it is a
series without a final term, but rather by the characteristics
of the series as a whole. Dedekind defined the infinite not
as an unending series but rather as a definite type of
"system." Royce added the idea (central to his own voluntaristic understanding of the absolute as a self) that the
infinite system is purposive. He began by examining an
infinite series of discrete numbers. Between each of these
numbers there is an infinite series of fractions. The structure of the fraction series is a smaller scale reproduction of
the integer series, since both series are infinite. And the
infinite nature of the series, as Herbert Schneider points
out, is not based on its endlessness, but on "its very structure,
i.e., its members interpret each other in terms of the structure of the whole."[6] The infinite series of fractions between

any two integers keeps the integers an infinite distance apart, so that they have no direct relationship with one another. At the same time, however, the fraction series does provide a middle term between the two integers. Each integer is related to its neighbor in the same terms that it is related to the series as a whole, i.e., in terms of the infinite. The different parts of the series are thus representative of the whole series.

Royce applied this idea of the infinite to his metaphysics of the absolute, emphasizing that the infinite system constitutes a "community," and the means by which different members of the community are related is a process of "interpretation." Here he departs from traditional logic. Philosophy, in his view, is concerned with the antitheses of appearance and reality, the public and the private, the false and the true, etc. But the traditional categories of identity, noncontradiction, and excluded middle, while sound in themselves, do not help us to evolve one truth from another. The process of inferring one truth from another depends rather on another category, that of "relation." And the process of relating two things involves something more than the two things to be related; it involves the thought which relates them. A simple process such as the comparison of two objects is therefore not a "dyadic" relation, as had been traditionally assumed, but a "triadic" relation. Augustus De Morgan had put it this way:

> Any two objects of thought brought together by the mind, and thought together in one act of thought, are *in relation.* Should anyone deny this by producing two notions of which he defies me to state the relation, I tell him that he has stated it himself; he has made me think the notions in the relation of *alleged impossibility of relation;* and has made his own objection commit suicide. Two thoughts cannot be

brought together in thought except by a thought; which last thought contains their relation.[7]

Using the work of De Morgan and Peirce as a logical foundation, Royce set forth a metaphysics of relation, his famous triadic doctrine of interpretation. One of his better-known illustrations of the doctrine is the problem faced by an English-speaking archaeologist confronted by an Egyptian hieroglyphic tablet. The process of translating the text into English involves a three-way relationship among (1) the text to be translated, (2) the archaeologist, and (3) the English translation. These three elements represent three different priods of time: (1) the past: the hieroglyphic text, (2) the present: the work of the archaeologist, and (3) the future: the translation, prepared for some future English reader. Interpretation is not only the process by which we come to know the world, but also the key to knowledge of ourselves. A past promise or plan of action is remembered in the present where the self proposes a future fulfillment of the plan.[8] For Royce, interpretation is the key to all reality, which, in its simplest terms, is the process of the present interpreting the past to the future. And each interpretation will, in turn, demand its own future interpretation. The English text will need to be translated into German, for example, and so forth, ad infinitum; and the fact that the process pushes inexorably ahead is an expression of its purpose, best seen in the relationship between the individual and the community.

Any specific interpretation is admittedly performed by an individual, but Royce did not regard truth as an individual achievement. Because truth is finally established only as the accumulated result of human experience over a period of time, interpretation is ultimately a function of the community. The work of the scientific community was one of his favorite examples. In *The Problem of Christianity* Royce wrote: "The Individual has made his discovery; but it is a scientific discovery only in case it can become, through further confirmation, the property and the experience of the community of scientific observers."[9]

The scientific community is at work on a series of interpretations which is unending, i.e., it is an infinite series. This infinite forward push is as hard to explain as it is easy to recognize; somehow man "needs to know." Each individual member of the scientific community shares methods, values, and some vague goals which are characteristic of "the community as a whole," which Royce called, simply, the absolute. The interpreting work of each individual is a self-representation of the work of the absolute, which is the actual, purposive, infinite structure of the world.

Peirce had promised Royce that wrestling with mathematical logic would help to clarify his basic categories, and William James later admitted that he found Royce's logical prowess intimidating. The question remains, however, whether this adroit analogy really advances Royce's argument for a purposive "absolute mind." To say that numbers in an infinite series "interpret" each other in terms of the "whole" is to say that the structure of the individual number is formally comparable to the structure of the series. But to say that a human individual "interprets" the past to the future is not to define the formal characteristics of that particular mind; it is to note the unpredictable result of its creativity. A scientific discovery is never necessary. It is not an inevitable manifestation of a given characteristic of the mind of the individual. It is an historical event, often accidental, regularly resulting from an illogical stroke of genius. One might argue that what is discovered has always been

true, and is only now being made manifest. Perhaps God
and/or the absolute have always known it, but we have not
known it. In the serious philosophical sense, therefore, it has
never been true before. We do not make truth, we find it;
but in the method used, the context established, and the
lines of relationship drawn there is room for genuine creativity. The interpreting work of the mind is quite different
from the work which a discrete number in an infinite series
does in interpreting another.

This discrepancy between the way mind works and the
way numbers work also calls into question Royce's assertion
about the "purposiveness" of an infinite series. Granted that
such a series is characterized as much by its total structure
as by the fact that it is unending, still the work of the human
community is purposive in response to man's need to know.
A number system, however, harbors no hopes and labors
under no responsibilities. To credit the forward thrust of an
infinite number series with "purpose" seems arbitrarily
anthropomorphic. On the contrary, the inherent formal "motions" of mathematics, like the mechanical motions of physics,
only serve to remind us that most of the doing and undoing
of the world around us goes on without the immediate benefit of any conscious purpose at all.

Hocking's concern for integrating the worlds of the self,
nature, and society found much that was fruitful in Royce's
triadic logic of relations. But he used this triadic epistemology to develop a dialectic which was quite independent of
Royce's theory of interpretation. Individuals in Royce's
community are like discrete numbers in an infinite series.
They have no *direct* contact with their neighbors. Each discrete number reaches out to its neighbor only to find that
there is an infinity (the infinite series of fractions) between
them. The basis for the relationship between the discrete

numbers is the participation of each in the infinity of the absolute, the overarching structure of the communal whole. When applied to the community of persons, this theory produces two important doctrines. One is that we have no intuitive knowledge of ourselves; the other is that we can have no direct knowledge of our neighbors. As to the first, Hocking argued, contra Royce, that before the knowing self can know anything, it must assume a self that knows. One must therefore have a knowledge of oneself before knowledge of any other kind is possible. On the more crucial issue concerning our knowledge of other selves, Hocking notes: "We have, he [Royce] maintained, no direct empirical knowledge of ourselves nor of other minds, and hence, in substance, of our entire social environment on which his later philosophy so essentially turned."[10]

For Royce, individuals are like the monads of Leibniz, except that they are not entirely windowless. They have a skylight open to the absolute. The absolute makes available a set of universal symbols (language and science are the most important of these) for communication with one's neighbors. These communications are real, but only on the basis of the reality of the absolute. The line of communication between Royce and his neighbor is always indirect. It is only because they both participate in the absolute that Royce can say that he "knows" the other person. When we actually meet our neighbors, of course, common sense tells us that our knowledge of one another is direct and immediate, not mediated. Royce agreed that indeed our knowledge of one another *seems* immediate. He further agreed that for practical purposes we must live *as if* we have direct relations with one another. But he never overcame the solipsistic view that individual minds can know only their own states, and cannot directly experience the reality of another person.

Hocking chose to explore the instinctive response of common sense. If our common experience convinces us that our relations with our neighbors are direct, while philosophy tells us that they cannot be, perhaps we should call our philosophy into question. Is a consistently subjectivist theory logically possible? For example, Hocking notes that Leibniz' theory that all men are monads *must* be false—at least in the case of the monad Leibniz. For Leibniz escaped his subjectivity, experienced the world of others, and brought back the report that all men are monads. Hocking suspected that all solipsisms—even the "mutual subjectivism" of Royce—were self-defeating. With the rude eagerness of graduate students who set out to attack the views of their professors, he announced in the introduction to his doctoral thesis that he would seek:

> . . . to remove the ground from that epistemological idealism amounting to monadism, whereby God and the philosopher know our real communications to be essentially different from those apparent to experience, so that human intercourse on its cognitive side has a purely representative character. No such idealism fails to give us real connections, to demonstrate that we are one in the absolute, but this juncture is by way of the ineffable in each of us, not by way of the overt movement of intercourse. In opposition to such an idealism I would hold that our juncture is by way of our common foreground, that our dealings are as real as we mean them to be, that a communication of minds not experienced by the communicators is a logical not less than moral mockery. Idealism has been exercised to rediscover the outer world which the individual self has absorbed: I wish to restore the stinging reality of contact with the human comrade which this same idealism obscures.[11]

When James returned to Harvard, Hocking was deeply involved in Royce's idealism, and he found himself critical of James' method, or—as it seemed to him—lack of method. But James brought with him the manuscript of *The Varieties of Religious Experience,* and in his lectures from it he expressed his sensitivity to alive human nature, and his openness to irregular expressions of human vitality in life and religion. His treatment of the oddly reported mystical experiences which make up so much of *The Varieties of Religious Experience* appealed to Hocking, because of James' intuitive perception of their genuineness and significance.

James saw that feeling, purpose, and *charis* all have a metaphysical significance which cannot be absorbed by psychology, although psychology was his major tool in analyzing them. He also argued that the conventional religion of the ordinary religious believer was a secondhand form of original religious experience. This original experience, which sets the pattern for conventional imitation, is to be found, James said, "in individuals for whom religion exists not as dull habit, but as an acute fever rather." Despite their "symptoms of nervous instability," these individuals are " 'geniuses' in the religious line."[12] The religious experience of the mystics is therefore not to be regarded as an aberration, radically distinguished from the religion of Everyman. It is rather the "original source" of ordinary, conventional religion.

Hocking did not accept all of James' material as illustrating this continuity, but he did accept his general thesis and used it in *The Meaning of God* to argue that the "true mystic" is the one most acutely aware of the "original sources" of Everyman's knowledge of God. In so doing, he joins James in opposing a traditional Protestant prejudice against mysticism, which argues that the mystic, in his "negative path" to God, in the ineffability of his experience, and in his concern for absorption into the Divine, cuts himself off from the mainstream of historical religion. Hocking's metaphysics argues that the mystic is a radical empiricist, dealing with the stuff of experience in its most profound dimension. His theology argues, in opposition to the usual contrast between mysticism and prophecy, that the mystic is both the "true worshipper" and the "true prophet." He is the one who combines the most perceptive religious insight with the most effective religious activity in the world. Hocking is critical of the "negative metaphysics" of much mysticism, on the ground that a spiritual experience which amounts only to zero has a value for life which is also zero. But when mysticism is understood as one pole in a necessary "alternation" of religion between worship and work, it recaptures the value that its negation seems to have lost.

Hocking was already well schooled in Hegel's dialectic when he renewed his interest in James' thought. James' dealing with experience convinced Hocking that Hegel was right in seeing a bond between the give and take of abstract thought and the give and take of experience. The man of action finds the direction for that action in a motivating "idea"; and that idea is molded and hardened on the anvil of experience. Great achievement involves the overcoming of great obstacles, and the motivation for hard achievement has secret sources of ambition and responsibility which require nurture if they are to maintain their vitality. This nurture is what Hocking means by "worship" in the broadest sense. In this communion of the individual with his vision a basic purpose is reconfirmed. For Hocking, as for James, the crucial value judgment concerns the kind of purpose involved in this communion, and both men were essentially worldly. If worship does not feed one's work in the world, then there is something immoral about it. If he had had to choose between worship for its own sake and work for its own sake, Hocking would have chosen work. In this he is thoroughly American. He did not like people who were concerned only to save their own souls. A mystic who just sits is denying his own insight; the value of sitting still for a season is to summon up new resources for doing something. Hocking's philosophy is involved with the endless adventure of becoming. For him, the realms of "being" are only such as to give shape and purpose and meaning to that adventure. He is concerned with the demands of the coming world civilization. He sees a need for men of well-cultivated inner spiritual resources who will act out of a deep rapport with the powers that be in a universe which is essentially spiritual, not material.

No Indian would find William James a typical mystic, and yet James, as a Westerner, was able to make room for the kind of insight which is peculiarly characteristic of the East. He influenced Hocking profoundly with his religious sensitivity and the manner in which he expanded his "worldliness" to include it. This same capacity for relating transcendentalism and humanism forms the bond between Hocking and Arnold Toynbee and is the inspiration for Hocking's special regard for Radhakrishnan. The "true mystic," who is also the "true prophet," as Hocking sees it, is a man characterized by a new universality in spiritual matters. He is neither solely Western nor solely Eastern in his response to the world. He is a man ready to effect a new synthesis out of an age-old antithesis. It was from James that Hocking got one of his first inklings as to what manner of man this might be.

James had written of *The Varieties of Religious Experience* that it sought ". . . to defend . . . 'experience' against 'philosophy' as being the real backbone of the world's religious life . . ."[13] By "philosophy" he means the tradition of "natural religion" so beloved by the absolute idealists of his day.[14] They had reduced the varied richness of religious living—its institutions, "cult," festivals, theologies, etc.—to a set of philosophical ideas. Their religious activity was speculative, fulfilled by a knowledge of God which was the fruit of the particular philosophical system. In the Hegelian manner, they had smelted out the primitive stuff of religious myth and custom, leaving the pure metal of thought. James knew this traditional intimately. It was represented in his family by his father, and his colleagues Dickinson Miller and Josiah Royce were its able advocates. James was robustly anticlerical, but he was equally repelled by this kind of "gnosticism." For him, "natural religion" was too abstract, too cerebral, too bloodless, faint, and cool to satisfy the earthy requirements of what he liked to call man's religious "appetites."

But can the "dull habit" of the conventional congregation's worship satisfy the "acute fever" of the individualistic "religious genius" any better than philosophy? It was several years before Hocking came to a tentatively affirmative answer. The experience of conversion in the evangelist's meeting had led directly to his joining the Methodist Church. As a student at Harvard, however—perhaps under the influence of Royce and Dickinson Miller—he spent his most characteristic Sunday mornings in a little discussion group gathered by his friends Richard and Ella Cabot in their Boston house at 291 Marlborough Street. Cabot was a great admirer of Royce's. The Sunday morning seminars were held at the symbolic hour of eleven o' clock, and were for the purpose of discussing "Friendship." Hocking was also instrumental in forming a short-lived "Union for Ethical Action" during his student days which he describes as a kind of "church substitute."[15] He never completely resolved this tension between the institutional church and the philosophically conceived "Christian community." On the other hand, he had always believed in "belonging," on the Hegelian ground that "idea" must be concretely embodied in order to be both real and effective, and he applied this conviction to the life of the Church. During his years on the Harvard faculty, while he regularly attended Harvard's Memorial Church, he established a membership, which he continued until his death, in the Old South Church (Congregational) in Boston.

The issue came up again in later years when he was asked to chair the Laymen's Commission investigating foreign missions. His Harvard colleagues were not enthusiastic about the venture for a variety of reasons. Despite the fact that Hocking had, by that time, published *Human Nature and Its Remaking,* which argued that the Christian mission gave a creative direction to man's instinctive "will to power," he was not convinced of the value of Christian missions as they were then being carried on. He was convinced, however, that something of the sort was necessary, that "religion in general" was no answer to the need for a positive religion, which must be institutional if it is to carry on its work in the world. On the basis of this conviction, he decided to accept the Laymen's Commission chair. The decision was a victory for the James in him. For James, as for Hocking, adventure was almost the good-in-itself. James combined adventure with a high degree of tolerance. His example stimulated a similar sense of adventure and sympathy toward religious zeal in Ernest Hocking and gave him an openness to the problems and possibilities of Christian missions.

Insofar as pragmatism was a systematization of James' emphasis on the emotive and purposeful side of life, Hocking was drawn to it. But he shied away from the full implications of pragmatism, convinced that truth has a structure which cannot be exhausted by its active relation to our feeling and planning. Hocking did, however, retain an element of James' pragmatism in his conviction that a "negative pragmatism" is valid.

> The pragmatic test has meant much in our time as a principle of criticism, in awakening the philosophic conscience to the simple need of fruitfulness and moral effect as a voucher of truth. It is this critical pragmatism which first and widely appeals to the intellectual conscience at large. *Negative pragmatism,* I shall call it: whose principle is, *"That which does not work is not true."* The corresponding positive principle, "Whatever works is true," I regard as neither valid nor useful. But invaluable as a guide do I find this negative test: if a theory has no consequences, or bad ones; if it makes no difference to men, or else undesirable differences; if it lowers the capacity of men to meet the stress of existence, or diminishes the worth to them of what existence they have; such a theory is somehow false, and we have no peace until it is remedied. I will even go farther, and say that a theory is false if it is not interesting: a proposition that falls on the mind so dully as to excite no enthusiasm has not attained the level of truth; though the words be accurate the import has leaked away from them, and the meaning is not conveyed. Any such criterion of truth is based upon a conviction or thesis otherwise founded, that the real world is infinitely charged with interest and value, whereby any commonplaceness on our part is evidence of a lack of grasp. Upon this basis (not apart from it), a negative pragmatism must be an effective instrument of knowledge.[16]

Hocking's major disagreement with James was over the idea of the absolute. James felt that Royce's absolute made a steel fence enclosure for a world bursting with novelty and adventure, and Hocking had complete sympathy with the view that the world cannot be thus enclosed. But he insisted that the novelty and adventure of the world must have some context of ultimate meaning, a finality in which alone one can find the conditions for a necessary certainty in both thought and action. He was convinced that unless there is an ultimately-real, there can be no ultimately-true.

Fact and Destiny, Hocking's Gifford Lectures for the academic year 1938-1939, had closed with a discussion of the meaning of history and the conditions for an integration of selfhood: "If there be an objective unity, an Absolute, . . . these requirements could be met. Thus in the Absolute rests the final over-rule of history. Without it, no conviction; and without conviction, no courage."

Rereading this passage in the summer of 1964, he acknowledged his debt to James with the comment: "And now I would add: 'without courage, no adventure.' "[17]

James' famous outburst—"Damn the Absolute!"—made a considerable impression on Hocking. He felt the force of James' argument that an idea must have pragmatic value, and can therefore be conceived as a plan of action, or an expression of our purposes. James' adventuresomeness is constantly looking ahead to the future. He admitted that the absolute might help us in categorizing what had happened to us in the past. It could do this precisely because, like the past, it is static, completed, unchangeable. But life looks ahead; it is dynamic and unfinished; it faces the new and unexpected. It was wrestling with the human "prospect" which made life interesting for James, and he did not see how the absolute could help.

James' challenge is so keenly felt that when we come to examine Hocking's doctrine of the absolute we shall discover that he begins with James' objections and concedes their point as a criticism of the subjectivism with which the absolute has regularly been associated. He then goes on to state his own case for the absolute precisely in terms of its practical value.

Hocking freely states his debt to both Royce and James in the Preface to *The Meaning of God*.

> If I have taken frequent occasion in this book to express dissent from the views both of Professor Royce and of William James, it is but a sign of the extent to which I owe to them, my honored masters in these matters, the groundwork of my thinking. I have differed freely from both, in the spirit of their own instruction, but not without the result of finding myself at one with both in greater measure than I would once have thought possible—or logically proper![18]

A running philosophical debate like the one between Royce and James (combining truth-seeking with a touch of sport, as a good debate should), emphasizes disagreements, thus polarizing opposing views. The polarization per se is a distortion of the total relationship between the two; but polarization eases the work of thought by enlarging distinctions, and we perpetuate this exaggeration by cementing it in the shorthand of typology: James is a "pragmatic, pluralistic realist," while Royce, in sharp contrast, is an "absolute idealist." True, but never true enough. Despite his outbursts against absolute idealism, James' pluralism made important concessions to monism,[19] and Royce, accepting a good deal of pragmatism, was ever mindful of James' views as he shaped his own.[20] In our eagerness to find the point at which a man differs from his colleagues—for it is here that he makes his unique contribution—we overlook those convictions which they share in common. Even in the present contentious age, there is more philosophic agreement than is publicly acknowledged. It is the ironic fate of common ground to remain unemphatic. It is the business of philosophers to argue, but fruitful debate is possible only on the basis of preliminary agreement which is often both considerable and unrecognized.

To be sure, Royce and James had permanent and significant disagreements;[21] but their differences are not such that a student must resort to the patchwork of eclecticism in order to admit influence from both. Hocking's metaphysics examines the relationships among the self, nature, and society in terms of a dialectic between experience and idea which grew out of a unique personal experience. It is to a preliminary survey of this dialectic that we now turn.

Chapter II

DIALECTIC

HOCKING, WITH ROYCE, BELIEVED in the absolute as a "self," a living reality; but Royce gave no satisfactory account of our knowledge of other human selves. In opposing Royce by affirming the intuitions of common sense against the philosophies of monadism, Hocking was, however, faced by several thorny problems. Descartes' *Cogito* had given the Western philosophical tradition a compelling argument for self-knowledge, and philosophers from Locke through Kant had carefully analyzed our perception of physical nature. However, Hocking noted that another person is neither oneself, nor merely a perceivable physical object. Like oneself, he is a "mind," (personality, spirit); but, like the objects of nature, he is "other." How can one know "other mind"?[1] He agreed that another person's face can be a marvelous mirror of his thoughts and feelings, but he pointed out that it is still only a mirror, a physical characteristic, and not selfhood per se. He was perplexed that there doesn't seem to be any way to "get at" him. Selfhood seemed to be a bastion against the world's intruders, but against the sharings of love as well. Hocking saw further that the problems involved in knowing the absolute as self are of the same order as those involved in knowing other persons. To destroy solipsism would be simultaneously to build the cornerstone of a religious philosophy. This was the task which he had set himself.

Knowledge of another self, whether absolute or finite, involves a number of problems. For example: what is the relationship between our ideas of others, and our feelings about them? What is the relationship between the physical characteristics of another person's body, and the characteristics of his mind? And, by the same token, what is the relationship between the physical characteristics of the world of nature and the spiritual characteristics of the absolute mind?

In *The Meaning of God in Human Experience,* which is his major statement on the problem of knowing other minds, Hocking develops his argument discursively, dealing first with the place of religion in the history of culture and its role in the life of individuals, and then outlining his case for the role of ideas in religious life, on which any idealistic philosophy of religion must be based. He then approaches his idea of the absolute, considering first the nature of a monism which can include a necessary pluralism, and then going on to consider man's need of an absolute and of God in relation to the traditional problems of happiness, evil, freedom, etc. Then comes what he calls the "refractory kernel" of his argument, the discussion of "How Men Know God," the hinge on which his entire metaphysics turns. With this established, he concludes with a discussion of worship and the fruits of religion in man's creative work.

We are dealing here with a philosophical system, which is, I take it, what has usually been meant by "a philosophy," in both West and East, until very recently. This does not mean that Hocking has a framework into which his different ideas about God, man and the world have been fitted. This is the image which spurs critics of system *qua* system. They assume that system is necessarily prior to its separate doctrines, and that systematization requires trimming the ragged edges of experience in order to stuff living ideas into cramped intellectual cubbyholes. The systematizer, fascinated with the hobgoblins of patterned consistency, overlooks the fact that his ideas have all suffocated and died; so the argument runs. Hocking finds it a good criticism of one kind of system, "system-from-without." But, he queries, are these admitted defects inherent in system *qua* system? To be sure, a deductive system such as Hegel's does tend to be mechanical, arbitrary and confining, precisely because the systematic structure precedes and controls the idea content. The deduced "world" which such a system deals with is "produced" and largely artificial. If, however, in a purifying burst of anti-Hegelianism, one rejects system altogether, one flirts with disorganization (which sometimes has a cavalier charm), and downright incoherence (which does not). Even if a man presents his collected views modestly, claiming only that they seem to him, individually, to have merit, the question arises for Hocking as to whether or not the fact that they have all recommended themselves to *him* doesn't imply that the group has at least as much integrity as one requires of selfhood. Indeed, more, for our ideas are constantly under review, and the mind instinctively adjusts, picks, and chooses, seeking an inner coherence. For Hocking, the systematization of one's point of view is the process of finding this necessary integrity. There is such a thing, he claims, as "system-from-within," a natural outgrowth of the interaction of experiences which have been sifted, clarified, and mutually understood.

It remains true, however, that whether system is imposed (illegitimately) "from without," or develops (legitimately) "from within" it does result in a conceptual totality, a "system of the world." Some such working unity in a philosophical point of view is inescapable, but perhaps we need not claim that it is anything more than a useful summary (subject to inevitable change), of how the world looks to a self at the present moment. In debating the issue with Gabriel Marcel,[2] however, Hocking claims that a systematic, conceptualized version of "the world" can be real. Marcel rejects such systems of the world because system closes in and rounds off a world which must be open to the future. For him, a valid ontology must always lie just beyond any system. Marcel speaks from experience. Having planned a systematic treatise from notes collected over a period of years, the final result defies fixed delineation, and must be published, not as a metaphysical system, but as a metaphysical "journal"; not an objective, public conclusion of final, established results, but as the autobiographical report of a private *itinerarium mentis*.

Hocking asks: "If it is *purely* private, why publish it?" Spinoza answers that we have an obligation to announce whatever truth we find, for its own sake. But, Hocking counters, in openly asking others to be interested enough to read it, are we not urging that there is worth for them in pursuing that interest; that this truth is being announced also for their sake? In the simple act of publication Hocking finds "faith in a *potential universality* not wholly alien to that of conceptual reason." Again, why should men feel a responsibility to labor over their most intimate and "inexpressible" convictions in order to express them to others?

The autobiography of passion, like the literature of confession, is of perennial human weight, not for its psychological interest so much as for its revelation of the meaning of human existence, the most promising source of light on the nature of being for other seekers and gropers. If this is the case, is it precluded that this light also, as well as the light of science, shall find sooner or later its own conceptual expression?

I am inclined to the thesis that all meanings, including the wordless meanings of music and the other arts, are destined to meet the relentless and ultimately successful assault of the concept. For, after all, the concept imposes no constraint on that which is conceived. Changeless as the concept is, there is a concept of change, quite as valid as the concept of the static; there is a concept of the conceivable, another of the inconceivable. A concept of "the whole" builds no fence around what is meant by it. Conceptual structures must be coherent, but psychiatry is bound to build coherent concepts of incoherent mentalities; and any lover of mankind must try to gain an orderly view of public disorder and moral descent toward chaos, as Marcel does in *Man versus Mass Society*.[3]

He acknowledges, however, that even system-from-within runs the danger of proliferating "connective tissue" which is the "notoriously non-nutritive . . . gristle that spoils the steak." Some compromise will have to be worked out between structure and content. He believes that "system-from-within is simply a man's necessary concern for his own mental integrity, and for his good faith with his fellow-enquirers."[4]

The discursive approach to the problem of our knowledge of God in *The Meaning of God in Human Experience* and his other books clothes the bare bones of the system with the flesh of experience. This makes his work more alive, but, since it also makes the bones harder to see, it is worth glancing briefly at his systematic method, its structure, and its basis in experience.

The method is dialectical. Two elements are emphasized in Hocking's dialectic. One is the fact that there are two different points of view represented; the other is the fact that they are talking together, therefore sharing common ground. Dialectic is not a formula for deriving truth automatically from any problem; it is a description of the manner in which the mind works. It is analagous to the way conversation is carried on between two people. Dialectic is another term for the learning process in which an experience confronts a seemingly contradictory experience. Out of this confrontation comes a rethinking of each experience in the light of the other. As a result of this rethinking, elements of both become part of a complex of thought and experience which is larger in perspective and more inclusively true than either of the other two. Dialectic is both conservative and progressive. It is conservative in that some element of a thesis is carried over for rethinking and remaking in the synthesis. Dialectic never loses touch with tradition; it always has roots in the past. On the other hand, it is endlessly progressive in that it is never finished. Each synthesis becomes a new thesis. The conclusion of every discussion is: "We must talk more about this," for there is always more to be learned. So Hocking concludes *The Coming World Civilization: "Opus hic terminatum sed non consummatum dico."* Dialectic insists on certitude about some things and a continually open mind about the rest.

Hocking's dialectic is summed up in a portrait of himself which is in a corner of his library, a separate building next to his home in Madison. Done originally by a friend, the portrait was not a success, and Hocking took the liberty of touching it up. In the original, both hands had been open on the arms of the chair in which he was sitting. He noticed this immediately and it made him uncomfortable. In the retouched picture, one hand remains open; the other has become a fist. In showing the picture, he referred to the then current crisis in Berlin: "This is how we must deal with the Russians. A closed fist—and an open hand. We make it clear that our support of free Berlin is firm and not at issue in any discussion; but that we are open to negotiation on ways and means."

Dialectic is an epistemological method, but it has metaphysical implications. One thinks immediately of Hegel's "absolute spirit" going forth from itself into the concrete world of matter and then returning fulfilled to itself again. Hocking's dialectic is appreciative of Hegel but concerned, for its part, with what this symbolizes about our experience. Hocking comments:

> There are two stages of knowledge of one's own land, for example, or of one's own language: the knowledge one has by living in the land or using the language, and the knowledge one has when after travelling in foreign lands one returns home. It has been said that he who knows only one language knows none: it is by comparison with something else that one appreciates the *meaning* of a thing.
>
> In a similar way, Hegel suggests, mind must, as it were, abrogate itself in order to appreciate itself; it must wander in a world alien to its nature and come to itself again. Nature is this foreign land; nature is the "otherness of the spirit." . . . With these truths in view, we grasp the general meaning of Hegel, when he describes the development of life and mind out of nature as the Odyssey of the Spirit (Geist) coming to itself. The ultimate law of the world Hegel declares is the paradox, Die to live: He that loseth his life shall save it. There is a "dialectic" in the structure of the world and of history.[5]

The strength of Hocking's dialectic lies in its inductive emphasis. He sees it as the natural method by which the mind sorts out conflicting experiences. He softens the rigidity of dialectical theory by couching it rather casually in terms of a principle of alternation, indicating that he is as much interested in the give and take of thought as he is in defending a schematic pattern and the syntheses which it produces. I think it was T. R. V. Murthi of Banaras who once pleaded for "a reasonable use of reason" and Hocking's dialectic seems to me to respond to that plea. At the same time, however, dialectic is almost inevitably a seductive device. It tempts one to the assumption that everything turns out cogently in the end, if only you keep at it assiduously enough. Dialectic cannot suffer gaps; vagueness or cleverness tends to creep in to cover them over. This is the great pitfall for idealisms of all sorts, and Hocking stumbles into it occasionally. Better, I think, to confess perplexity than to be overly loyal to any schematic pattern.

The structure which Hocking's dialectic explores is the antithesis between objective nature and the subjective self. If we begin with nature, we are impressed with its otherness and its tangible objectivity. It seems to represent the really "real." This is the thesis of the dialectic. On the other hand, when we stop to think about our actual knowledge of nature we realize that it is *our* knowledge. Nature, with its seeming objectivity, is really encompassed by the subjectivity of self. When we say "nature is objective" what we are actually saying is "*I think* nature is objective." So the initial thesis of "natural realism" as a valid philosophical explanation of reality gives way to "subjective idealism." The resolution of these opposing views comes with the insight that nature is necessary to mind. One cannot simply think, one must think *something,* and nature is the realm of objective content and concrete action. Nature is necessary in order that mind may have content, and may qualify as will. The synthesis of the dialectic is therefore that nature is an objectively real realm of mind, but of mind other than one's own. This affirmation is the cornerstone of Hocking's work as a philosopher. The synthesis becomes a new thesis as he explores the question: "what kind of other mind does nature repre-

sent?" We realize that our minds know nature only empirically and passively. We must take nature as it presents itself
to us—objectively. If all knowing is empirical, however,
there can be no genuine social experience, and no genuine
knowledge of any other mind, since empiricism is passive and
knows only physical objects. But we do know nature as a
realm of mind. So the final synthesis discovers nature as the
realm of an active mind—the absolute—presenting itself as
content for subjective thought and therefore creative of one's
own mind.

These are only the bones of argument—the abstracted
statement of a theory. The dialectical method and the structure of nature in relation to the self are rooted in experience.
This experience is the direct evidence for the theory which
is then tested by analysis. Hocking describes the experience
this way:

> I have sometimes sat looking at a comrade speculating on
> this mysterious isolation of self from self. Why are we so
> made that I gaze and see of thee only thy Wall, and never
> Thee? This Wall of thee is but a movable part of the Wall
> of my world; and I also am a Wall to thee: we look out at
> one another from behind masks. How would it seem if my
> mind could but once be *within* thine; and we could meet
> and without barrier be with each other? And then it has
> fallen on me like a shock—*as when one thinking himself
> alone has felt a presence*—but I *am* in thy soul. These things
> around me are in thy experience. They are thy own; when
> I touch them and move them I change *thee*. When I look on
> them I see what thou seest; when I listen, I hear what thou
> hearest. I am in the great Room of thy soul; and I experi-
> ence thy very experience. For *where art thou?* Not there,
> behind those eyes, within that head, in darkness, fraternizing
> with chemical processes. Of these, in my own case, I know
> nothing and will know nothing; for my existence is spent
> not behind my Wall, but in front of it. I am there, where I

have treasures. And there art thou, also. This world in which I live, is the world of thy soul: and being within that, I am within thee. I can imagine no contact more real and thrilling than this; that we should meet and share identity, not through ineffable inner depths (alone), but here through the foregrounds of common experience; and that thou shouldst be—not behind that mask—but *here,* pressing with all thy consciousness upon me, *containing* me, and these things of mine. This is reality; and having seen it thus, I can never again be frightened into monadism by reflections which have strayed from their guiding insight.[6]

This experience, and the logic which surrounds it, is what Hocking calls the "refractory kernel" of his central metaphysical argument in *The Meaning of God.* In explaining the religious meaning of this experience in a letter to a friend Hocking wrote:

If we could understand the mystery of our human communication, we might get some light on the Divine Mystery at the same time. Now it seems to me that we perceive each other by the aid of objects which we have in common (meeting in a common place and time, under a common sky, having some common interests and ideals, and most fundamentally, common love of truth). And before we met each other, or anybody else for that matter, we knew that these objects and interests were not our private property, but were sharable—yes, already shared with a companion who does not come and go. In short, it is God who from the beginning shares all our objects, and so God is the real medium of communication between one person and another. That is all.[7]

Perhaps the simplest way of putting the point of this experience is to ask: Where do we look for the mind of another? Hocking begins by looking at the other's head. But then he thinks of his own mind, and realizes that the things which occupy his mind (quite literally)—friends, books, house, mountains—his "treasures," exist not behind the "wall" of his forehead, inside his head, but in front of it, out in the world. This is the world of his mind, where "my existence is spent." This insight makes him add this to the Cartesian *Cogito*: Mind cannot simply think; it must think *something.* Thought requires objects; therefore the world of objects is essential to mind. This question was at issue when Hocking rejected Royce's view that we know each other primarily through our *inward* awareness of the absolute. The common "background" of our experience, as Royce had outlined it, Hocking does not deny. He argues only that it is not the chief basis of community. It is not the place where our contact becomes "literal." Our chief meeting place is *outward,* in the "foreground" of our experience. "I can imagine no contact more real and thrilling than this; that we should meet and share identity, not through ineffable inner depths (alone), but here through the foregrounds of common experience. . . ."[8] Hocking adds:

> I do not say that knowing thus the objects of another mind is equivalent to knowing that mind; I say that such knowledge of the objects is a necessary, an integral part of social consciousness, even of ideal social consciousness.[9]

This is not a retreat from his euphoric affirmation that one can actually enter the mind of another; but it is a retreat from the implication that he can get there simply by sharing common objects with him. Common objects are necessary for social consciousness; this is obviously affirmed here. What is not so obvious is that—by implication, although not explicitly stated—the objects have to be shared in a particular way. Hocking never made this clear, partly, I think, because it would have required a modification in his central thesis which might have obscured the point he was trying to make. Because he was bringing idealism into closer touch with the realism and pragmatism of his day, his emphasis was on the empirical element in our knowledge of other minds. He is willing to go a long way with those environmentalists who insist that the "hard facts" of our experience determine who we are. The kind of body we have, the kind of surroundings we are brought up in, the places we have been, and the people we have met—these are the constituent elements of selfhood, Hocking agrees. Man is largely what he experiences. But precisely because this is the case, by knowing the empirical data of another's experience, we know something which is a constituent element of his selfhood. Hocking never wavered from this insistence on the necessity of knowing the objects of another mind in order to know that mind, and there isn't much to argue with him about on that score. We know another person largely through knowing the kinds of things he is interested in. But the experience which Hocking describes has more to it than that. In the first place, not any object will do. When he refers to these objects as "treasures," he gives us reason to think that the objects he has in mind are those which are of interest and value to the other person. In the second place, not any other mind will do either. The situation which he describes has a rather nice dialectical balance. The other person is one with whom we already share a certain measure of "common mind," or at least common interests and fellow feeling. On the other hand, he is one who sees differently than we do. Hocking's experience is notable for the fact that he seems suddenly to see the objects which surround them in a new light. The other's different angle of vision helps him to see more in the object than he had seen before—as when a botanist explains a familiar plant which we had never looked at carefully before—and, at the same time, the newly perceived object tells us something about the person who helped to reveal it to us.

Ernest Hocking once mentioned to me, rather casually, that the "comrade" referred to is Agnes Hocking. He felt that this fact was incidental to the metaphysical argument. While I agreed with him at the time, I am increasingly convinced that the experience makes more sense when one knows that the comrade was Agnes Hocking, and realizes that, in his dedication of the book, he prizes her as "an unfailing source of insight." The point of the recounted experience and, I have come to think, the point of dedicating *The Meaning of God* to Agnes, is not just that he loves her, but that she has helped him see things he wouldn't otherwise have seen. Remember that the test of reality, for Hocking, is creativity, and that therefore what counts in life is novelty, adventure, and the experience of seeing and learning things which one had not seen or learned before. His belief in what counts inspired both his far reaching travels and his wide ranging interests. When he writes on love in *Human Nature and Its Re-Making* he makes a particular point of the fact that the beloved is a "window on the world," and that the true lover is therefore constantly learning and growing. Loving is the most creative thing which man does, both biologically and spiritually. But creativity is dependent upon a measure of inspiration; it needs some person, or place, or event to trigger it.

I agree that the experience which Hocking describes is universal. Still, it is only occasional, and depends upon certain conditions. Hocking seems to be saying that it is the inherent power-to-be-known of the objects which relates us. But this is true only of those objects to which we are attentive in a special way. This special attention requires motivation and involves a certain quality. Without this motivation and resulting attentiveness the object lacks the binding quality which Hocking claims for it. One need not be in love. The scientist in his laboratory attacks only those objective issues in which he is interested. No merely casual experimenter gets anyplace until an interest is aroused which claims his attention, demands responsibiilty, and elicits devoted labor. I suspect that Hocking would say that anyone incapable of an interested attentiveness to some part of his world simply lacks humanity—and on this basis he can call the experience which he has in mind a universal one.

The implication that any object can become common mind stuff for any two observers can be justified theoretically perhaps; but for any two finite observers, this is never the case. The world may indeed be endlessly fascinating, but our individual capacity for interest is limited and specialized. If it is true, as I believe with Hocking that it is, "that we perceive each other by the aid of objects which we have in common," it is also true that this perception of other selfhood through common objects relies on a prior attentiveness, without which the object is powerless to introduce us to the mind of the other. If he overstates the case for the empirical side of this experience, it is because he was concerned to establish the point that material objects are the stuff that mind is made of. The metaphysical issue here is whether or not Hocking has simply restated the Berkeleyan thesis that the world is an idea in the mind of God. But let him first work out his dialectic to its final synthesis in the idea of an absolute mind.

A crucial problem which Hocking faces here is precisely what we mean by an "idea," and how our feelings are related to our ideas. Henri Bergson had argued that an idea is a limited piece of consciousness, like a coin or a bucket. An idea *must* be limited and unchanging or it becomes a different idea. If it doesn't include some definite things and definitely exclude others, it doesn't give us very good service. If my tree-idea, for example, is not such that I can recognize both pines and jacarandas as trees, and still distinguish trees from telephone poles, then obviously I need a better idea. To suppose an idea to change must be to suppose it to become a different idea. But our most interesting and important ideas are ideas of living things—wife and poetry, democracy and faith —and these things are dynamic, constantly changing. It is this contrast between the fixity of ideas—a necessary fixity if they are to be clear and distinct—and the fluidity of living reality that drives Bergson to his assertion that intuition is a higher authority upon which ideas rely. Hocking feels that the problem lies with ourselves as idea-makers, rather than with the structure of ideas themselves. He insists that our ideas do *in actual fact* maintain their identity in the face of such change. Bergson himself speaks of "fluent reality" in contrast to "fixed ideas" and for Hocking this raises the question: What is this "fluent reality"? If one knows what one means by "fluent reality" then one must have an "idea" of it. The necessary definiteness of ideas does not keep ideas involving change or growth from having meaning. Hocking's principle is that anything we can experience we can think—even something like a revolution, which is constantly changing—for an idea is simply "selected experience, in shape for memory and communication."[10]

He begins with brittle little idea-pieces, and succeeds in loosening them up. If we admit, then, that ideas are flexible, and thus adequate to changing reality, we are faced with another question, which is particularly important for the philosophy of religion. How far will ideas stretch? Religion, after all, is primarily concerned with things infinite. Isn't reality in its infinitude constantly breaking away from our ideas, precisely because they are finite? With a courage bolstered by his mathematical studies with Royce, Hocking asserts: "All ideas contain an infinity,"[11] albeit an uncounted infinity like that of the uncounted points in the face of a circle. Even if our bucket-idea be that of the smallest imaginable entity, it must serve constantly in the mind for an endless number of recurrences of its object, and therefore has an infinite character.

This is interesting, but not quite what we wanted to know, since infinite recurrence isn't the same thing as having an idea of an object which is, in itself, infinite. Our concern is with "world" and "God." Can one really have an idea of "totality?" Particulars, yes; infinite recurrence of particular contents, perhaps; but "the whole"? Surely this is only a feeling, a "sense" of the infinite. How could "the whole" be a legitimate object of knowledge? Hocking's reply lays the cornerstone of his epistemology, the idea of the whole of reality. Knowledge, he tells us, is not only built up empirically, bit by bit; it also proceeds from the whole to the parts. Take our idea of space. We begin modestly; our early experience is of crib-space and room-space, yard-space and town-space. But does our idea of space unfold bit by bit? Our understanding of the *size* of space develops. But does our understanding of the "spaceness" of space per se—i.e. what space *is*—change? No. What space is for us now it has always been. "We do not learn *to see space little by little*. The child's space is as great as the man's,—namely, whole-space. He who comes into the world at all comes at once into the presence of the whole world."[12] Space, of course, is only one aspect—along with time, order, particularity, and all the rest —of this world, this whole, this real in terms of which we

live. This he believes is the one thing—the only thing—
that is permanently known. Subjective idealism says that the
one thing that is always with us is "consciousness." Hocking
counters that the one, permanent, objectively real thing
which consciousness continually encounters is the total
reality within which consciousness takes place.

This idea of the whole contains an obvious danger: it may
kill the life of thought. It gives us everything before we even
begin. If we have the whole, what more can we need? And
how do we explain growth and change and error in *this*
idea? How can there be any genuine novelty, or development, or fun in thought, if thinking begins with an idea of
the whole? But Hocking argues that the whole-idea is where
thought begins, not where it ends. It is the indispensable
context for our thinking. It has no content in itself; it is
rather the necessary possibility of content. It is that framework within which growth takes place. When he speaks of
growth in knowledge, he is speaking of the "under-standing"
of all this. The growth takes place in what he calls the
"middle-world" between the self and the absolute. Every new
bit of experience, as it becomes idea, requires new reasoning-
connections with other ideas and their idea-connections.
This idea-weaving in the middle-world of daily thought always takes place against a constant, stable background within
"the Loom . . . the simple-total frame of things."[13]

Hocking's view is that we begin with this frame; we cannot weave idea-connections without the "loom." Every idea
which we have is a possible predicate for this primary subject—a quality or aspect of the whole world. And these
predicates are all relative, because our thinking is finite, not
absolute. Our ideas are all subject to change, all requiring
constant readjustment and development within the framework of the whole. (Hence the importance of "rethinking"

in Hocking's philosophy.) There is no absolute stability to any of these predicates; only their framework is absolutely stable. And because this idea of the whole is what we think *with*, and not usually what we are thinking *of*, it is unobtrusive and can easily be called into question when the predicates we attach to it become entangled or discordant or insecure. But all of our thinking—however entangled—presupposes it. And although the reasonings of our middle-world are complex, the subject of our middle-world predicates is itself both simple and everpresent to the mind.

Chapter III

THESIS AND ANTITHESIS:
NATURAL FACT AND PERSONAL WILL

THE WHOLE-IDEA IS THE CRUCIAL CONCEPT in Hocking's battle for an idealistic (or what he calls, more accurately, an "ideaistic") philosophy of religion; a philosophy which holds that we can have an "idea" of God and not just a feeling for him. His view is challenged, on the one hand, by Positivism, which concentrates on the empirical stuff which mind thinks *about,* and therefore, sees no unifying idea that mind thinks *with.* On the other hand, the whole-idea is challenged by representatives of what William Bartley has called *The Retreat to Commitment*[1] in contemporary religious philosophy. They hold that even if there were such an idea, it could not be crucial to religion, because all ideas are secondary and relative to feelings derived from one's social and economic position (Marx), one's psychological history and attending neuroses (Freud), or simply the relative and unique individual peculiarity of one's existence. No commitment in love, or politics, or anything else, is rational—so the argument runs—and therefore the religious commitment is as irrationally valid as any other.

Hocking does not believe that ideas replace feeling in religion. There remains an organic relation between feeling and idea, but neither does feeling displace idea. In spite of his "mysticism," or perhaps because of it, the thrust of Hocking's meaning is always toward the specific and the concrete. Since knowledge of the objects of another's mind, including the mind of God, is "a necessary, an integral part of social consciousness," the "sense" or "feeling" of God's presence which man has in the elemental experience of nature and society is also in relation to an object.

> . . . God has been known for the most part in connection with other objects; not so much separately, if ever separately, as in relation to things which served as media or as *mediators* for the divine presence. We find the early knowers of God worshipping him under the guise of sun, moon, and stars; of earth and heaven; of spirits and ancestors; of totems, of heroes, of priest-kings; and of the prophets themselves.[2]

Unlike Friedrich Schleiermacher, who analyzes feeling directly and deals with God indirectly as the "whence" of feeling, Hocking analyzes the knowable aspect of God (i.e., the absolute) directly and deals with feeling in terms of the God-given objects which mediate it. He can therefore speak of the feeling-for-God, which is inseparable from the idea-of-God, as "literal." The first page of *The Meaning of God* announces the need for "literality at some point in [one's] creed,"[3] and this emphasis on the "literal" is a recurring theme in the book.[4] The starry heavens (to take a traditional example) mediate something of the grandeur of God. What shall we say about this feeling? To describe it purely subjectively is to turn one's back on its source, and therefore on much of its content. Purely subjective experience is always an abstraction; this is Hocking's criticism of the "eidetic" phenomenology of the early Husserl. The feeling "belongs" to the feeler; but it also "belongs" to the starry heavens. It is a "starry-heavens feeling." How, then, does he avoid pantheism and affirm the objective reality of nature? By arguing (a) that the natural object in connection with which God is felt and known is given by a transcendent God; and (b) that while nature is objectively real, it is not independently real—an argument which, as we shall see in Chapter VI, has some affinities with Radhakrishnan's neo-Hindu reinterpretation of the Advaita Vedānta doctrine of the natural world as *māyā*. Nature is a symbol of the reality of God, and hence mediates this reality. The "mysticism" which knows that God is the giver of nature and the problem of the precise definition of the natural object will be dealt with in a later chapter. It might be noted here, however, that Hocking's metaphysics can be read as an interpretation of Methodism's "mountaintop experience" of God.

Hocking finds, however, that if we examine the relation of our "middle-world" ideas to the idea of the whole, a tendency for idea to pull away from feeling in order to establish itself independently results; this tendency threatens the organic relation between the two. The scientific thinker, for example, has an emotional relationship with the hypothesis on which he is working. This may be nothing more than the necessary hope, requisite for all hypothesizing, that the idea "may have something to it." Beyond this, there are aesthetic considerations which exert a subtle and, Hocking thinks, usually valid influence.[5] When the "moment of truth" arrives, however, feeling is excluded in favor of "objective" analysis. The thinker may love his theory dearly, but, when the testing begins, he forsakes all attachments in order to answer the question: "Is it true? Is it a real part of the world—the whole world—in which we live?"

Ideas need to establish their objective reality *before* they can be combined effectively with our desires. Hocking insists that this objectivizing is an important step that is missed in some theories. The pragmatist "action-theory," for example, conceives of an idea as a plan of action, a means to an end, and thus immediately and inextricably involved in whatever values and desires cause the action. Hocking agrees that idea is always a cue for action, but also something more; or better, it is something else first. By the pragmatist principle, for example, wine would be defined as "something-to-be-drunk." And, of course, it is. But the prior reality of wine is bound up first with the reality of the grape and ultimately with the total reality of nature. To define wine in terms of our purposes is to miss its prior participation in a reality —nature—which couldn't care less whether we press the grapes or leave them for the birds.

We cannot divorce our ideas from our purposes in the long run, nor do we desire to. Hocking admits, therefore, that the thrust of the pragmatist's theory is valid. But he finds that we require of our ideas something prior to value and usefulness. The first thing we want to know about them is whether they represent something real, apart from our values. And reality, the "that which exists," which nature typifies, is not first the impulsive world of purpose and value; it is first the "nonimpulsive background" to this purposive world. In itself, it is indifferent to our purposes.

> To lodge meaning somewhere in Nature seems to guarantee [an idea its] genuineness; as if all meanings must be made to touch base in a *region of indifference* before they may spin lawful alliances with feeling and action.
> Nature is the typical region for the feeling free anchorage of the meanings of ideas.[6]

Whitehead used to say that no man knows anything about reality until he has been knocked down. Descartes' demand that our ideas should be "clear and distinct" is met by the model of clarity and distinctness which is provided by physical contact with the natural world. Hocking finds nature the source of definiteness, vividness, and pungency in our ideas. An important reason why extrasensory perception cannot satisfy our desire for knowledge of another person is simply that it lacks this definiteness. He has already noted that knowledge of another mind includes knowledge of its objects. No one is interested in an empty mind; we want to know a mind thinking. We want to know what things our friend is interested in. To ask "What is he thinking?" means "What is he thinking *about*?" We want to know him in relation to the tangible objects of nature.

At the same time, Hocking tells us, we want to know another mind as other than our own; this too is a criterion of our interest in the other person. And once again it is nature which supplies the standard for all thought of "over-against-ness." We have not only an instinctive confidence in the objectivity of nature, we also have an intellectual and spiritual need of the qualities it provides. God Himself is of neither help nor interest to us if he is merely a projection of our selfhood. He cannot save us unless he is both real and other than we are. At least in the West, Hocking notes religion has developed alongside an empirical science in such a manner that the scientist's value of literality became part of the religious conscience. It has never been content —as the East has—with a religion of myth. Faith for Western Christianity means, among other things, belief that the object of one's devotion is real, not-myself, not-imaginary. Whatever is purely mythical in our religion we label as such, and, I would add, much energy has been given by the older liberal theologians of the last century and the biblical form-critics of the present day to the task of "demythologizing."

The need for literalness shows itself again in the renewed quest of the Historical Jesus. Hocking is right, I think, in arguing that Western Christianity has not been content with anything less than a genuinely historical revelation; and its empirical conscience will not allow it the dogma of revelation-in-history without supporting tangible evidence that dogma finds support in historical fact. This literalness of nature has thus left its mark on our religious thought.

At the same time, however, there is much distress today in religious circles over the influence of the natural sciences on our culture and its way of thinking, and there has been much religious polemic against "scientism." Hocking endorses the polemic, up to a point. He recognizes that the I-It relationship of sense experience, which is the model of valid knowledge for natural science, is incomplete in seeking our knowledge of God. God is not an object which can be taken into the laboratory and tested. When scientism, viewing man, announces "There is no such thing as a soul," Hocking is quick to point out that the statement is unscientific, and should read: " 'We do not find any soul,' an assertion not open to doubt, and leaving always open the hopeful question, 'Do you know where to look for it?' "[7]

But is a pure personalism the answer to scientism? Shall the I-It be totally displaced by an I-Thou? Has the confrontation of religious knowing with scientific knowing no yield from the scientific side? The "biblical personalism" of recent Protestant religious philosophy has unfortunately cut itself off from the epistemology of the natural sciences. John Dillenberger, in his *Protestant Thought and Natural Science,* points out that none of the major twentieth century Protestant theologians has come to grips fundamentally with the movements and methodology of the natural sciences.[8] Can Protestant religious philosophy, with its concern for relevance to the "human situation," actually claim that relevance and, at the same time, disregard the scientific concern for Nature which looms so large in the present "human situation"? In contrast to this one-sidedness, Hocking, as we have already discovered, is in the midst of an experience in which the I-It relationship of the self with its world serves as a mediator of the I-Thou relationship of one self with another. The service of nature to this relationship among persons is to provide the specificity, distinctness, and vividness without which mind is at a loss to display that variety and concreteness which alone make us interested in knowing it. Hocking argues that in order to insure the over-againstness of objective reality, nature is encountered as totally devoid of that which characterizes us as conscious subjects—i.e. purpose. By way of background to this affirmation, a historical note may be helpful.

Our science is built on an understanding of a world operating according to laws. This is a modern achievement. Modern science was free to develop only when it divorced itself from the medieval combination of Christian theology and Aristotelian philosophy. That theology understood nature as the realm in which God was working his purpose out; and the "final cause" of Aristotelianism provided a philosophical category which readily lent itself to the theological interpretation of natural purpose. When modern science refused submission to the preconceptions of theology and philosophy and submitted itself afresh to the empirical facts of the natural order, it discovered that nature had no empirically discernible purpose at all. Inherent purposes are limited to conscious living beings. Empirical nature is dead.

The discovery of the inanimateness of nature has been a problem for religious philosophy ever since. If God is entirely separated from the natural world, religion becomes irrelevant to life in nature. This elimination of purpose from the purview of science has led some—Whitehead among them—to suggest that we must reinvest nature with some of those elements of purpose and meaning which modern empirical science has taken away from her. Hocking, for his part, prefers to leave well enough alone. To reinvest nature with purpose is, for him, to forget that man needs a realm of the purposeless—in thought as well as action—in order to have an area for the exercise of his own purposes. We cannot dam rivers and fell trees unless we are confident that our purposes violate no hidden purposes of the river or the tree. The realm of the purposeless in nature makes technology possible, and with it some definitive features of the modern world. By the same token, he thinks, we shall not be free in our thinking unless we can root our ideas in a realm of purposeless factuality which then makes possible the purposive and emotive destiny of our ideas.

It should be noted that this indifferent nature of empirical science triumphs over the superstition which plagued "spiritual" conceptions of nature. If we hear a bump in the night it may be a branch falling on the roof or a thief in the family silver; but we know that nature is not alive—there are no "ghoulies and ghosties and long legged beasties" to prowl our dreams. Nature is dead and indifferent; we may press the grapes or leave them for the birds, she couldn't care less. But whichever we do, Hocking tells us, we must recognize that this purposelessness of nature is a *necessary* purposelessness, if *we* are to think and act purposively. And that thought leaves us with a hint that the dialectic of experience may move on to a point where the purposelessness of nature takes its place within the purposes of an absolute will.

Thus far we have been exploring Hocking's view that

reality is objective. But now we must consider the subjective dimensions of truth. Ideas, he has said, become real when they establish themselves in that realm of objectivity which nature typifies. In religion this principle assures the transcendence of God as a reality other than ourselves. He has already said that faith—in the West, at any rate—has always included a note of this realism, and he has made it clear that we cannot do without it, either in philosophy or religion. The question which his dialectic faces here is whether natural realism is sufficient: indeed, whether—as it stands—it is even genuine philosophy. Hocking has refused to invade the purposelessness of nature in order to save it for some spiritual—and therefore seemingly religious—interpretation. This is the metaphysical root of Hocking's sympathy for modern secularism. He will not quarrel with empiricism or natural science as such. But philosophical realism is another matter. It stands opposed to Hocking's idealistic conviction about the reality of idea. He notes the difference between realism and idealism succinctly:

> One way of thinking holds that our ideas, though not now adequate, are in principle adequate to facts, since facts are ideas in disguise—an 'idealism.' The other holds that ideas are in principle inadequate, since ideas are themselves but facts in disguise—a 'realism.'[9]

This definition of realism is admittedly broad and unsubtle, but I continue to use it in this sense in the discussion which follows.

Realism—"scientific philosophy," especially in its positivistic forms—is primarily concerned with a description of the workings of the world. This is an important task, Hocking admits, and philosophy is dependent upon its success. But it is not, in itself, the specifically philosophical task. Philosophy, he believes, can never be content to describe. Its goal is understanding. If reason is not compelled to ask *why* factuality is there, and whether or not the purposelessness of nature may be *necessary*, then genuine philosophy remains unborn. Every genuine philosophy is, he insists, a kind of idealism. Realism in its more extreme forms is not so much a philosophy as it is a branch of science. Idealism goes behind natural fact and asks: "Why should there be a world? Why should it be *this kind* of a world, and not some other kind?" Or, as the weighty simplicity of the classical formulation puts it: "Why is there something and not nothing?" The suspicion that irrational fact may ultimately be dependent upon rational meaning is, one must admit, already contained in the rational "Why?"; and realists insist that this preconception is philosophically illegitimate. It may, they say, lead to much beauty in thought and feeling, and perhaps even a measure of incidental truth. But it cannot be more than intellectual poetry, because it forsakes the "substantial," which is natural fact. This, the realists say, we know—empirically—to be the real. All else is speculation.

Hocking laments the realistic tendency of much modern thought:

> ... There are brash souls who enquire "Why these facts and not others?" But typical modernity is wise-dog-mindful-of-his-bacon; it is first of all 'empirical,' it will master Nature, but by way of perfecting its obedience. No one can doubt the tactical and also moral sense of this policy; yet I challenge the total capitulation which has gone with it. The strange antithesis between our proud engineering projects reaching beyond the skies and the pseudo-virtuous desertion of man's will to understand I must consider a liability of our great epoch.[10]

What he believes to be "pseudo-virtue" is illustrated in

a comment by a logical positivist on this same issue of realism versus idealism:

> Only when we . . . recognize the grandeur of the metaphysical vision and the depth of its joy, only then can we measure the shocking horror caused by the positivist denial that philosophy can justify the vision of reason. This denial is for the metaphysician sheer blashphemy, an infamy, a vilification; for a logical positivist it is a matter of honesty and of release from harmful illusions.[11]

But empirical objectivism in modern philosophy is counterbalanced by a new inwardness, which explores the implications of the credo: "Truth is subjectivity." In this subjectivism, Hocking sees natural realism meeting its inevitable antithesis: at one moment, we are convinced that the world is entirely objective, apart from ourselves; but we are reminded, in the next, that all we can ever know of the world is what each person knows subjectively. He muses that we are prisoners of our self-consciousness. We cannot jump out of our skins and be immersed in the real. We never meet reality except within the bounds of that self-consciousness. All of our assertions must be preceded, and therefore encompassed, by an "I-think." We are always limited to the real-as-it-seems-to-me. If we are ready at one moment to assert with utter assurance, "I am in the world," we are, at the next, driven to its opposite, "The world is in me."

To these controlled logical considerations of "inwardness" we can add the personal feeling of intimidation and loneliness which has become widespread in the Western world. Postwar affluence in Europe and America has produced a variety of machines whose overwhelming power makes human individuality appear impotent. There is something insidious about all these machines and their gradual replacement of manual labor, threatening us with the fact that we are creating a world which no longer needs us. Something of this threat permeated the intellectual atmosphere even a century ago. Kierkegaard's bitter objection to "system" in Hegel's philosophy is not primarily an objection to logical argument—a point sometimes missed by Kierkegaard enthusiasts. It is a rejection of the philosophy-machine. His famous comment about the system swallowing up the man who created it, so that in the end there was not even a "dingle-dangle of a philosopher left," is the cry of the individual against the mechanical world that threatens to destroy him.

In turning in upon ourselves to find some reality we can affirm, some power with which to fight the depersonalization of the world around us, we are not disappointed. We find reassuringly that the individual will is the creator of much truth. Hocking begins his examination of subjectivity with this observation: "What I believe of my fellow men goes far to determine what my fellow men are."[12] The relationship between oneself and another person is more biological than mechanical. Friendship must grow, and depends on one's will for its reality. Turning to the state as an illustration, writ large, of the workings of the mind, Hocking points out that the state is not ready-made and mechanical, but constantly dependent upon the good will of its citizenry. So, he finds, with the good will of religion. The brotherhood which religion preaches is something which that preaching creates. Religion is even more responsive to the touch of will than friendship or the state. The difference between the religious man and the nonreligious man is not that one has a whole-idea and the other has not. The difference lies in the different predicates which each attaches to his whole-idea.

Religion, in interpreting the whole as divine, makes the transition from the idea of the whole to the idea of God. But does the religious world view fit the facts any better than a nonreligious one? Believe in God and the world everywhere confirms that belief; lose it, and suddenly the facts confirm that there is no God. Even the mystics, the experts in faith, are subjected to a dark night of the soul where it is impossible to see the world as God's world. Perhaps, after all, the inner world is the only real one. Perhaps will is the whole of truth. Hocking suggests an imaginative voluntaristic recreation of the subjective mental process by which we might come to believe in God.

The modern world threatens us, but Hocking's point makes it clear that this is not solely a modern threat, even though the modern machine gives it particular force. There has always been

> . . . a grim and menacing aspect of reality which remains commonly unemphatic as our lives go but which events may at any time uncover. . . . The merciless processes of nature, of disease and death, of fate generally, are not impressed by entreaty or effort. . . . But in the human creature at bay there are other depths; the recognition of futility is the beginning of human adequacy. For despair ends by calling out a certain touch of *resentment*—resentment having a tinge of self-assertion in it, even of moral requirement directed against reality. . . . In that deep impulse of self-assertion there was involved, though I knew it not, *the will that my reality should be a living and responsible reality.* . . . The God-idea thus appears as a postulate of our moral consciousness.[13]

It does indeed tend to make itself good in experience, he suggests, because experience has this plasticity. Without the act of will there would be no discovery of God. And the ideas of God and of value do go hand in hand, because—so it seems—they are the same thing. From this perspective, faith is no longer the recognition of an objective quality in the world; faith is the loyal, moral energy which sees the world as plastic, and thus as capable of becoming something better. The religious creed turns out to be neither an empirical discovery nor a revelation but simply an "ideal" in the sense of an emotional commitment to what we believe ought to be.

If Hocking is right thus far, then the literal-mindedness of the West, of which we have already spoken, may be simply a lack of imagination—and perhaps even of humor. There is an imaginative freedom in religion's purport to be not only a world-maker, but a God-maker. Perhaps the empirical conscience of the West is, after all, only yet another form of that worldliness against which religion must always fight. God is transcendent and spiritual. The truth of God must be known only by that which is spirit in us. In the contact of spirit with Spirit isn't the interjection of "the things of this world" merely a hindrance?

So say those small sects whose poverty-stricken adherents have little to hope for in this world, and who rivet their attention on the after life. But arguments against a literal and historical approach to religion take other and more sophisticated forms. One of the issues in the "demythologizing" program of Rudolph Bultmann is its emphasis on the Lutheran principle of justification by grace through faith alone. Bultmann regards the doctrine of the resurrection of Christ as central to the Christian faith; but, if asked "did it really happen?" he responds by defining "really happen" in terms of the religious consciousness of those who believed. The event which is the resurrection is the coming-of-faith to the early church. Bultmann is not concerned to speculate on its possible historical grounding; he argues rather that biblical evidence does not tell us that it "happened" in the literal, naturalistic, historical sense. It tells us only that Christ claimed the church in the "faith-event" of the resurrection. To base our acceptance or rejection of this claim on the literal details of history is to demand evidence which simply does not exist. And more importantly, such a demand is an attempt to avoid the religious issue. Bultmann's doctrine of the incarnation is not without elements of literality, so that one cannot fairly call his theology "subjectivistic" without serious qualification. In the central doctrine of the resurrection, however, the question arises as to whether, by his own definition, the resurrection is not a "myth," and why this myth should be more acceptable to modern man than those which Bultmann feels must be rejected in order to make Christian faith and thought relevant to modern experience.[14]

Our question here, however, is whether either philosophy or religion can afford to reject naturalism *in toto*. Is the empirical conscience entirely irrelevant? Hocking's own early conversion was strongly subjective, and the energy with which he follows the threads of his early subjectivism in his dialectic indicates not only the rigor with which he is willing to test his main hypothesis, but also the appeal which its antithesis has for him. For all its appeal, however, the lesson which he draws from subjective idealism is that the world can be shaped by our inwardness—especially our wills—only because *the world* allows these developments. Subjective idealism as it stands is false.

It is only fair to note that "idea-ism" is readily drawn into a moral "idealism" by its own metaphysics. If mind is the stuff of the real, then the area of plasticity which we experience in our immediate world must extend, in some sense, to the whole. Realism, on the other hand, insisting that the world is *not* mind-stuff, emphasizes that the factuality of the world is obdurate and stubborn in response to our purposes. But, for the idealist, the venture of moral re-making begins with the conviction that the stuff of his visions is real; he is on the world's side. It is no accident that revolutionary movements regularly trace themselves back to idealistic sources. Marxist materialism, for example, is not so far from Hegel's idealism as it supposes, despite the fact that it "stands Hegel on his head" in insisting that the determining force in history is economic law, not reason. Marxism finds its touchstone not in the fact of economic law, but in the fact that it *knows the secret* of this law. It is confident that the Communist revolution is "on the side of history." This item of faith, which gives communism its "religious" character, is an indulgence which any pure realism abhors.

Hocking cannot accept subjective idealism as it stands.

> . . . I must believe that the great heave of the West to get a literal and objective grip upon its major religious objects is an advance, and not a retrogression. We only drive men to make their religion all prose, when we threaten to make it all poetry and postulate. . . .
>
> The destiny of religious truth to become universal and imperative must detach it at last from all salient subjectivity; and must state and define the *scope* of our creative possibilities *within the frame of that which independently Is.*[15]

His dialectic therefore insists on those elements of naturalism which we have already discussed as part of the "empirical conscience of the West." But it insists equally on the emphasis which subjective idealism gives to creative possibilities for the self. In his individualism, his idealism, and his "mysticism," the influence of subjective idealism is felt.

In his doctrine of the prophetic consciousness the insight of inwardness becomes a creative force in history. In politics, this doctrine has been directed in recent years to the conflict between the United States and the Soviet Union. Hocking points out, in *Strength of Men and Nations,* that the struggle which seemed so inevitable and desperate in the ten years after the war, does indeed have areas of plasticity which responsible men are honor-bound to explore. In religion the prophetic consciousness has been devoted to a subtle and often misunderstood attempt—in *Re-Thinking Missions, Living Religions and a World Faith,* and *The Coming World Civilization*—to outline a minimal basis for understanding and cooperation among men of different positive faiths, and to define the role of Western Christianity in the coming world civilization.

Prophecy, as Hocking understands its role in both politics and religion, is not only learning from the past, and discerning the signs of present times, but also an envisioning of the future which is not mere ideal, but the expression of man's creative power. This must be a power over facts if it is to be relevant to the real world; but it comes only to those determined to have power over recalcitrant facts. Given the limited areas of experience which prove themselves responsive to the working of our wills, Hocking feels, we have grounds for hope that the leaven of our ideal ends will infect increasing areas of the historical lump. From the political realist's perspective, of course, the crucial fact is the vast area of social life which the leaven has not yet touched. Realism rejects idealism as ever-hopeful and over-hopeful, and makes a sharp distinction between the ideal and the actual in history. The ideal appears as practically irrelevant —i.e. relevant in theory but not in practice. But if idealism tends too readily to think that we can build the kingdom (of economic equality, religious righteousness, or whatever), one notes in Hocking's defense that realism tends too readily to think that we do well just to hold the fort. I have always found Hocking's social and political thought too optimistic. Still, history must always be the judge of prophetic power. When *Strength of Men and Nations* first appeared in 1959, it seemed to many to be stronger on pious hope than on practical possibilities. Five years later, its case was strengthened by President Kennedy's historic address to the graduating class of the American University in June 1963, in which he argued that areas of common ground between America and Russia were real and must be expanded. Hocking's conviction turned out to be more "realistic" than it first appeared.

If Hocking's idealism has tended to optimism, it is perhaps more appropriate for us to be grateful than cynical. There have been more than enough hands to man the oars on the other side of the boat. Great crises in history probably call for more hope and creative energy, not less. For himself he can say,

> In the course of a lifetime of imprudent undertakings, one maxim I have been led to adopt is that no task is to be evaded merely because it is impossible. The relevant questions are: whether it requires to be done, and whether the circumstances point a finger in one's direction.[16]

His maxim is that "the criterion of reality is creativity, both for the world and for the individual."[17] The area in which this creativity is tested is fact as it exists in the objective reality of nature. Hocking's dialectic must now relate the separate worlds of nature and mind, and ask the crucial question concerning the reality of the absolute.

Chapter IV

MONISM, PLURALISM, AND
THE ABSOLUTE

BEFORE PRESENTING A SYSTEMATIC DEFENSE of his own adaptation of absolute idealism, Hocking asks two questions: "Do we need the Absolute?" "Would it do us any good if we had it?" He is too American to be caught succumbing to the weakness of German scholarship which, "though it be prolific of the Very True, must sweat to provoke an interest."[1] If the absolute is only an abstract theory, irrelevant to life as we live it, then it is best forgotten. Ideas have to work, because philosophy is concerned with what we really believe.[2] Hocking didn't need William James and the pragmatists to tell him this; he turned to James after his interest in Herbert Spencer precisely because Spencer didn't work. Spencer didn't explain what Hocking knew in his experience to be true. By the same token, no technical eclecticism, no neat theorizing about the absolute will do. It has to be something which we need, and something which we are interested in. There is a democratic spirit to Hocking's thought.[3] Although he wrote only one "popular" book (*What Man Can Make of Man*), he is obviously indebted to the tradition of *Lebensphilosophie*—the view that philosophy grows out of life-concerns and must meet the problems which they pose.

Ideas have to make a difference; they have to "cut some ice."

But who cares about the absolute today? Even before *The Meaning of God* was published, George Santayana had written an epitaph for absolute idealism: "Nothing will be disproved, but everything will have been abandoned." There is much evidence that Santayana was right. The Western world is increasingly secularized, and secularism—concern for the here and now, and a rejection of all that is beyond—is as much opposed to metaphysics as it is to religion. Short views are the order of the day, and the absolute (that longest of all possible long views) is out of fashion. Hocking himself admits that the modern era is over, that we are now involved in a "passage beyond modernity."[4] How can he argue that the old certitudes are still relevant? Haven't the Grand Conceptions and High Ideals of the recent past been chewed up in the grinding gears of this cultural shift to an unknown and as yet unformed post-modern world?

Not entirely. The movement for racial equality, interesting enough, is thoroughly absolutist. It does not admit any qualification of its guiding principle that civil rights are rights for all men. Even as personal ethics become more relativistic, social ethics become increasingly tied to absolutes, not only in civil rights, but in matters of war and peace. In philosophy, too, the absolute survives. It has prudently adopted more fashionable aliases, such as "reality," (humbly presented in the lower case) or—more bravely—"ultimate reality," or "being." "Metaphysics," hoping to escape its checkered past, now often answers to the name of "ontology." In all this a basic idea persists, however, and that is the idea of a stable, knowable reality which is the source of both meaning and value in the universe. Hocking continues to insist on the significance of the absolute, but he is keenly aware of the problems posed by the widespread disillusion with the traditional formulations of absolute idealism.

We have already found anticipations of the absolute in an epistemology centering in an idea of the whole. Philosophical realism inclines to accept this whole as a working element in our thinking. But whether a useful epistemological tool represents an objective metaphysical reality is another matter. Realism argues that we know only the whole-*ness* of our own experience. James A. Martin, Jr., agrees that the whole may be "a *co-implicate* of gross experience *when interpreted in a certain way*"[5] but not an independent metaphysical object. At issue here is Hocking's monism. Why should the unity of one's thought processes imply a metaphysical unity in the world? Or, put in terms of dialectical method, do thesis and antithesis necessarily come together in a metaphysical synthesis? We might argue that life requires a rough synthesizing in both our thoughts and our actions. The American college girl who spends a year in India and finds her thinking challenged and upset by entirely different ideas of, say, marriage and social responsibility, must synthesize the thesis of her America-self with the antithesis of her India-self before she can call her soul her own. But her own personal solution will not be the same as her neighbor's. We each need whole-*ness* for our moral integrity, but on what basis can we say that the world requires this of us?

We have become familiar with the fact that the world is full of loose ends which we cannot tie up neatly, either in morals or metaphysics, and we have learned to see real value in this pluralism. Even if we admit the necessity of principles, or behavioral norms, we must recognize that these are many in number and changeable in character. Is there any evidence, then, that our world has an ultimate, stable, and moral unity?

In reply Hocking points out that monism can be either optimistic (as with Hegel and Royce), or pessimistic (as with Schopenhauer). But he argues also that any truly hopeful view of man's prospects in the universe implies a kind of monism. A world without pluralism would indeed be a boring place. But,

> there is no pluralist who does not limit, and very profoundly limit, the sort of chance and accident which he admits into his world picture. Change occurs, new things are born, forces of many kinds drive at large, free individuals assert themselves freely: but all this variety and novelty takes place in *digestible quantities.* New creations are to be noted; but they begin small, in a more or less considerate manner, appearing in homes and other places where they can be taken care of. The pluralistic universe does not blurt and burst out in erratic and unmeasurable Facts, or unheard-of Kinds. The most revolutionary things that happen there are *revolutions:* each quietly contained for a time, in the form of a new idea, within the compass of some man's head. *The Mind* is in fact the hearth and brooding place of such wild Force and Novelty and Freedom as the pluralist most wishes to make way for. And the fortunate circumstance that these things have any brooding-place at all shows how important it is, even in pluralistic eyes, that the new should come with some reference to the old; the Many be not too fatally disruptive of the One.[6]

Hocking argues that we do, in fact, assume that the world is good.[7] It is only on the basis of this assumption that the presence of evil constitutes a problem. If we did not assume goodness, evil would be merely part of the varied content of experience. But the world-unity which mind makes possible must be substantial, and not merely formal. Hocking rejects the argument that even chaos has a unity in the idea which encompasses it. This formal concept of unity may satisfy the subjective idealist's intellectualism, but it is small comfort for the business of living. Purely "metaphysical" monism, and the deism which is its theological counterpart, Hocking maintains, makes sense of the universe for the absolute, or for God—but not for us.

By way of contrast, he notes that the monism of science deals with the processes of becoming in a way that purely formal monism does not. Natural science is an attempt to reduce the practical problems of man to one problem—the world problem—through an interlocking system of causes and effects. The unity thus achieved means that each fragmentary individual success solves an aspect of the world problem. This kind of unity does not eliminate freedom and variety; rather it makes them possible. Unity is the condition of freedom, for freedom is not mere indeterminateness; it is the possibility of creativity. Creativity seeks to establish something, and needs some ground of unity to receive this effort. Subjective idealism solves the problem of evil in a purely formal manner in which Hocking finds no existential relevance. The scientific reaction to the world problem, however, refers the particular evil to causes. One assumes that the problem was formed under definite conditions; the task is to master those conditions. Applied to morals, the task necessitates our discovering the good and working it out in every situation. But the scientific type of monism cannot solve the problem of evil by giving us a grip on the world's unity. The evils we face are simply too numerous to be taken on one by one and disposed of individually. Hocking points out here "the overcrowding of possibilities of choice" which Kierkegaard once called "the education of infinite possibility." We must each of us choose that aspect of the world which we will live and work in, leaving the rest. And we must work out our destiny on the assumption that the real is the good and that this can be known in that finite slice of the infinitely possible encompassed by each individual's experience.

This does not mean that one can make a conscious principle out of ignoring evil; Hocking does not intend that. Evil must be genuinely disposed of by whatever it is to which we turn our attention.

> If I assume of my neighbor that the reality of him is good, and that his faults are relatively non-real, this assumption is justified only as I actually grasp his faults as the seamy sides of his virtues, having their reality and their ultimate relief in the heightened life of those same positive qualities,—his wrath as part of his *spirit,* his hesitation as a phase of his self-consciousness—to be relieved by more self-consciousness, his shiftlessness an accident of his ideality—to be remedied by a more vigorous ideality, not by mere battle against shiftlessness.[8]

Ignoring evil is justified when the evil is known to be part of a total reality which is good. Hocking retains an element of the scientific reaction to evil in referring to this known evil as an "alterable aspect" of that ultimately good reality. Given the plurality of evils in our world, he contends, we solve our personal problem of evil only by giving ourselves to some cause or aim in the belief that it participates in the character of the *one* reality which is ultimately good and enduring. We must "let go" the majority of moral discontinuities in our experience, simply because we cannot hope to master their infinite complexity. We must get on with the business of living with the ones which directly concern us.

But we cannot do it with any ultimate hope, Hocking tells us, unless we do so on the positive ground that the good does and will prevail; that evil as such is ultimately alterable and will be altered. If unfinished moral business is constantly lurking on the rim of our world, threatening to break in on us and destroy our hope, we are not free and our hope remains unestablished. Without an element of monistic optimism, our failure to fight all the moral battles of the world is immoral. And, Hocking notes, the attempt to fight all of them results in despair.

> The only hope of finding the Real to be one and good is in . . . sifting-right, in the circumstance that the universe is not utterly organic, and that we are not compelled to absorb into our structure all the false scaffolding we have raised. Unless our monism were thus saturated with pluralism and absolute death, we should have no power to move under the burden of our past. . . . Whatever the ultimate goal of Reality there is leisure for working it out; the creator has been generous with time, with the material of existence, the cloth of history, and most of it is wasted. It looks at times as if he had been equally prodigal of men. Only the Nature of things is One and Good; all the "empirical stuff" is as yet unmeasured and unjudged. . . . The monism of the world is such only as to give meaning to its pluralism; our belonging to God such only as gives us greater hold upon ourselves.[9]

As an answer to "the problem of evil"—i.e., Hume's wonderfully perplexing question as to why a good God would make a world with evil in it—the preceding discussion is not very helpful. Hocking offers no evidence that the real *is* one and good. He does not indicate what sort of evidence might prove his thesis, nor does he deal with the methodological question by showing us how to go about "sifting right." He is so far from coming to terms with the problem in its traditional formulation that one gradually realizes he is not attempting to deal with the problem in these terms at all. The traditional formulation centers on the logical contradiction between a good Creator and an evil creation. Later in his life Hocking did suggest a line of attack on this contradiction, noting that Hume's formulation of the problem of evil assumes that God could, if he chose, eliminate evil without changing anything else in the world or could have made the world as we know it without its evil. This, Hocking argued, was a false assumption, inconsistent with current findings in theoretical physics. He came to believe that any alteration within a space-time field would alter the entire field. The question which Hocking is addressing himself to here, however, is a pragmatic question, and the solution which he offers is largely voluntaristic. The question is: "What kind of attitude toward evil is logically required if we are to live creatively in a world where evil exists?" If he can show, pragmatically, that a certain minimal optimism is necessary for a creative life in this admittedly evil world, then he can conclude that the world, in spite of its evil, necessarily embodies the good which makes that optimism possible. This is an application of his negative pragmatism. Like Royce—who taught that the best way to know whether or not you had hold of an absolute was to try getting along without it and see whether or not it worked—Hocking tries to show that without optimism we are subject to a despair which cuts down our capacity to live and work creatively.

This is a graceful, even charming way of dealing with the problem. The argument begins with so little—man's need to hope—and conjures up The Good itself. Subjective idealism in its optimistic form specializes in such effortless evaporations of other men's difficulties, however, and one wonders whether Hocking isn't saying only that if you want goodness, and believe in it, then its yours. That would be too clever by half, and this is not an issue on which we can tolerate people who play games. The problem of evil provides a good test of philosophical seriousness. Is Hocking dealing seriously with evil in a way that helps, or is he just being clever?

An English colleague of mine who survived the blitz in London once said of Hocking: "He seems never to have gone through an air raid." That is a fair comment. Hocking was something of a Victorian. His dress, his manners, the style and extent of his letter writing, the special quality of his friendships are all those of the Victorian gentleman. He was not easily deceived by other people, and his expectation of what life had to offer was almost never extravagant, but he was a successful and genuinely happy man, and optimism came more naturally to his generation than it does to ours. This accounts for a touch of glibness in an argument which was first shaped in 1912. It would be niggardly to begrudge him his good cheer, however; nor is glibness the issue. The issue is whether or not his view is shallow, and the critical criterion for a voluntaristic approach to evil such as Hocking's is psychological rather than purely logical. Do we really need a minimal optimism in order to live effectively (creatively) in a world which often seems intent on destroying us? The faintly romantic despair of popular existentialism insists, with Sartre, that we must go it alone in positing our own good in spite of the world's evil. This is subjective idealism in its pessimistic form, but does despair really work?

Hocking insists that despair is the subjective option because it says, in effect: "I must act as I do *in spite of* the way life is." Hocking counters: "I must act as I do *because of* the way life is. Life itself *requires* that I should act in this way." Like the late medieval voluntarism of Ockham, and in the pragmatic tradition of his own day, Hocking takes the will of God as the definitive element in the ultimate being and comes to a knowledge of being through will. Hocking denies that we can "make up" a direction for our own purpose. We must find it, and it is dictated to us by experience. But, he says, the experience is not merely personal. It is human experience if we deal with it at its deepest level. From such experience, so understood, we discover not only what we are to do personally, but what life is like objectively. This is what he means by the assertion that "experience is metaphysical." Its demands are our window on the world, on the nature of being itself. Because the touchstone of life is creativity, Hocking says, the discovery of the direction in which one's own creativity must run is a discovery of a truth about the nature of things. "For the good of men, for their good-hope as also for their rightful darings and commitments, some concrete conscious monism is a necessary condition."[10]

The question remains, however. Does metaphysical despair work as a creative way of life? The question of man's most basic instinct for meaning-in-survival probably lies beyond laboratory experiment or questionnaires. In spite of his Victorianism, my experience is that Hocking is essentially right. I suspect that only the very great and the very sick can declare the world basically meaningless and evil and survive on the resources of meaning and value generated from their own isolated inwardness.

William James had argued that the absolute is "useless for deductive purposes. It gives us absolute safety if you will, but it is compatible with every relative danger. Whatever the details of experience may prove to be, after the fact of them the absolute will adopt them. It is an hypothesis which functions retrospectively only, not prospectively."[11] Hocking takes this to be the basic criticism of the absolute. He agrees with James that principles which make no difference to the detailed practical business of living are irrelevant. Idealism, too, is concerned with workability. Nothing seems more "idealistic" than Hegel's famous mistranslated dictum that "the rational is the real, and the real rational."[12] Yet reality here is *wirklich,* from the transitive verb *wirken* (to work), indicating an element of realism in Hegel's speculations.[13] And James himself, for all his tough-minded pluralism, was not entirely immune to the idealist's concern for a knowable unity in one's working world. Nevertheless, James' pluralism has a point which Hocking is quick to admit: the absolute, the real, the substantial, does have a certain barrenness to it, as implied in the phrase "non-impulsive background" with which he has characterized the idea of the whole. But if the absolute is "compatible with every relative danger," perhaps, he suggests, it is also compatible with every relative advance. Can we have relative truths without some ultimate truth which relates them to one another? Are we free to judge the achievements of others, positively or negatively, without the assumption that we are all concerned with the same world, and therefore have an objective, substantial basis for judgment?

Eternal truths by themselves are barren. The loom of our whole-idea comes alive only with the weaving in of minor premises. But Hocking argues that this empty major premise of eternal truth has a necessary minor premise in the self, and that reality is known at that point where the character of the self meets the objective nature of the world. The uselessness or barrenness of the absolute results from the subjectivism with which it has been associated, a subjectivism which Hocking labels the "reflexive turn" of thought. In epistemology, for example, we ask what we can know with certainty, in order to avoid error. Descartes pursues uncertainty to the point where it yields an absolute assurance: that because I doubt I cannot doubt that I am doubting; therefore I exist. But does Descartes *use* this truth? The answer is "no," because the truth has no bearing on the objective world, which is what our epistemology seeks to know.

A similar irrelevance plagues Kantian ethics. In a world of relative moral principles it proclaims as absolute the law that there shall be a law. For the Kantians, absolute morality lies not in the world of actions, but in the reflexive turn which insists on duty for the self. And in metaphysics, when ideas of matter or force or energy dissolve, on analysis, into mere formulae for what can generally be expected from experience, Berkeley finds consciousness the reality upon which all other reality depends. Here again, the absolute is contained within the self, and the objective reality of a "world-not-myself" has escaped us. Hocking tells us that these convictions—along with the religious affirmation that heaven and hell are within us—are heirs of stoicism, that "first pure case of the reflexive turn in history" (or, at least, in Western history) arguing, as it did, that I myself am the source and power of my own absolute good. And none of them answer our need for objective reality. The absolute of the "reflexive turn," he concludes, is an irrelevant universal.

To say that the absolute is useless is to argue that it is indifferent—without value for us. But is it possible, he asks, that this realm of the indifferent does make a difference to us that is valuable? Take our example of the scientist. Hocking has been arguing that nature is that area of pungency, particularity, and otherness which sets the standard of the objectively real. The scientist subjects his hypothesis to the test of reality and forsakes it if it does not meet that test. He wants to know whether it is factual—true for any observer.

He may be working on a theory which, if true, would provide a cure for cancer; but the worthiness of his purpose is irrelevant to the objective test. The real is indifferent to our purposes; it judges only whether the theory in question fits the facts.

Why does the scientist submit to this test? Because, Hocking answers, he has a passion for this "reality-that-has-no-passions." He has need of a judgment which will take no account of how long he has worked on the problem, or whether he is a good man, or whether his theory is clever and original. Such judgments make a difference to us as men, but the one thing which makes the greatest difference is the judgment of the indifferent on our work. If the theory of the scientist—or whatever object of interest to any observer—meets this test of indifferent reality, then, by virtue of meeting that test successfully, it becomes valuable. Reality, per se, is a value, he insists. Or, take the love of life for its own sake. Men have a passion for simply being that seems to defy all rational explanation, particularly when the contents of life are tragic and full of evils. But can this "instinct of self-preservation" perhaps be explained as attachment to the source of all values?

Again Hocking reminds us that our idea of the whole—the world-reality and life-reality which religion finds to be personal in the God-reality—is easily ignored since it is regularly what we think *with,* and not what we are thinking *of.* To say that it is the reservoir of all values seems a bit far-fetched. But consider: If we support Jones for President rather than Smith, it is—we say—because Jones is the better man. And what is the measure of this value? We approve of Jones' policies; he agrees with our foreign-policy-idea and our what-is-good-for-America-idea. But such agreement inevitably, although unobtrusively, involves our what-is-man-idea and our what-kind-of-a-world-are-we-living-in-idea. In shocking us into seeing that our whole-idea is in constant use and is the source of our values, Hocking casts about, somewhat impishly, for a strikingly ridiculous illustration.

> With what idea, pray, do I think hat? With the hat-idea, to be sure. Yes, but is the clothing-idea unconcerned?—or the city-street-idea? or the civilized-society-extraordinary-require-ments-idea? or the whole mass of aesthetic notions, and po-litical, historical, even religious opinions? With all these, and with all other ideas summing themselves up currently in my whole-idea, hat is thought.[14]

Because the real is the active criterion of value in our thinking on everything from hats to presidential candidates and beyond, Hocking is free to draw a conclusion which il-luminates the problem of knowing both God and the people around us: "Love itself . . . is not a thing apart from knowl-edge."[15] People, admittedly, are not scientific theories; the scientist whose love of truth makes him abandon an idea that does not work will not be justified in abandoning a wife who does not produce his dinner when he wants it. But I think Hocking is right that the love of the scientist for the real is not unlike our love for other people. Love and sympathy are not pure emotions. The helpful counsellor is not one who supports our every misconception about our-selves, but one who helps us see the truth—however hard—of who we actually are. And in times of crisis—such as those brought about by a death in the family—sympathy which is lacking in knowledge of what is real about the people in-volved is sentimentally irrelevant. Worse than that, it is demonic, since it tries to shield us from something which we must face—the real fact of death.

The saying is that all the world loves a lover. Let us expand this saying, it is always the lover whom we love; *we cannot love anyone except the lover!* The intrinsically valuable thing about a man is his capacity for love—whatever form it takes, whether of persons, or beauty, or truth. . . . Perhaps the reality of the object of your emotions does not matter, since the emotion itself is what counts? No. Poor mankind, impoverished for the substance of worth, does in fact sustain itself largely by its enjoyment of enjoyers, and sets an inordinate value on these temperaments which spontaneously flow out in affirmations of value. But underneath lies the craving for *reality in appreciation.* . . . The ultimate question cannot be evaded: Is the world worth our devotion? If you say, "No," the whole system of values is in for slow collapse.[16]

Here Hocking admits James' point: the absolute must be compatible with every relative evil and danger, since it could not otherwise be the absolute. The absolute must be that which continues to hold good, no matter what happens. What, then, are we to say about the goodwill or justness of an ultimate reality which "maketh his sun to rise on the evil and the good, and sendeth rain on the just and the unjust"? Shall we say simply that this is part of the mystery of God's hidden purposes? Or can we say that divine indifference to relative evils is an expression of absolute justice? If so, how could one escape James' criticism that such an absolute justice is the supreme example of irrelevance and uselessness for deductive purposes?

Stoicism uses absolute indifference as a defense against the slings and arrows of a world which it cannot trust and from which it retreats into the haven of the self. Hocking's response, so seemingly similar, is precisely the opposite. Because the world is to be trusted, one is freed from fear and able to see absolute indifference as an expression of absolute love. Royce had said that divine attention is equivalent to divine love. Hocking finds in this "care-full" consideration of the world by the absolute the secret of human creativity. He would agree that "what is" makes no difference to us as it stands. But when the self becomes conscious of what is— i.e. the absolute moral unity of reality—it grasps a principle which is "the only radically creative attitude yet known to humanity."[17] Assured that the good is real, man is free to create the good in his world, knowing that this work is substantial. In so saying Hocking implicitly rejects both the demand of the "verification principle"—that we establish an empirical proof for the absolute, and the demand in its inverted form, the "falsification principle"—that we indicate what empirical conditions could prove the absolute false. The premise on which these demands are based is that truth is limited to empirical facts. Such an assertion about truth is itself beyond the test of empiricism, indicating that even radical empiricism must go beyond itself in order to establish its guiding principle. The absolute, if it is truly absolute, cannot be verifiable or falsifiable in empirical terms. But it is relevant to empirical facts, in both the present and the prospective future, in setting the standard for a creative *modus vivendi,* in its attentive concern for the world.

God's attention and our consciousness of it in a "sense of the presence of God" are widely thought to be only a preliminary to God's real value to us, which is found rather in his differential work. Hocking's theology makes much of this differential activity of a personal God in the incarnation and the sacrifice of the cross. His philosophy of religion, however, emphasizes the importance of the simple fact that the real source of all being is constantly attentive to us and our world. The work of religion, after all, is to redeem lost souls. And what is a lost soul?

Our life is a process of conversation between ourselves and the whole of the world in which we live. It is possible for human beings to talk to one another with their lips and be remote from one another in their hearts. Falsehood and selfishness create chasms between man and man; and the professions of friendship have always to be tested by the inner facts of sincerity and love.

These principles of human intercourse are also valid for this continuous conversation between the individual and his world. A man may be at odds with his world and he may be in harmony with his world; but there is everything in human experience to give us, as we look at the facts of nature and at the facts of history, a sense of loneliness in the presence of the great unknown. There it is in its immensity, operating according to natural laws, opaque, silent, inscrutable, frequently cruel, and apparently uninterested in the lot of us poor human beings.

Then, too, in the group which we call humanity, there is something massive, something immense, something in the pre-occupation of individuals and of social wholes, which makes the individual person feel that he is alone and uncared for, and that his only possible policy is one of struggling with might and main to gain for himself by snatching from the whole what he can.

Now in so far as a person maintains this picture of the universe, he is a lost soul: he cannot see beyond that horizon which closes his life in nothingness and means the ultimate wiping out of the race. He cannot see any meaning in his own life beyond what he can enforce by dint of his own self-assertion. In so far as we feel in ourselves this absence of confidence, this absence of certainty, this fear of calamity and of death, this servitude to chance, this rebellion, this poor guesswork of questions thrown into the void and receiving no answers, we are lost.

The only thing which could come to us to make it possible for us to deal in full honor and trust with the world, and with each other, is some assurance *that these appearances are not true;* some assurance that out of the silence there is a voice which speaks, and in the callous machinery of the cosmos there is a heart which cares and a purpose which plans. *Whatever brings this assurance comes as a saviour.* The saviour, to you, is that event, that person, that word, in which you can say, "The Universe speaks to me"; "God speaks to me."[18]

This discussion serves to reopen the question of the absolute. Perhaps it is, after all, a useful concept. But desire and need do not insure reality. Sartre, for example, wants God and needs God but has the courage of his atheistic conviction that God is gone. What we now require is some proof that what we need actually exists; for this proof we return to the problem of knowing other minds.

Chapter V

SELFHOOD, NATURE, AND

OTHER MIND

HOCKING'S METAPHYSICS DEVELOPED in response to a particular challenge, the challenge of solipsism. As he had announced in the preface to his doctoral dissertation, "I wish to restore the stinging reality of contact with the human comrade which [monadism] obscures." His is a social philosophy, a "philosophy of communication," concerned with establishing the terms of genuine dialogue between man and man. To know an "other mind" would be to know its world and the content of its thought, precisely as being known by an other. We have noted Hocking's experience of shock when he realized that he occupied the "great room" of the other's mind by virtue of sharing a common world. Hocking's defense of this experience begins with the question whether social experience is, as it seems to be, an intermittent thing (are not social occasions interspersed among moments of solitude?), or whether it is, like our experience of nature (which we never entirely escape, since we are always in the world, even in sleep), a continuous experience. His argument is that social experience (in a minimal sense) has to be continuous; that if it were not, we would be unable to begin it. It is true, of course, that other people come and go—or at least their bodies do. But if we recall the embarrassment of looking for the mind of the other behind his forehead only to discover that his thought was literally "out here" in the world, we will be prepared for Hocking's statement that "his body appears and disappears to our sight; but his environment does not disappear."[1] The immediate objects which we shared when we were together are no longer perceived by him once he goes away. Immediate objects, however, are knowable only in a context of space, time, energy, causality, etc., which remains constantly known, wherever we move within it. Thus Hocking asserts: "If, therefore, at any time I have known an Other; and in knowing him have known Nature as his object; then this same Nature,—with its Space-field, Force-field, and the like—does not cease to be *his Object* when he disappears."[2] In order for any two beings to communicate, they must already have a common field through which to approach one another. This common field (space, time, etc., or, more simply, nature) implies an element of contact or presence between two communicators—out of which the varieties and intensities of specific communication develop. Without the possibility of communication inherent in the common medium of communication, social experience would be impossible. "If then, experience ever becomes actually social, it has, in more rarefied condition, always been so; and hence is, in the same fundamental sense, continually so."[3]

Hocking is attacking the current "double-translation" theory of communication, which holds that all communication from A to B comes through sensation in a process which requires two translations. The first is from A's thought to some physical sign capable of affecting B's sense receptors, and eventually B's brain. The second is from this physical image to terms of comprehension in B's thought. Hocking, however, remembering his experience of sharing a common mind, asks, "what would happen if someone meditating on the wonder of human communication should conclude that double-translation itself would never have arrived—that speech itself would never have been thought of—without some directer experience of other mind to sustain the working out of the code?"[4] He answers his own question by examining Whitehead's assertion that factuality is the point of departure for thought, not an area to be explored or "explained." During the joint seminar which Hocking and Whitehead taught at Harvard in the spring of 1934 (given to the topic "What do we mean when we appeal to experience?") Whitehead had objected to any rationalizing of factuality by saying: "Hang it all, *here we are!* We don't go back of that, we begin with it."[5] For his part, Hocking insists on asking what it means that facts are as they are in our experience; it is through an analysis of factuality that he establishes his thesis concerning direct communication.

Hocking is one of those philosophers who made up his mind what he thought when he was relatively young. When *The Meaning of God* went into a fourteenth edition, fifty years after the first, it was still the major statement of his philosophy. While he never published the systematic metaphysics which he long planned, he nevertheless clarified two of his basic categories, those of fact and destiny, and quite radically recast the third, that of self.[6] *The Meaning of God* is full of the objectivity of nature as space-time continuum, but Hocking does not there attempt to make the factuality of Nature a rounded-out metaphysical category. It is, however, obvious from his numerous references to Whitehead that their work together helped him to refine his categories. Several key essays of the past twenty years bear the fruits of that work.

Generally speaking, a fact is "the existent object of a

single act of intention."[7] A fact can be as big as a war or as small as a snowflake; but either way it is exclusive. It leaves out the total context in which it takes place in order that we may fully come to terms with the particular datum which is the fact itself. The implication of the term "datum," like that of Hume's term "impression," is that there is an outside force which gives the fact or makes the impression. And "force" is just the word, since there is no escaping fact. In this sense, all facts are hard facts, even though they are largely enjoyable.[8] The hardness of fact refers to *what* the fact is; but the existence of fact, showing simply *that* the fact is, has its own importance. Factuality in this sense is the test of truth against falsity, the reality of being against non-being. What's more, fact is, it would seem, impenetrable. It is not to be understood, but only accepted. As Whitehead says, it is where we must begin. But Hocking queries: "Must we also end with it?" For him, this is "the issue on which philosophy as distinct from science stands or falls."[9] If fact remains impenetrable it turns "brute" because it continues "dumb." And, of course, radical empiricism, and all the forms of logical positivism, linguistic and analytical philosophy which have rallied under its banner, insist that it is precisely factuality in this sense which is the final test of all truth. They insist that we must "accept the facts"—as though we could do anything else! But the "scientific" approach, in creating a science of man, has aroused an opposite response from existentialism. The scientific attempt to describe, predict, and control the human phenomenon produces, in reaction, the existentialist insistence that man's existence precedes his essence—i.e. that man makes himself. *That* he is determines *what* he is, for man is free. This fact, at least, is neither "brute" nor "dumb." But let's go back to Whitehead.

"Here we are." Whitehead offers it as a ground for all further judgments. The observation is basic, rock bottom, empirical. But Hocking wants to know the function of the word "here" that provides the context for the "we." The "here" is the crucial "third" element, the meeting ground of the first "I-exist" with the second. He has already argued that this common ground is necessary for any social experience, and that the continuing presence of the ground makes the social experience (in a rarefied condition) also continuous. If we accept the necessity of this ground, then we can agree that Hocking has brought nature into the orbit of social experience, which is not, after all, a very difficult task. The difficulty lies in the fact that this "third," the "here" of Nature, now stands *between* the two communicators, both joining and separating. Searching for a direct social experience by making natural fact the coin of communication, Hocking has, at this point, made intersubjectivity clearly indirect. (And, we might add, he has landed himself in the same fix for which he criticized Royce.) He recognizes this, admitting that "much, perhaps most, human intersubjectivity *is* indirect."[10] Most close friendships are made by common endeavor, the sharing of common goals and values, the common memories and hopes which Royce explored so expertly. A "fellow" is one with whom we have shared something. We are friends because we rowed together in college, because we are professional colleagues, because we took a trip together. It is this "third" which associates us, binds us together.

But is this binding ingredient in our association entirely external to us? Is it totally refractory, obdurate? We could not have become friends without it; Hocking is clear about that. That is to say, our coming together requires that the "third" should be genuinely "other" than each of us, so as to take us "outside" ourselves and "into" a new relationship. Yet the "third" is not totally "other," as witnessed by the fact that the experience is binding; it is a "common" experience; it "unites" us. We can even say that association is possible because, in some sense, we share a "common mind" about the purposes, goals, values, delights, interests of the association. As long as we continue using quotation marks in this description of our social relationships we can command wide agreement. These are terms of everyday speech used by people of every philosophical persuasion and no philosophical persuasion. Hocking, however, is looking for something more than an agreeable metaphor. He wants "literal" truth. Let's dispense with the quotation marks. Do we actually share a common mind?

A large part of Royce's failure to solve the problem of solipsism centered around the discrete character of individuals within the infinite community. Each individual fact, whether natural or personal, is exclusive. Hocking's attack on the problem is to ask where this discreteness comes from and whether fact is only discrete. He has indeed been saying that fact is exclusive. The outline of fact, in the act of attention which defines it, is necessarily discrete. Attention discovers fact by plucking a definable piece from the totality of experience. At any given moment experience is a torrent of sensations flooding over us. We derive factuality out of this torrent by narrowing the scope of general awareness to concentration on a particular item. We pick a bit of flotsam out of the stream of consciousness. Since the purpose of the fact-finding venture is to define and analyze the fact itself, Hocking says, we concentrate on it and not on the context from which it was taken. In itself, the fact is indeed refractory, atomic, "hard" in its *what*-ness. But *that* the fact is takes us back to the original context of which it is a part. Our con-

sciousness of fact, Hocking suggests, has a double character.
Having deliberately renounced wholeness in order to make
the discrete fact possible to consciousness in the first place,
the whole remains "as present to thought, and as pertinent
to the nature of the fact attended to."[11] We always deal with
the facts in their particularity or in the limited groupings
which serve scientific explanation. Yet the larger fact of the
context is always there as the shadow accompanying all particular factuality. The fact is always itself, but it is also the
total context with something left out. "In a journey of 100
miles, we have to say of each intermediate point that we
have come (say) 40 miles, and that we have (say) 60 miles yet
to go. This negative or reciprocal aspect of fact may be the
more important aspect, as when a cashier whose books call
for $100,000 can show assets of [only] $90,000."[12]

We know particular facts as belonging to a whole, and we
know this whole as a common object of interest to other
minds, and therefore a common content of other mind. We-
consciousness in society is based on common tasks and loyalties, but this indirect bond is itself based on an awareness
which is an ever present groundwork of intersubjectivity.

> The groundwork must be non-occasional. To discern it
> we must look away from specific symbols, interests, messages,
> transactions, the enormous volume of the day's give and
> take, to a more pervasive level of experience. It must be less
> a trans-pathy of ideas than a trans-pathy of existence or
> presence. We approach that ground-level in our constant
> undertone awareness of "the world," never as "my" world,
> always as "our" world knowable by all on the same terms.
> Or again, in our awareness of such truth as you or I may
> light upon not as "my" truth but as "our" truth,—truth for
> man as man.[13]

It is this "truth for man as man" which is the presupposition of all science, as Hocking understands it. Science is possible only as it imparts preliminary knowledge—i.e. that experiments carried out in Boston are also valid for Bombay, given the same controlled conditions. It is this availability of "my" truth to other minds who, in confirming it, acknowledge it as "our" truth which makes it objective. When science talks about objectivity, it means that the declared truth is true for any observer. Objective truth is public truth. "Physical experience, taken as solitary experience, has no very perfect independence of my Self," Hocking notes.[14] It dissolves almost instantly from sensation into memory, which is entirely internal to the self and reliant on its mental capacities. There are, for example, innumerable isolated individuals who say they have had the physical experience of seeing a flying saucer. The newspaper reader is not inclined to credit the report as objective, however, even if a reputable citizen makes the claim. It becomes objective when it has been publicly attested and made available for whomever wishes to test the claim for himself. In other words, other mind is guarantor of physical objectivity. We experience nature not as our private experience of the world, but as shared experience. The other mind who shares it is not identified, and therefore this intersubjectivity is only partial, latent, impersonal. But we could not know the objects of our experience as common, unless one knew that other mind existed.

It is on the basis of this latent intersubjectivity that Hocking was able to say that solipsism is a tenable, almost impregnable, philosophical theory—but a theory that has never been believed.

It is not merely inconsistent with our natural behavior, as when solipsists commune with their fellows, or when Mrs.

Ladd-Franklin, solipsist by logical conviction, writes to Bertrand Russell expressing "surprise that there are not more of us." It is further inconsistent with its own assumptions. For the proposition "I am incurably alone" implies that I know what being-alone is contrasted with: the proposition is significant only if I know what it would be like to be not-alone. But if I were constitutionally alone I would be unaware of that fact, having no conception of the opposite condition of being.[15]

This is perhaps a bit too adroit on Hocking's part. More compelling, I think, is his fascination with the fact that Descartes felt his *Cogito* a discovery which he wanted to publish. Admittedly, Descartes clearly does not mean "René Descartes thinks; therefore René is." To make such an assertion the theme of a philosophical publication would try the patience of even the most admiring reader. But no; the fact that Descartes *announces* it is evidence of his assumption that he has here uncovered an element of universality in the human situation. It is this assumption that Hocking is exploring.

A clarifying word is needed on the "thirds" or the "between" things which unite disparate minds in common endeavor. The issue is whether the occasional intersubjective work of these thirds is possible apart from a constant, minimal intersubjectivity between oneself and one's world. The establishing of this intersubjectivity is the point and purpose of Hocking's metaphysics, not only because it leads to the religious conception of God, but because it provides the divided human communities of our contentious world with the metaphysical assurance that we do in fact live in a community, and that all movements for peaceful cooperation can rely on this bond as the cornerstone of the coming world civilization. Hocking's thirds fall into two distinct groups, roughly distinguishable as universal and particular. The universalistic thirds are those items of common experience which are most characterized by selfhood and idea—for example, a political creed which unites us in a campaign for that poignant universal, peace. The particularistic thirds are those items of common experience most characterized by nature and empirical factuality—for instance, the space and time context of a geology field trip which unites us in an exploration of igneous rocks.

To Hocking, "universal" in this context does not imply either logical inclusiveness or extensive generality; rather it suggests a qualitative claim on human concern. In this sense we say that peace is a universal human value, even though there are political units extant which welcome inevitable class warfare. This universal is not only *my* good, but *our* good. Thus Hocking says, "with this understanding, it is evidently a matter of simple identity to say that as one finds and serves the universal he promotes community; or obversely, that there can be no genuine community among men except through this their several hold on the universal. And it is equally evident that this hold, as a function of human freedom, is and must be variable through an enormous range."[16] It is this universal which Gabriel Marcel sees as the solution to the problem of community posed by contemporary mass society. In modern technical society mass man is related to his fellows functionally, as one part of a machine to another. What he needs is to find his bonds in some universal human goals and values. His functional relationships are more or less compulsory; the businessman must submit to the demands of the organization. The universal, on the other hand, is an invitation. The values and ideals of the American civil rights movement are not given, for example; they do not "pre-exist as salient mental property."[17] They are uncovered through the give and take processes of historical development (dialectic). These universals are vulnerable insofar as they depend upon the existence of individual wills which appropriate them; but they are not destructible. In another context which we shall deal with in detail when we come to his philosophy of history, Hocking speaks of historical development neither in terms of the old liberal idea of progress nor in terms of modern skepticism's idea of a more or less meaningless historical flux. Hocking argues that there is a ratchet built into history whereby some things, once achieved, are not lost. Discover technology and it stays discovered; you can develop a better technology, but there is no going back on it to a pretechnological medievalism (despite its lures of cultural integration) or pre-industrial romanticism (despite its lures of pastoral peace and oneness with nature). Those universals which foster intersubjectivity, however, are rather less firmly established than those which bring material gain. We give up peace for a season if we feel we must; but under what circumstances would we give up our automobiles? Only if some better form of transportation were immediately provided. The intersubjective universal can be realized only in degree, and Hocking agrees with Marcel that it

> . . . can be achieved in depth only in smaller groups. . . . It can enter into the empirical datum only to the extent that it cannot be wholly absent while the human will is still human. It is therefore partly a fact, a discoverable datum. But it is only partly a fact, and partly a passionate need whose nature is a search for brotherhood, a wish for intimacy, and whose generic name is 'love,'—love as the child of Poverty rather than of Plenty but never ceasing to hope and now and then tasting fulfillment.[18]

A second group of universals, according to Hocking, is made up of those "enveloping particulars" which characterize our lives as physical beings. The most comprehensive of these is simply the world. He calls the world the most particular of all particulars, claiming: "Make this world different in any one of its indenumerably infinite specifications and you alter its impingement on each of us, probably altering each particular self in the process."[19] The world is indeed a common fact; we can all agree on Whitehead's "here we are" and on a set of general factual terms which govern our being here, and on the conditions under which we must all operate. These facts are beyond the scope of individual preference. They are "given" and we must accept them. But precisely because of this inescapable givenness, these facts are irrational; they just are—or as Whitehead puts it, "we don't go behind that." We have already noted that man is capable of a certain resentment at this situation. But have we done justice to fact by making the negative judgment that it is irrational, or, as the existentialists have it, absurd? Hocking offers some considerations:

i. That every particular world, unless someone discovers a necessary particular, must be in the eye of the universal an irrational;

ii. That since every human existence must be particular or nothing, this same irrationality inheres in our own being.

Thus far he is squarely in the existentialist camp. But alienation from the world of fact is not the total picture. There is one more consideration, which for him is crucial:

iii. That when love supervenes, it is precisely the particulars that become significant, and indeed beyond price.[20]

What does this dual emotional context of absurdity and pricelessness say about the fact of our received sense data? Hocking knows that particularity is (among other things) the price of love. There is philosophical perception in the ballad's insistence that "I know my love by her way of walking," and the identification of mind and body which distinguishes us, makes us separate, is crucial to life itself. "Without our particular insertion in space and time there would be no historical journey at all, with its particular hopes, adventures and partial achievements."[21] Whitehead's "here we are" requires no further vindication as a direct empirical datum except the implication, hidden within it, that we could not know that we are here, apart from our prior knowledge in experience that the here is itself a social ground of communication between selves, and not simply a physical theater which is unmindful of the seating of the house or the drama enacted on its stage. The key consideration here is Hocking's argument that nature is to be known as an area of mind because it is creative of mind in oneself. Let the Walter Mitty imagination run riot; it is physical fact that brings us back to earth with the sobering truth that "here we are" in a less exotic world. Let the grip of tragic drama fill us with foreboding; it is the sunshine or the reassuring street noises outside the theater that bring us back to earth with the glad truth that "here we are" in a more hopeful world. In an age when neurosis has infected cultures and nations, Hocking suggests that the tangible realities of nature, as much as any other single force, keep us sane. To be cut off from nature—by a loss of sight or hearing—is to be diminished *as a self* and requires a major struggle to reestablish oneself, largely through enhancing those senses which are still intact. It is the outer reality of nature which sustains us, which indeed makes us who we are by constantly supplying mind with that something without which it is unable to think at all. Hocking asks,

Is not that outer activity then essentially *creative* in its constant action (as probably also in its original action)—creative of *me?* My dependence upon Nature, my momentary submission to its independent, obstinate, objective decision of what Fact and Truth shall be, both in principle and in detail:—is not this a finding of my own mind? It is here, in this momentary (as well as permanent) creation of my Self that I begin, I say, to find Nature taking on the aspect of an Other Mind.[22]

We have already noted that the term datum or given implies a gesture from nature toward the perceiver. The factuality of nature is, on the one hand, objective and indifferent; on the other hand, it is creative of mind. Since the fact of mind is impossible without Nature, Hocking finds it impossible to clear nature of selfhood, although not the selfhood of any particular self. For it is not necessary that man should think a world. Sensation, per se, does not constitute a world; world-building requires energy and implies a motive. Part of the motive is aesthetic or recreational; not all the protestations of reluctant school boys can hide the fact that thinking is part of "the *élan vital* of the thinking animal."[23] But, Hocking realizes, since one cannot exist without sense experience, the giving of sense experience is also a giving of one's own existence. This is a creative action, creative of mind in the perceiver. To be thus given a world through the creative action of sense perception is, for him, to call forth a response to the giver on the part of the receiver. The thinking of a world is precisely this appropriate response. The primitive and immediate intersubjectivity of this process goes unnoticed because it is not marked by sur-

prise or any sense of attainment, for there has been no prior
solitude to contrast it with. But to Hocking the felt responsibility to *think* a world—rather than simply to enjoy
sensation for its own sake—marks our first venture of re-
sponsbility in discovering that the infinite shadow cast by
finite fact points the way to a destiny.

> The emotional impulse of that response is as little trans-
> latable into conceptual terms as the *élan vital* that enters
> into it: something like this, we might hazard, "This way,
> and not in sensing alone, lies my destiny." But there is also
> in it, I surmise, a tinge of obligation,—"I ought to become
> what it is in me to become, a thinking being, for my own
> sake and for ours,"—discerning a wraith of summons from
> the world at large!
>
> However we translate it, from a pre-Cartesian level the
> Cartesian "I think" is born, but born as a "We think," and
> therefore thinking an intersubjective object-world suitable
> for the uses of science. The realm of "nature," science itself,
> is thus the product of an elemental moral act, in which the
> incipient human will commits itself to a destiny of inter-
> subjective truth-seeking. It does so in response to a Thou
> immediately present in the creative activity in sensation,—
> and presumably in other levels of awareness as well.[24]

This fundamental reality of nature is both experience and
idea at the same time. We are all simultaneously experiencing space, and it is the same space for us all. Yet at the
same time, each of us has an idea of space. Space is "the
activity of each finite thinker,—but an activity held empirically in place by the active decisiveness of Outer Reality."[25]

There are two reasons for my dwelling on the relationship
between self and nature, idea and experience, mind and the
body of fact which makes up our world. One is the obvious

importance of this interrelationship for Hocking's metaphysics and, through it, for his philosophy of law, politics, education, religion, the state, and civilization. Hocking once wrote, "the eye of any philosophy is epistemology"; and the grounding of any philosophy is in metaphysics. Once we have firmly in mind how he knows what he knows, and the basic categories which his epistemology establishes, then his particular views on the basic objects of man's interests have been provided with their necessary framework. This does not mean that the particular views follow automatically. The fact that a man is an idealist does not mean that he believes in a "block universe."[26] It means, rather, that a man has been willing to engage in what Ernest Hocking calls "the hard work of thought," insisting that "system-from-within" is an obligation placed upon one by thought itself, as well as one's responsibility to other thinkers to draw the rightful lines of communication between one's several ideas and the basic categories which make them possible.

The second reason for this extended treatment of the problem lies in my attempt to lay to rest the ill-informed view that Hocking's philosophy is somehow eclectic. Whether one accepts his dialectic or not is another matter. One can legitimately argue with his categories and/or with his method, and we shall consider several of these arguments in our next chaper. However, no philosopher whose writings evidence a careful study of Hocking has taken the charge of eclecticism seriously. A dialectical system-builder may be guilty of making ideas fit too neatly, and he may gloss over certain problems in the cause of systematization; but it would be a feat of criticism to show that he had been too systematic and unsystematic (i.e. eclectic) at the same time.

We have come through the first synthesis in Hocking's dialectic. In earlier chapters we have considered at some length the claims of natural realism and subjective idealism as philosophical alternatives; here we have explored a number of detailed problems within the antithesis. Hocking will support neither; nor will he totally reject either or both. Each has something to say; neither will do as a complete perspective.

We are ready, now, for the second movement of the dialectic. We know that natural realism and subjective idealism have come together in an awareness of other mind. Who and what is this other who makes possible the human community?

Chapter VI

OUR KNOWLEDGE OF GOD

MATERIAL FOR INQUIRING INTO THE NATURE of this other who is the fundamental social object is already at hand. Hocking has noted that the other cannot be identified with any particular other person, since individuals in one's subjective world come and go. Their presence at any given moment is more or less accidental. More important, knowledge of another person is always, in some degree, uncertain. We have already noted (Chapter III, above) that love includes areas of unknownness and unknowability which it can neither penetrate nor do without. Friendship, loyalty, love: all are adventures. About any other individual human person we may, conceivably, be mistaken at any given moment.[1] The key consideration, Hocking realizes, is the fact that man, whether taken individually or collectively, knows nature empirically, and therefore passively. Natural fact is a datum; it is given, and we have to take it as it is given. If, however, passive empirical knowing is the only knowledge operative in the world, then by virtue of this passivity, the consciousness of each knower must remain "self-enclosed," and a genuine social experience is excluded. Hocking has already argued that our experience of the world is always social or it is never social. Any attempt at communication with an other begins with a search for some common coin of conversation. And simply to know nature as other mind is not, in

itself, enough; for even if some cosmic other is, like ourselves, passive in his knowing of nature, then nature, as the
frontier of thought, will be a common barrier, not a common bond.[2] But if, on the other hand, the givenness of
nature, in all its objectivity, is giving me the content of my
mind, then nature has about it an active and intentional
character. Behind the fact of givenness is the realization of
an active and intentional giver, and "nature wins its further
meaning, and is found as an intentional communication of a
Self *wholly active.*"[3] As noted earlier, the other mind of
nature must be creative; it is, in fact, creative of mind in
oneself. This fundamental social experience, on which all
further communication is built, is a common, pervasive, constant experience of an active, creative other mind, which, by
virtue of its scope and power, we recognize as the mind of
God.

But if this idea of God is an experience of God—as it
must be in Hocking's terms—where do we find this experience? If it is both pervasive and permanent in common
experience, why should we need an argument to prove it?
Wouldn't it necessarily be the most obvious of all truths, and
therefore universally acknowledged and accepted? One
might argue that God-consciousness is a "common human
experience" in the sense that there have been precious few
established human communities without religion of some
kind; but a literal universality, such as Hocking argues for,
must go beyond general cultural considerations of this sort.
He recognizes that such knowledge is not "conspicuous."
Like the whole idea, or absolute, (which is part of the meaning of God), the idea of God is what we are thinking *with*,
not what we are regularly thinking *of*, and is therefore in-
conspicuous by nature. The experience is the substratum for
all other experience, and its contribution to our specific

transactions in the world will be as vague and difficult to pinpoint as it is crucial to the business of living. We do not, for example, regularly think about the source of that stability and certainty, that self-assertion and even self-confidence which assures us that the world and life in it is good; yet what would life be without this assurance? Would it be at all? (Isn't it precisely the loss of this assurance which alone explains suicide?) Hocking speaks of "my disposition to take experience with full *empirical openness*, breast-forwardly, originated by the universal or common eye which the fundamental God-consciousness gives me. In whatever rigid scientific acceptance of fact I may accomplish, I detect the degree of this experience."[4] "Breast-forwardly" is not a current metaphor, but it has a current translation in Paul Tillich's phrase "the courage to be." The courage to go on, in spite of all that threatens the human adventure; the recognition that one's dependence on the world of given fact also involves one in a sense of responsibility derived from the simple fact of one's existence—a consideration upon which existentialism dwells so fruitfully—this elemental thrust of the human will to live depends for its force on the indistinct awareness of an absolute other.

But there is a crucial difference between Hocking and Tillich at this point. Tillich, rooting this courage in the reality of God, defends the statement "God is the Ground of Being" as the one literal assertion possible to the philosophical theologian.[5] Hocking, for his part, never says that the absolute is God.[6] The absolute, or "Ground of Being," is *that which* explains the world, on which the world depends. This transcendent fact is, as we have already noted, part of our initial awareness of God as absolute. Continuing theological debate over the nature of God also indicates that we are always more certain *that* God is than *what* God is.

> But the starting point of this development . . . is no mere
> That Which, without predicates. Substance is known as
> Subject: reality from the beginning is known as God. The
> idea of God is not an attribute which in the course of ex-
> perience I come to attach to my original whole idea: the
> unity of my world which makes it from the beginning a
> whole, knowable in simplicity, is the unity of other Self-
> hood.[7]

The absolute, the loom within which our idea-weaving takes
place, and without which the work of thought is impossible,
is the grammatical subject for all our conceptual predicates.
The transition from the idea of the whole to the idea of
God, however, requires that this grammatical subject become
personal subject, self or mind. God is not the absolute as
such; God is the Other Mind or Self which is the source of
the thinker's whole or absolute.

Both Tillich and Hocking have affinities to Brahmanism
on this issue. (By "Brahmanism" Hocking has in mind especially the Advaita Vedānta of Saṅkara). In this tendency to
equate the Absolute and God, Tillich is closer to Brahmanism than Hocking. But for Tillich, while the Ground of
Being contains within itself those dichotomies which exist
within the ground (e.g., essence and existence), it is not to
be identified literally with either half of the dichotomy. The
most dramatic example is, of course, his insistence that "God
does not exist. He is being-itself, beyond essence and existence. Therefore to argue that God exists is to deny him."[8]
Brahmanism, on the other hand, sees the original dichotomy
as *māyā* "illusion"; but since the individuated, empirical
world of *māyā* must be dealt with in its own terms, at least
until realization comes, it is possible, for example, to speak
of God as both *nirguṇa* (without "guṇas" or qualities or
predicates) and *saguṇa* (with "guṇas"), depending upon one's

point of view as within the empirical world, or released from it.[9] On this point, Hocking is closer to Brahmanism than Tillich, for Hocking, while agreeing that the mystic experience of God is *nirguṇa,* insists that the route to the absolute is an empirical one, and that the inductions gathered in along the way are reliable reports of God's ultimate nature.

Whereas Tillich denies that contingency and novelty can apply to God *literally,* Hocking is closer to the "panentheism" or "di-polar theism" of Charles Hartshorne in arguing that the selfhood of God, like our own selfhood, faces an open future. He does not deny God's all-inclusive consciousness, but argues that the selfhood of God includes time and mutability within God's infinite and immutable nature. Hocking has always been fond of saying, "God does not know what I am going to do this afternoon." Hartshorne's dipolar metaphysics takes its fundamental inspiration from Whitehead, and also Pierce; but it was in Hocking's metaphysics class at Harvard that Hartshorne first discovered the view that finitude is contained literally in God.

I shall never forget the day when, after class, I objected to Hocking's statement of the temporalistic view of God, and he convinced me on the spot that my objection was ill-founded. I suggested that if the future were outside God's awareness this would compromise His status as the all-inclusive reality. But Hocking brought me, in but a moment or two, to realize something like the following: as "outside" God's awareness the future is really nothing, since insofar as genuinely open or indeterminate the future is not a definite object of knowledge. It will be fully definite only when it is no longer future; but then its definiteness will be entirely embraced by the divine experience. I thus saw that my supposed difficulty was unreal. It will perhaps scarcely be denied that much—the best-reasoned portion—of the opposition to idealism, was due to idealism's apparent denial of the reality of time and contingency, its identification of the real with the rational, necessary, or eternal. From this Hocking did at least as much to save me as the "realists."[10]

For Hocking, then, knowledge of God as other mind or self makes possible our knowledge of our fellow men, because our most primitive awareness of nature is an awareness of God's mind actively communicating with us. Of course we know the mind of another person; for knowledge of other mind is precisely that knowledge with which all human knowing begins.

> Nature is not, as I experience it, a consensus effect, due to the wills of my fellow finite spirits, conscious or sub-conscious: but I dare not say that their presence has no part in making Nature what it is, even to my experience. For Nature, we may say, is the region where this system of minds does actually *coalesce*. Space does not reside in me, nor in any mind; but in all minds at once. In space and time and their contents we have not merely common *objects,* we have a region of literal common Mind. It is not that we are each so constructed after a common pattern called Human Nature, with certain *a priori* ideas or forms of arranging experience, that given certain stimuli at our nerve ends we all do, as a fact, turn out the same world, each in his own private copy. I do not in my growth make up a new space and a new causal system for myself. I *adopt* them. Space and Nature are numerically one, and I, by my community with Other Mind, am born inheritor of that one identical object. In my experience of Space and Nature I am experiencing identically all that Other Mind which is contemplating that same object; in so far, I have an infallible element in my knowledge of my finite comrades, as well as in my knowledge of God.[11]

This claim—that there is an infallible element in our knowledge of God—takes us to the logical defense of Hocking's dialectic, an adaptation of the historic ontological argument.

What Cyril Richardson calls "The Strange Fascination of the Ontological Argument"[12] is really not so strange. Philosophy is concerned with the relationship between ideas and reality, and as long as there is the disposition to take this relationship seriously, the question which the ontological argument seeks to answer remains *the* philosophical question: Is there any idea whose essence necessarily involves real existence? In more general terms, Hocking finds the ontological argument asking whether there is any bridge between the world of essence and the world of existence. He finds the force of the ontological argument dependent on something unique in a particular idea which forbids it being taken as a mere idea. Traditionally the attempt to bridge essence and existence has concentrated on the special case of the existence of God, arguing that the idea of God is just such an instance: the essence of this idea is peculiar in containing the essence of existence. To suppose this idea to be unreal would be an admission of the contradiction "my idea of the real may possibly be my idea of a non-real."[13] Hocking considers it the most important aspect of existence—and perhaps its only philosophical meaning—that it is the field for the realization of essences. The problem, then, is one of this relation, the process of realization, whereby essence crosses over into existence.[14]

This realization is something which happens to our essences in the midst of experience. If one asks whether our experience is real or not, Hocking counters with the question: "What is your standard of reality, and from whence do you derive it?" Is it not necessary to assume some a priori principle, and, if so, are you not already assuming an essence of the sort that must necessarily be realized? He does, in fact, follow Royce at this point.[15] The realistic assumption that there is an unbridgeable gulf between the world of essences and the world of existences is, Hocking argues, a self-defeating argument. If one knows that essence is not existence, one must know what existence *means,* i.e. what it is, its essence. The argument which sets out to prove that essence is on one side of the gulf and existence on the other ends by finding essence on both sides.

Hegel had argued that the essence of existence could not be described without bringing immediacy into the picture. Hocking adds that a true description of the essence of existence also requires something very different, i.e. objectivity, the not-self.

> I can only be as actual as the things I am at any time dealing with; I get my reality in part from what is over against me. On the other hand, nothing can be more real than the self: that which is over against me gets its actuality from the fact that I am dealing with it. Reality implies an intercourse between the self and the not-self.[16]

I realize myself, then, in dealing with my objects, and therefore I find the standard of reality in the not-self. When I realize the significance of an event in the world, I am finding this same standard of reality in my own world of meanings. In both cases I am using a standard of reality that is necessarily prior to the events of either self or not-self; prior, indeed, to either the world of essences or that of existences. God, in these terms, means the "reciprocal of self" which is, at the same time, inseparable from self and self-consciousness. God is the external factor of a single reality which includes both and consists in this intercourse of one with the other. The essence of God is not merely infinity, perfection, or even reality, since these would make the ontological argument a tautology. The function of the argument is rather to show that there is an essence which is not merely subjective. Hocking raises the question and answers it himself. To the question:

> Is the idea of God merely subjective? comes the answer, "In forming the essence 'merely subjective' you have at the same time formed the essence 'not merely subjective' as in contrast thereto; and 'God' as essence belongs to the 'not merely subjective.' Whatever artificiality there is in the argument hails entirely from the artificiality of the question." The natural situation may be stated thus: the essence of God must be real, because it is an essence inseparable from my continuous consciousness or experience of reality.[17]

In both thought and experience the whole precedes the two partial aspects of ego and non-ego. Thus, too, the real as self and other self precedes the distinction between essence and existence. That by which we distinguish essence and existence is better known than either. Our knowledge of the real is the logical basis for that instinctive assurance of man that there is a lack of finality in the mode of being in nature and history, where we are possessed by essence and existence. For Hocking, this instinctive assurance is, in its negative form, "the heart of the metaphysical problem,"[18] for the history of religion indicates that man begins with nature and finds himself dissatisfied with it. Suddenly he seems to possess the real, the good, the self-sufficient.[19] What has happened is "some leap from idea to reality that constitutes the essential historic movement of the mind to God."[20] Our natural realism begins with the assertion that objects are more real than subjects, more substantial than any meanings one may give to one's own being or one's relations to others. Our subjective idealism counters with the reflection that nature, as known to one person, is always within that person; and so one asserts that oneself is more real than nature can ever be.

From this dialectical confrontation comes the synthetic view that nature is "neither self-sufficient nor illusory; it has *derivative* reality. As over against me, it is real; as over against the Creative Spirit, it is not real."[21]

Hocking's contribution to the ontological argument is the framework of experience in which he sets the problem.[22] Rather than argue that the problem is purely logical, he asks where this assurance comes from. Because experience is an encounter of the self with the absolute, "reality itself is present to me in experience; and all of the process of judging this and that thing to be unreal or less than real is made possible simply by the grasp of that reality which at any moment I have."[23] On this basis he can say, "The whole tale of Descartes' discovery is not told in the proposition, I exist, knowing. It is rather told in the proposition, I exist, knowing the Absolute; or, I exist, knowing God."[24] Rejecting the cosmological argument (which moves from the reality of the world to the reality of God), and the moral argument, both of which discover a being who is only *as* real or *as* great or *as* good as the world, he insists that it is precisely the insufficiency of the world which prompts the movement of the mind beyond the world to God. *"Because the world is not, God is."*[25] The major point on which he stands is not the traditional assertion that I have an idea of God, therefore God exists, but rather: "I have an idea of God, therefore I have an experience of God." This discovery of God's priority as an object of knowledge is always made *in medias res*. It is in the process of knowing selfhood, nature and other mind that we know God. But it is not because we know these three basic objects of experience that we know God; it is in the midst of our experience of these three that we realize our knowledge of God as the prior item of knowledge which makes it possible for us to know them. God is the relatedness of these three items, the ground or context which makes them real. On this basis Hocking can say:

> The object of certain knowledge has this threefold structure, Self, Nature and Other Mind; and God, the appropriate object of the ontological proof, includes all three.[26]

As a result, the ontological argument also applies to selfhood and nature. As Hocking reads him, Descartes was right in his *Cogito ergo sum,* but he did not go far enough, or did not include enough. In *The Meaning of God,* Hocking puts it this way:

> . . . the Cartesian certitude may with greater validity be put into this form:
>   I think myself, therefore I exist; or
>   I have an idea of Self, Self exists.
> For in thinking myself I find myself in experience and thus in living relation to that reality which experience presents. So may it be with Nature:
>   I have an idea of physical Nature, Nature exists. That is, in whatever sense I conceive Nature, in that sense physical nature is real. Idealism has wavered much in its judgment regarding the reality of Nature, and of "material substance." It has said that we have no idea of matter; and again it has said that matter does not exist, which implies that we have an idea of it. Some meaning, however, we do attribute to the word matter; and without enquiring what that definable meaning may be, we may say in advance that whatever idea is framable corresponds to reality as experienced. We need not fear that this realism of Nature will detach Nature from God; though if we could think it so detached it would doubtless so exist. For of independence also, in whatever sense I can think the independence of beings, in that sense independence obtains between them. That which is most

independent of me, namely the Other Mind, has been the first object of our ontological findings.[27]

Later, in *The Coming World Civilization,* Hocking proposed a more economical statement of his adaptation of Descartes' *cogito:*

> In order to be valid the Cartesian certitude requires to be enlarged: *cogito aliquid ergo sum, et aliquid est:* I think something, therefore I exist, and something (else) exists. It still remains true that my thinking involves my existence; the point is, it involves more.[28]

In his doctrine of God, Hocking differs from both classical absolutism and classical theology in maintaining a polarity *within* God, a view which, as I have already remarked, brings him close to what we now call panentheism. He argues, for example, that it is a crucial error to think of God as an object among other objects, and, on this basis, he is sympathetic with Tillich's motivation for insisting that God does not "exist." But he italicizes his own insistence that even this error *"is not all error"* for God is both objective and incarnate in his works. The absolute "sanctions both the one and the other of [man's] divergent ideals,"[29] and it is its function to maintain this balance. So, too, with the problem of God's transcendence and immanence and the contrast between the personal and the impersonal. "Here again, the direction of religious progress is not single, but twofold."[30] Hocking shows considerable appreciation for the way in which Brahmanism deals with the transcendence-immanence problem, and the personal-impersonal problem. Brahmanism is too abstract; nevertheless, " . . . these Brahman pietists who most clearly recognized and defined the otherness of God from all things phenomenal and even conceivable were the ones who first asserted (so far as history knows) the immediate unity between the ineffable without and the ineffable within."[31]

Having fought for the selfhood of God as other mind, Hocking nevertheless expresses his lack of affection for the term "personality,"[32] finding in the word a brittle ring, remininscent of the Roman Code. God as Law seems to him, by contrast, more of a piece with the totality and warmth of the universe as we experience it. (Here is an interesting reversal of the conventional contrast between the coldness of law and the warmth of personality.) Acknowledging the dichotomy between the concepts of God as personal and God as impersonal, he says:

> God is not falsely judged in experience to be *both the one and the other*. The negation of any one such attribute by the other is only for the enlargement of the first, not for its destruction. Until I can perfectly conceive personality, God must be for me alternately person and law; with the knowledge that these two attributes of one being are not, in truth, inconsistent, and that their mode of union is also something that I shall verify in some present knowledge, as by anticipation of an ultimate attainment.[33]

When Hocking says, "Because the world is not, God is," he seems to have forsaken the element of realism which his dialectic has struggled to maintain, and even sympathetic readers have found this an overstatement of his case. Taken simply as it stands (i.e. out of context) it is indeed an unhappy statement; in context it is reasonably clear that the concept of the world's unreality is dialectical through and through. Hocking is really saying that vis-à-vis God, the world is not independently real; but because God is also in the world, the world is as real as we want it to be. Here I am reminded of Radhakrishnan's neo-Hindu re-interpretation of the Upaniṣadic doctrine of the world as *māyā*. Radhakrishnan comments:

> We admit that according to the Upaniṣads, plurality, succession in time, co-existence in space, relations of cause and effect, oppositions of subject and object, are not the highest reality. But this is not saying that they are non-existent. The Upaniṣads support the doctrine of *māyā* only in the sense that there is an underlying reality containing all elements from the personal God to the telegraph post. . . . *Māyā* represents at the conceptual level the self-distinction residing in the very heart of reality, propelling it to develop itself. The particular things are and are not. . . . Measured by the perfection of the absolute, the unlimited fullness of the one reality, the world of plurality, with all its pain and disruption, is less real. . . . [But] Even if we look upon the persons and things of the world as shadows of a substance, still, so long as the substance is real, the shadows also have relative reality. Though the things of the world are imperfect representations of the real, they are not illusory semblances of it.[34]

There are, then, two different perspectives on reality: the particular, empirical perspective; and the absolute, ideal perspective. How are they related? Radhakrishnan, in the tradition of Indian idealism, begins with the absolute and deduces a world in which persons and things are "shadows of a substance" and which is known essentially through an intuitive, or mystical perception. But for Hocking, neither persons nor things are mere "shadows" of anything, nor is any methodology valid which deduces a world from a synoptic intuition. He shares, with Radhakrishnan, a synoptic intuition, but he discovers it in the immediate world of physical experience; he will not present it philosophically except as the beginning of an induction. It is the intuition that gives him his hypothesis. Modernity, however, requires that all guiding principles must have a home *in medias res,* and, in turn, requires Hocking to take his stand on the thesis that substance lies within the experience of the particular. His argument is that when those particular objects "out there" are taken into our own minds, we find ourselves knowing them as already known by some other. Here Hocking runs into trouble.

Describing this experience of knowing in the central passage in *The Meaning of God* (pp. 265-266), he says that participation in the mind of another person places us literally within that mind. The logical extension of his argument would seem to be that if we were thoroughly within the mind of another person, that mind would be completely known. Hocking, of course, will not make this claim. He leaves us with unanswered questions: Granted that meaning cannot be divorced from fact, how do particular facts become meaningful? If meaning is inherent in factuality, why is it not always apparent?

In his later years Hocking recognized that the spatial metaphor of *The Meaning of God* was not a success; but he was at a loss to suggest a better one. Marcel, noting that for Hocking "to be is to *be with*," suggests a musical analogy —that of two notes in harmony—to explain the interrelatedness between minds.[35] This allows for a unity-in-difference which is in keeping with Hocking's insight; but it falls short of the literal description which Hocking sought. The difficulty of describing the relationship between minds is part of the price which Hocking pays for his insistence that modern philosophy must accept Cartesian dualism and work it through to a viable solution. One might have expected a religious man and an idealist such as Hocking to try to work his way around a radical dualism. I think he was forced to meet dualism head on because of his conviction that both religion and idealism must be integrated with our experience of nature to be relevant. That Nature must be taken as *res extensa,* in keeping with the Western philosophical tradition, is important to Hocking. His emphasis on a secularized conception of nature is particularly notable, for nature has not always been regarded as entirely objective.

Renaissance science rejected the Aristotelian-medieval notion of "final cause" or purpose because its empiricism discovered a more detailed and accurate explanation of the world in terms of mechanical operations and their laws. Aristotle's "final cause" is, after all, a sophisticated version of the primitive idea that the world is essentially a person since rational purpose is a human characteristic. This conviction fits neatly into the medieval view that ultimate knowledge is knowledge of a personal God, making it logical that theology be regarded as the "queen of the sciences." Theology, after all, explained the ultimate reason why things are as they are in the world. The entire creation participated in the purposes of a living God.

For the new science, however, the world was not a person; the world was a machine. Aristotle and the medievals had spoken of things as though they were people. Aristotle spoke of the *desire* of the seed to become a mature plant, and the medievals spoke of "the love of God which kept all things eternally aspiring to be themselves, the love of the flame for the fire that caused it to strain upward, the love of the stone that is its hardness, of the grass that is its greenness. . . ."[36] Descartes, on the other hand, divided reality into two radically different kinds, *res extensa* and *res cogitans.* "Extended things" were material, subject to physical laws, empirically verifiable, mathematically predictable. "Thinking things," on the other hand, provided a source of certainty that the world of matter existed, (*cogito ergo sum*) but they were distinct from the material world, and their personal characteristics were no longer allowed to invade the realm of matter and its motions.

As a twentieth century philosopher, Hocking is involved in two battles simultaneously. On the one hand, he is opposed to men like Hobbes who, in his *Leviathan,* applies the physical principles of matter in motion to the affairs of government and the state. Hobbes thus turns the tables on traditional philosophy by interpreting the laws of living society in terms of the actions of dead matter. On the other hand, Hocking is opposed to men like Hartshorne, who argues that nature is really living, composed of tiny "creatures" whose aggregate mass makes up what, to our unsubtle observation, appears to be an inanimate, individual "object." Hocking is prepared to fight these battles because he believes that Cartesian dualism has made possible the two major achievements of modernity: scientific technology and the free individual. As long as nature participated in the "purposes of God" its uses were limited to an orthodox interpretation of those purposes and the laws which were thought to effect them. As long as the individual was bound by medieval Christendom's hierarchical concept of society, his freedom to live out the creative possibilities of his thought was restricted by a hereditary social class which did not recognize this freedom as his right. The values which Hocking seeks to protect are the freedom to use a purposeless nature for human purposes, and the creative rights of the free individual. In developing these themes, however, Hocking finds that modernity overstates them both. In the philosophy of nature, the overstatement asserts that a purposeless nature implies a purposeless universe. In the philosophy of the human person, the overstatement asserts that a free individual implies an isolated individual cut off from any clear knowledge of other selves and therefore without substantial bonds to the human community. Hocking's understanding of the meaning of God in human experience is that He reveals the purposes for which a purposeless nature was created, and provides the elemental knowledge of an other self which makes a human community possible.

This dialectical treatment of nature leaves us with a certain ambiguity. If a material object is seen, on reflection, to be an expression of communication from the divine mind, is it not ultimately an idea in the mind of God? If so, what is the difference between Hocking and Berkeley, for whom nature is a pattern of ideas through which God speaks to us? Doesn't Hocking's dialectic finally rob nature of the purposeless materiality which he has tried to protect?

Charles Hartshorne has criticized the ambivalence of Hocking's dialectical theory of perception.[37] Hocking insists that knowledge is constituted by its objects, and that these objects, because of their objective reality, must be discovered. They are not products of our own thought. They are there in their own right. Hocking's objects are initially dead and powerless, only to stand revealed in the second movement of the dialectic as content of an other mind. Hartshorne wants Hocking to fish or cut bait. Is God the creative agent in the perceiving process? If so, what is the status of the object, if not that of an idea in the mind of God? For his own part, Hartshorne, following Leibniz, argues that "nature consists of individuals which as such are not distinctly perceived, since what we seem to see or tactually discriminate as individuals are in reality aggregates, masses of indistinctly given individuals, *the nature of which therefore cannot be known from direct perception.*" Thus, "the cells of plants and animals can be viewed as self-creative units of experience, and so can molecules, atoms, or even particles. The rest of nature consists of masses of individuals, for instance a tree or a cloud, whose active units fall below the threshold of our discriminations."[38] On this analysis, the notion of "mere stuff" is a confusion arising from the lack of distinctness in our perceptions. Nature is composed of experiencing individuals or creatures. When, in perception, mind unifies experience, it is accepting antecedent factors which are indeed "given." But these experienced individuals "more or less consciously *expected* to be taken into account somehow by future experience." On this basis Hartshorne builds his "contributionism," arguing that "to be, as a singular concrete event, is to anticipate as inevitable the status of being appropriated as datum by suitable future experiences."[39] All experience is social because the world is entirely made up of sentient beings who are themselves experiencing, even while they are being experienced.

From Hartshorne's point of view the Cartesian bifurcation of nature into *res extensa* and *res cogitans* is entirely unfortunate. Hartshorne stands with Fechner, Paulsen and Whitehead in denying the independent concept of matter and the subsequent radical distinction between the mental and the non-mental. Hocking demurs:

> I believe . . . that while the Cartesian dualism, like all other dualisms, has to be overcome, the cleavage can only be cured by being first clearly seen; so that the Cartesian stage has [to] be gone through in every philosophical tradition, sooner or later.[40]

The Cartesian dichotomy is important for Hocking's analysis of perception in that it highlights the ambiguity of the perceiving process. Hocking finds that the scientific, or realist, or sensationalist account of perception, honoring the objective independence of the "it," analyzes the brain-events which *underly* the mind's perceptual awareness; but how the brain event *becomes* mental awareness remains unexplained. Behaviorism, for Hocking, is not an explanation, it is a flag of defeat. The "bifurcation of nature" stands. Rejecting this "sensationalism," Whitehead offers a theory of prehensions which has stimulated Hartshorne and others to bring the "it" within the unifying scope of the "thou." Hocking agrees with Whitehead and Hartshorne that sensationalism is inadequate, since "the several private images [perceptions] somehow accompanying these brain effects are *all we per-ceivers have* of that presumed-objective world with which the doctrine starts. The subjective terminus contradicts the premises. A doctrine thus at odds with its own consequences cannot be true."[41] On the other hand, the Whiteheadian rejection of scientific realism tends toward a universal subjectivism, and cuts us off from the valuable pragmatic thrust of that realism, seeking as it does to narrow the gap between perception and the brain events which underly it. "We shall, for example," Hocking says, "never desist from perfecting our optical instruments by the aid of close correlation between inferences from that theory and our visual experiences. And for this task, so far as I can see, neither the theory of families-of-perspectives nor the theory of prehensions offers tangible help."[42]

For Hocking the factuality of nature, as we have seen, is a concept with a "double-boundary." Nature includes the brain processes, but "the knowing of that Nature is not part of the Nature then-and-there known." He insists that the mutual otherness of the "it" and the "thou" is a natural relation, implying a larger concept of nature, known through a "wider empiricism," which includes both the nature-of-physical-science *and* the nature-of-the-knower-of-physical-science. The unity of this "con-natural" relation between the perceiver and nature is to be found in that common mysticism of everyman, in which he knows his world to be *the* world—its reality present in experience, even while the full character of that reality is endlessly sought through scientific investigation. Contra Hartshorne, Hocking holds that matter is real, but not independently real; thus he finds himself back in close company with Radhakrishnan once again. Hocking has never said that the world is *māyā*. What he says, rather, is that nature is a symbol, and that the seeming ambivalence of the dialectic is due to the richness of symbolic forms. He does not say, as Radhakrishnan does so clearly, that there are two radically different perspectives on reality. But he agrees that the mind's capacity for inspiration, insight or realization, is due to something which Tillich called "ecstatic reason" and which Hocking broadens into a common "mysticism" of everyman. In terms of his own doctrine of perception, this "mysticism" is for Hocking simply the capacity of any observer to recognize the symbolic dimensions of natural objects.

Two major categories of Hocking's metaphysics remain to be explored: selfhood and human destiny. These are dynamic concepts, best understood in relation to those social institutions whose business it is to direct the development of the individual and his society. Hocking is particularly interested in problems of education and in the philosophy of the state.

Part Two

MAN IN SOCIETY

Chapter VII

THE HUMAN INDIVIDUAL

OURS IS A COLLECTIVISTIC AGE. The orientation of world politics has swung to the left in the past twenty-five years, and this leftward swing has won from conservative and liberal alike a new loyalty to the claims of the community on the individual. Hocking found himself generally sympathetic to this shift. After all, a man whose philosophical work seeks to overcome solipsism cannot be counted a friend of untempered or rugged individualism. A philosophy of communication must be, and was for Hocking, a philosophy of community. And yet, as a philosopher who swam against contemporary currents in much of his professional work, Hocking has obviously set his compass by private, inner bearings. Perhaps one can say, in a manner which only seems paradoxical, that his sense of being with that absolute other who is God has strengthened his own individualism. Indeed, it may well be that individualism, as we have regularly understood it, is a misnomer. Was anyone more individualistic than Joan of Arc? Yet wasn't her individual power the result of her conviction that some other had called her and was giving her strength; and that what she was doing had nothing to do with her own particular individuality? We must acknowledge that even those individualists who lay no claim to being on God's side do regularly claim to be on some side other than their own; the side of some idea, some common human value, in whose name they act.

For his part, Hocking argues that the creative individual is not a threat to community but rather its only hope for strength. In his philosophy of religion, for example, he rejects the conventional assumption that there is a basic difference between the mystic and the prophet—one oriented to his own inwardness, the other involved in the destiny of a people.[1] It is not surprising, therefore, to find in Hocking a philosophy of community concerned with a careful examination of the individual self. He conducts his examinations first from the angle of psychology and then in terms of contemporary physical theory. *The Meaning of God* is fundamentally concerned with a reinterpretation of the absolute. But the absolute, as major premise in the basic syllogism of human knowing, needs the self as minor premise. The absolute is "the quintessence of Eternal Fact,"[2] but the self is the field in which that fact becomes significant for action. In his second book, *Human Nature and its Remaking,* published six years after *The Meaning of God,* Hocking turned his full attention to selfhood, the second major category of his developing metaphysics, in a study which he calls "an individualistic theory of society."[3] Later, in his Terry Lectures at Yale on *The Self, Its Body and Freedom* (1928), he explored the mind-body problem in detail. *The Lasting Elements of Individualism* (1937) went on to explore the role of the individual in the state. The essays in the forties and fifties on what he called a "new route" to an idealistic metaphysics examined the interrelationships between psychology and quantum mechanics; it was at that time that he put forth a fully worked out conception of the self as a "Field of Fields."[4] *The Meaning of Immortality in Human*

Experience (1957) continues this discussion—in the light of religion and the problem of physical death.

Man has always been fascinated with himself, and is more eminently qualified to speak on himself than on any other subject. Yet the self-confident fascination and authority harbor an element of discontent. In the scores of epigrammatic attempts to capture the essence of human life (as opposed to that of other living beings), man has been defined variously as the animal who thinks, or laughs, or engages in politics. But more important he is, perhaps supremely, the animal who invented the future. Man needs a future because he is not wholly satisfied with what he is. The future is necessary for achievement in what is perhaps the most crucial of all human ventures—man's remaking of himself. The broad name for this venture is education. Whether one concentrates, pessimistically, on the mistakes which man wants to correct; or, romantically, on the desires which he longs to satisfy; or, ethically, on the good he wants to accomplish; or, religiously, on the destiny which he seeks to fulfill—this remaking is one of the basic activities which distinguishes human nature. Man is the animal who goes to school. But before this remaking process can proceed confidently, some solution must be found to the enigma of selfhood. Before a man can decide what he wants to be, he must have some idea of what he is. The enigma arises initially from the conflict between the self as a body, and the self as a mind.[5]

Clearly we are both mental and physical beings. But how? The Cartesian bifurcation returns to plague us. Are not body and mind radically different kinds? Our instinctive sense of ourselves makes us uncomfortable with any dualism; yet the history of thought illustrates the difficulty of articulating a felt integrity. We have tended either to make mind definitive, thus scorning the body as the prison house of the soul; or we have settled on the measurable activities of bodily behavior as the essence of selfhood, thus leaving unexplained the relationship between brain and mind, body and "personality." In *The Self, Its Body and Freedom,* Hocking is concerned with the construction of a philosophical psychology which will credit the distinctiveness of both mind and body and at the same time do justice to the felt integrity of the self. *Human Nature and Its Remaking* goes on to relate the individual's instinct and will to the problem of their fulfillment in society. The psychological problem of individual human nature thus inevitably becomes the social and political problem of corporate human careers and, ultimately, the religious problem of human destiny.

Hocking resists the temptation to see the body-mind problem as a battle between the behaviorists and idealists. Both Whitehead's prehensions and Hartshorne's creatures solve the problem idealistically by insisting that the concept of matter irreducible to mind in some sense, is meaningless. Hocking is no behaviorist, but he cannot take his initial stand with Whitehead and Hartshorne because of his commitment to experience. He must honor the Cartesian bifurcation because this is simply the way things are as we meet and deal with our here and now. The distinction between the body and the mind is not merely an appearance. It is real enough so that we are regularly aware of it, as when, in the last quarter mile of a boat race, I (my mind) keep telling myself (my body) to keep going. To tell me that the inanimate bodies with which I am surrounded are really groups of sentient creatures leaves me wondering why these groups are so very different from the minds which are said to constitute their microscopic parts. How can I know positively that they think and feel? Having gone through such a dialectic process, Hocking finds that man is neither body exclusively nor mind exclusively; he is both. And so it is with most other problems up to and including the transcendence and immanence of God. Rejecting both of the either/ or views of self—the behaviorist and the idealist—Hocking argues that the interdependent relationship between mind and body is necessary because the mind needs a body in order to become a self.

To be sure, Hocking's disagreement with Whitehead and Hartshorne is only provisional. Common sense also knows that body and mind are united, and "it would be easy to reflect that if body and mind are one thing, and if that thing cannot be body, nor any meaningless neutral stuff, it must be mind."[6] Fair enough, but does this really help us learn more about selfhood? Hocking believes that these shortcuts to monism, which take everything back to the incorrigible finality of mind, are not very nutritious; the pragmatist in him frankly prefers a provisional dualism to a hasty monism.

> If dualisms are delusive, finalities are unprofitable, and drive the pragmatic thinker back into the juicier inaccuracies of dualism or behaviorism. "Of what use is it," he argues, "to say that value is value and not fact? It is an axiom, if you like, but it throws no light on the nature of value." . . . The pragmatic interest is valid: thinkers must not be put to the impossible choice between truth and the usable or fertile hypothesis.[7]

In this manner, Hocking begins with a provisional dualism as his initial hypothesis. Mind and body are different, but they affect each other reciprocally—i.e., body changes cause mind changes, and vice versa. The problem is to find the point of contact between the two and to sketch the fundamentals of the relationship. Does body use consciousness for bodily ends, or does the mind use body for mental ends? In support of bodily dominance over the mind, Hocking recognizes a genuine chemistry of the soul. A deficiency of iodine can turn a clever man into an idiot—a minor variation on the familiar fact that a deficiency of oxygen turns a live man into a dead one.[8] One of the best known early formulations of the view that mental events have a physical source was the James-Lange theory which held that what seems to be the physical "effect" of emotion is actually a large part of its cause. James and Lange argued, for example, that we do not cry because we are sad; much of our sadness is caused by the tears themselves. Similarly, violent physical activity seems to arouse pugnacity. Even so, experiments on the relations among adrenalin secretion, muscular activity, and emotion have tended to confirm that emotion begins as an idea in the mind, and that physical expression of an emotion requires mental consent at a crucial point before it can reach full expression.[9] In recognizing the existence and function of this "threshold of consent," Hocking challenges two basic assumptions of the Freudian doctrine of "repression." Freud assumes, first, that impulse is outside conscious control. Secondly, and more significantly, Freud assumes that attempts at conscious control of impulse serve only to deflect it from healthy, overt expression to subconscious mischief. Hocking argues, contra Freud, that a given impulse, such as the sexual, reaches the stage where the problem of repression becomes acute only after passing the "threshold of consent." Psychoanalytic practice based on the two Freudian assumptions brings latent impulse to the surface of consciousness where it is expressed, thus releasing its otherwise psychologically destructive energy. Freud points out (notably in *Civilization and Its Discontents*) that freedom for natural expression of instinct throughout society would require radical changes in the traditional Western social order. Freud saw no indication that we were prepared for such a revolution, and argued that widespread neurosis is the price we pay for maintaining our traditional "civilized" middle class values and institutions. Freud is attacking Victorianism and all its ways. Hocking counters that the "confusion of repression with restraint or control reaches the dimensions of a social and educational humbug," and argues: "The thesis that a repression dangerous for mental stability is a necessary and general accompaniment of such a social order as our own has no scientific leg to stand on."[10] Siding with Julius Lippert he argues that the restraint exercised by the "threshold of consent" has the psychological status of a "secondary instinct," and that the breakdown of *this* instinct is more conducive to mental disorder than Freudian "repression." It is the Greek in Hocking, not any Victorianism, which makes him say that "The distinctive thing about human nature is not its gush, but its *balance;* and balance implies a harmony of restraints."[11]

Hocking's emphasis lies on the selective power of the self to entertain a particular stimulus from that flood of stimuli which constantly assault us. Hocking argues that in the process of tasting and testing we are admitting new forces into the moulding of our developing selfhood. We are discovering new powers and new problems, all of which become characteristics of ourselves. The career of impulse in this development of selfhood is circular. An impulse like thirst begins in the mind, solving its problem by way of the body. Close analysis, however, reveals a breakdown of the provisional dualism between mind and body with which Hocking's hypothesis began. When thirst is satisfied the causal series of events goes out of mind into body; and yet the mind experiences no loss of contact with the series. The sequence of events always remains generally intelligible. The process of pouring water down one's throat is a bodily event; but that does not keep it from being a mental event also. Hocking concludes that the body is not outside the reach of mind; that it is included within the reach of the self. When we drink we do not say, "My body drinks," but rather, "I drink." The body provides the self with certain characteristic features which are crucial even though often overlooked: a sense of particular and definite *being*, usually of well-being; the sense of capacity which comes through the exercise of bodily powers; the impetus of desire.

In summary, then, the body is necessary in the first place, in order that the self may make a clear distinction between thought and deed,[12] for a deed is required to complete a thought. Hocking puts it this way:

> In a way, the preliminary thought is more perfect than any deed can possibly be: when I try to execute what I have contemplated, I somehow fall short or spoil it. Yet the deed is what I mean; and anyone who means good will without doing good will, or who means opposition without fighting, is suspected of the disease of sentimentality, which consists in living in the too pretty world of inoperative meanings.[13]

In order to be a self, one's deeds must leave behind them what Hocking calls an "accumulation of power."[14] Creativity in the self is of no avail if the self cannot store its past experience and skill. Life moves on, but memory and habit build up certain skills. The resulting sense of capacity, of know-how—in basic activities like walking and the more complex business of dealing with other people, remembering ideas, etc.—is, in large part, a sense which the body makes possible. But not entirely. The heart of habit is not simply what it does, but what exactly is meant by what it does. Hocking even speaks of the "self" of a habit.

> It is because of this motive-kernel of habit that it is always something more than a mere ability to perform; it is to some extent a desire to perform. . . . By building habits, the self becomes a colony of included and latent selves.[15]

Finally, Hocking points out, the self needs a body in order to engage in give and take with the world beyond the self. If one thinks of the self as a system of purposive behavior, then it is clear that selfhood stands in need of a definable place which is identifiable and exclusive—one in which it can behave. Body, Hocking insists, is the inseparable organ of the self, the ever present fact through which the possibilities inherent in the self are actualized. The self needs its body in order to become actual, active, social, and historical. The difference between body and mind, which Hocking has no intention of denying, is the difference between a part and the whole. "The body is an organ of the self as the brain is an organ of the body."[16]

For Schopenhauer the body is simply the visible, objectified manifestation of the will. The tiger does not become a predator because he has teeth and claws and awesome physical power; his lethal equipment is an expression of his will to kill. The body, Schopenhauer says, has no substantial reality. It is only an *appearance* of the self, a spatial symbol of the will. Hocking asserts that the will cannot be itself without body. The process of willing something is the process of objectifying it. However, while the body is, generally speaking, the fit organ of the self, it is never altogether what our will would have it be. "In what sense," Hocking speculates "is Cyrano de Bergerac's nose an expression of *his* will to live?"[17] Are there not occasions when the spirit is willing but the flesh weak? These are occasions when body determines action which is against the will of the self. Schopenhauer dealt with this problem by proposing a behaviorism of the subconscious. For him, body never rebels, it only reveals the deeper hidden dimensions of the actual will. Hocking agrees with Schopenhauer that there are deeper dimensions of self beneath the level of immediate consciousness. His question is whether we are right in beginning with the will of the individual self. True, the self is to some extent its own architect through habit and exercise of the threshold of consent. But what of the mass of inherited selfhood? Are there no hereditary determinants of one's individual will? This question, of course, brings us, and Hocking, to the problem of instinct.

The most popular and influential writing on the topic has followed the Freudian view that instinct has its home in the subconscious. Hocking is wary. For him the subconscious, a murky area lying somewhere between mind and matter, is subject to question by a scrupulous empiricism. He warns that the subconscious is "a place for resolution in holding to what we know,"[18] but he readily admits that "Freud and his followers had lavished much shrewd observation upon the original sources of mental states, and I think not without valuable results."[19] In the spirit of Freud's own imaginative dealings with the psychological underworld, Hocking characterizes the Freudian doctrine of the "libido"—man's unsatisfied, restless will-to-power—as that of "a dark, unruly stranger whom we harbor as a secret guest while we live our overt life in a critical, suspicious and refractory world."[20]

Freud reads the psyche's story as a conflict between the underworld instinctive self and the everyday conscious self which is "rationalized" for purposes of normally polite social intercourse. Hocking is prepared to entertain the dramatis personae—id, ego, and super-ego—with which Freud has peopled his underground world. What he challenges is the scientific accuracy of separating the subconscious from the conscious self. As the provisional dualism between body and mind in the self is a dualism which must finally be overcome —for the self does what its body does—so too we must finally recognize that the conscious and subconscious selves are the same self. There are depths of consciousness to be sure. But is a purely subconscious craving—i.e. a craving which is not consciously felt or expressed—a real craving in an intelligible sense? The subconscious is a valid aspect of the whole self. For Hocking, however, it cannot be regarded as a sub-self, different in kind from the whole of which it is a dimension. It is the region in which inherited impulse enters a new life, but, as such, it is part of what the self affirms when it affirms itself. In this sense "to be . . . is to accept being."[21] Instinct, for Hocking, means that the self has a certain technique with which it begins existence. What this inheritance of instinct indicates is that selves actually overlap, not only in the physical overlapping of the child within the mother's body, but mentally in its inheritance of instinct-capital. In order to be, however, the individual self must claim this inheritance as its own and, in making this claim, adopt the instinct-capital into a total selfhood which is thereby unique and original.

There is another problem, however, which concerns the relationship of the individual self to the natural environment which seems to enclose it. Even if one argues that the wings of every fledgling are an expression of its own individual will to fly, and not simply a bodily or mechanical result of parental impulse, one must question the nature of the relationship between the individual self and the totality of nature which surrounds it and to which it is seemingly subordinate. We are already familiar with the general outline of Hocking's view that mind needs the objective reality of nature in order that idea may achieve the clarity, vividness, and particularity which nature provides. In laying claim to its own body, Hocking believes, the self also lays claim to nature as a necessary context for the fulfillment of its own needs. Again, this claim need not involve solipsism nor that subjective idealism which sees nature merely as an idea in the mind of the self.

> While the self is receiving, not making, the world it perceives, and is at every point in contact with a not-self, it proceeds at once to create after the pattern of what it perceives.[22]

The characteristics of nature which highlight its over-againstness—its given quality of sense data, its order, and its public openness— all these are characteristics which the self needs to qualify as will. The self is never static; it is constantly at work. Hocking sees selfhood as a venture, a task, a hope; it is a constant, purposive engagement with the world. Without the world there could be no selfhood, because there would be no engagement. At every moment the self is receiving not only the consequences of its own action, but also the consequential actions of countless others; it is in dealing with this problematic stuff that the self becomes itself, as Hocking understands it. The world of nature is real—opposite from the private, internal world of the Walter Mitty self, or the neurotic self, or the sentimental self— because it is the world of our common life. The impartiality of nature as a "non-impulsive background" to one's own impulsive, purposive existence—the dead character of its mechanical order—this is not a threat to one's own purposes and meanings, it is a context of opportunity allowing the self freedom to express these purposes. Hocking reminds us again:

> The inanimateness of nature confers freedom to exploit and reshape; the circumstance that it is a world of facts and not of meanings makes it the perfect receptacle for such meanings as we will to impose upon it. It can enter unobtrusively into works of public utility or beauty because its mechanical base is neutral and unconscious in its minutely lawful procedures. A world of conscious enterprise and especially of social enterprise would be impossible without such an impassive base: a world of meanings would necessarily include, and so give meaning to, such a world of the meaningless as abstract physical nature affords.[23]

Hocking's understanding of the individual's freedom takes us to his adaptation of contemporary field theory in the second major category of his metaphysics, that of the self as "a field of fields." This category developed gradually, from its first hints in 1928—well after the publication of *The Meaning of God*—until its most mature statement in *The Meaning of Immortality* in 1959.

At the regular post-Christmas meeting of the eastern division of the American Philosophical Association in December 1927, Hocking's presidential address asked, "What Does Philosophy Say?"[24] Without denying the basic disagreements for which philosophers are notorious, he nevertheless suggested that philosophy *qua* philosophy involves its various practitioners in a common acceptance of basic principles, among them the assumption that "things have a meaning." In the course of his paper he observed that meaning is a relative term, expressed in antitheses like good and evil, and that, for this reason, it was seemingly impossible to invest the idea of the whole or absolute with any meaning, since it is the ultimate synthesis. How can the whole of things be good, for example, since our experience of the parts within the whole is both good and evil? Or how can the whole of things be mental, since it is made up of both the mental and the non-mental? Observations of this sort have regularly led to what Hocking calls "neutralism" regarding any belief in an ultimate reality. Convinced, however, that the whole of life must have a meaning to insure real meaning in the parts, he proposes to move beyond this logical frontier. The most obvious route would be by way of Hegel's attack on the principle of noncontradiction. Rejecting this attack as philosophical suicide, Hocking suggested that there are some concepts which, while they are bound by their antithesis on one side, have another boundary which makes them applicable to the whole. Hocking explains:

> From my point of view, the concept of *self* has seemed the most perfect example of this class of concepts: for while the self has always a not-self over against it, it is always *taking that not-self in,*—its life may be said to consist in a process of consuming its limits. It has seemed to me to offer the best instance of a concept which could apply at once to the whole and to a part.[25]

This conception of the self as having a double boundary (which, as we have already seen, he later applied to the concept of fact) does not introduce field theory into his philosophy; but it does make way for this introduction insofar as it defines selfhood as having two different areas of operation —one in nature, and one beyond the limits of physical nature. Hocking admits the double boundary concept, and then wonders what can be said about those bounded territories within which the self operates simultaneously. In *The Self, Its Body and Freedom,* the metaphor of the bounded area becomes the metaphor of a field. Pointing out that "we cannot understand freedom by way of physics or chemistry, nor in spite of physics and chemistry," Hocking nevertheless felt "bound to enquire how, or whether, in view of the truth of physics and chemistry, freedom is possible."[26] The concern for freedom finds encouragement in the fact that physical laws are relative to a "restricted field of validity." He notes, for example, the law of the expansion of bodies by heat. The fact that ice, in melting, does not expand is an exception which illustrates the relativity of law to its appropriate field of validity. This relativity is characteristic of all physical law, and theoretically all such laws must be relative to an ultimate law of the universe. Physics pushes toward such a law but knows no assignable limit to the analysis of physical event and thus never deals with this ultimate law of events. And it does not need to as long as it keeps the relativity of its several laws clearly in mind.

For the self, in its pursuit and realization of value, however, there is a necessary, ultimate law of meaning to which the laws of physical nature are relative. This law of meaning implies the reliability and steadfastness of the laws of nature, for the self *needs* the steadfast unchangeability of natural law.

> Thus, the body as a thing of nature shows me my dependence on heredity and environment, my law of growth and decline, my fate, my certainty of death. Let it do so. This is what it must do as a faithful drawer of consequences. Unless it did this with complete fidelity it would be a worthless servant, like an erratic watch. So far as the body is immersed in the natural order, it presents me a stream of well-adjusted events which afford me a certain data for action. These data fit into their subordinate places in the hierarchy of action whose total result is directed simply from the seat of conscious will.[27]

Hocking is obviously feeling his way at this point. The relationship between the law of meaning and the relative physical laws of the natural world is not an issue on which he is prepared to be dogmatic, nor is he even ready to formulate a clear doctrine. He does speculate, however, and these admittedly metaphorical speculations indicate the direction in which his mind was moving.

> Now it is at least conceivable in a world in which space and time are to some extent functions of one another, that any control of the time-relations of events carries with it a control—it matters not how minute—of their space relations. It is conceivable that in the direction toward the future there lies before the self not space-one-and-absolute but a certain space-variety or space-spread, which the movement of life continuously reduces to singleness, and that this reduction is the essential business of life in the natural world.[28]

And again, in a comment which gave promise of future work on the same problem:

> On the physical side, if it were observable, [the] inner change which marks decision would show itself as a growing flush of activity in one of the waiting sets of action. It begins as an insensible change, a passage from zero to something, like the passage from a tangent into a curve or the fall of a raindrop on one side or other of a watershed. The physical issue lies in a physically indiscoverable alternative at the peak of the hierarchy of conditions of change. And my conjecture is that we have, at every instant of our lives, the choice before us which of several closely related future space-time-worlds shall become the continuous prolongation of the past-and-present space-time-world.
>
> These are speculations: let it be with them as it may. The enquiry is one for the physicist, the biologist, and the philosopher to work out in co-operation.[29]

The manner in which these speculations groped their way toward clarity is typical of Hocking's philosophical development, and makes an interesting case study in the birth of an idea. Characteristically, the problem surfaced in his mind in the midst of a vivid experience of nature. He was no longer a young man. His appointment at Harvard had been extended five years beyond the normal retirement age of 65, and he was already in the final year of that extension. It was the fall of 1941, and he was offering his seminar in metaphysics for the last time. The work of Nils Bohr had convinced him that metaphysical speculation and physical theory had become inseparable. The seminar was therefore concerned with a reconsideration of the problems of space and time, mass and energy. After the seminar meeting of Wednesday, October 21, Hocking took a lonely walk along the banks of the Charles River. The war in Europe was spreading, and America's involvement was only a few short weeks away. Perhaps metaphysical speculation was idle in the face of this crisis; yet relativity theory "seemed to carry us toward the center of things, since the unlocking of physical riddles must affect all human doings, including war itself." Hocking describes the event:

> The sun had already set. A new crescent was standing over the far end of Andersen bridge. The mass of Business School buildings was reflected in the river as a dimly waving blackness. Under the blackness the river was silver. Against the silver, a Harvard eight at belated practice was silhouetted, oarsmen and coxswain posturing rhythmically like gondoliers.
> To the west, over the line of gray-blue hills, a rim of brownish-red glow, shading upward into a sky-depth of luminous darkness. It was as though for the moment Nature were holding still—caught in a spell of quiet and tense glory, unwilling to fade.

. . . Here was quiescence—no seminar, no discussion, no
labor of categories, also no war. Time had stopped, and the
world was now drenched in unmoving space. Space was endless; it was *my* space, running out far beyond the solitary
evening star; running also through the earth, and out the
other side. There were armies at night, minds full of battle-
plans for tomorrow's action. Was it truly the same space?
Could that space, crowded with fighter's strategies, be the
same as my space, spell-bound in peace?

Yes, it must be the identical space; it is the same world for
all of us. Yet it cannot be the same. For no one else saw the
world I saw; if I had not happened along, that marvel of a
sky-moment might have passed unknown. It was certainly
not known to *itself*, was it? Those colors, lights, shapes,
shadows, could exist only for a creature with eyes, stationed
at or near where I was standing.

Our various spaces, all infinite, must be and cannot be
identical. The answer? *Space is not single, but plural.* There
is a world-space, identical for all included persons. But
for each one, there is also a private space, perhaps spaces,
holding private responses to qualities, holding also futuri-
ties, not yet existent—plans, battle-plans perhaps, plans that
can be detained, modified, cancelled, as events in the identical world-space cannot be.

Space must have a plural—this we were saying in the
seminar. And more than this, each person envisages plural
spaces. Then, the *position of the person,* the self, toward
this his plurality, how shall we describe it? Each space can
be called a "field," a continuum in which infinite positions,
potentials, etc., can be distinguished and held-together.
Could the self, as envisaging plural fields, be a *field of
fields?*[30]

That night an essay went off to *The Journal of Philosophy*.
It was entitled "Theses Establishing an Idealistic Metaphysics by a New Route,"[31] and in it Hocking stated a typically ingenious line of argument very briefly (the essay ran to
only two and a half printed pages) with the promise of

further development at a later date "in more intelligible form."[32] Hocking noted that the Kantian-Newtonian picture of the space-time world as necessarily singular had been upset by implications in the non-Euclidean geometries of Riemann and Lobatschewski that space could have a legitimate plural. He went on to say that Dedekind, Cantor, and others had developed conceptions of infinitude which now allowed for pluralities of the infinite. The relativity theory of Minkowski and Einstein drew on these developments in announcing that space and time were not only interdependent, but also plural and derivative. But what can we say, as a result, concerning the nature of space and time or space-time? Hocking notes that they are neither things nor relations, but "fields established by the relatableness which the concrete event implies."[33] Thus independent events x and x' both face an infinite possibility of relationships within their own space-time fields; but their infinitudes do not interpenetrate any more than the several non-Euclidean spaces clash with one another. Hocking illustrates with a puckish question: How far is it from where I sit in a room to the tip of a tree in an imaginary landscape painting hung on the wall of that room? Or we might add, how far is it (or how long does it take to get) from the mountain path down which a bear chased me in my dream last night to the bedpost which I found myself clutching when I awoke? An event at the landscape tree-top is independent in space-time from any event which takes place at a given point in the room. In two independent infinite fields, a position in one field will be spatially related to all other positions in that field, but it has no spatial relations to any position in any other field.

We wonder, along with Hocking, whether there is no way to break through this pluralism? Is there no basic unity among the different fields? One might argue that one's body participates in both the dream world of being-chased-by-a-bear and the waking world of clutching-the-bedpost. Hocking replies that body, as a member of the dream world, is numerically different from the body which is tossing fitfully in the bed, even though dream activity is sometimes symbolized by body movements during sleep. There is one point, however, in which this space-time plurality is broken through, and that is in the self which considers plural, space-time infinites and sets up plural geometries. The self is the "vinculum" between these various possible pluralities. "The self may therefore be considered as a 'field' in which the members are total fields: it is the field of fields."[34] But more than this: since *this* field is not a function of events within any of the particular plural fields which it encompasses, mind cannot be a function of events within any one nature-system, and "the self is not merely a field of fields, but a concrete event determining the field of fields."[35]

In his essay on "Fact, Field and Destiny," Hocking is consciously recasting the form of his earlier Gifford Lectures on "Fact and Destiny" to accompany his emerging understanding of field as the ground of relationship among the plurality of natural facts. This ground is not to be identified with the category of relation as such, as it figures in the work of Bradley, Russell, and Whitehead. Behind any set of relationships lies the ground or possibility of relation which Hocking seeks to bring forward for metaphysical examination. Removed in this way from any particular relations, and thus having no sense properties of its own, it seems at first glance indistinguishable from simple nothingness or void. With the advent of quantum theory, however, its characteristics have become newly significant because of the problem of continuity-discontinuity in nature. Hocking distinguishes his own use of field as a metaphysical category from the physical field-notion of Clerk Maxwell. Hocking points out that concentration on field as a background or "undifferentiated continuum" (F.S.C. Northrop) requires emptying it of all occupation-by-energy-functions such as gravity or electro-magnetism. The emphasis is on a "generalized, common sense" of field as field-emptiness. Even so, this ideal abstract field still has its nature, according to Hocking.

He asserts that "field has an all-or-none totality."[36] In other words, there can be no boundary to field, for this would leave a field-region beyond the boundary. Hence, space, as field, is all space; time, all time. Secondly, Hocking insists that "a Field is internally related to its contents."[37] Internal relation makes a difference to the being of the particulars thus related, so that the destruction of a time-field, for example, would simultaneously destroy the possibility of all events in time. Hocking also argues that the obverse is true. Common sense assumes that one can destroy an event in time without destroying time itself and that the elimination of a molecule does not entail the elimination of that space within which the molecule was positioned. Hocking's point is that destruction is not complete unless the part of the space-time field occupied by the particular event or thing is itself destroyed. On the basis of the all-or-none principle just cited, Hocking feels, the destruction of one segment would destroy the whole. It is on this basis that relativity theory denies the possibility of pre-existent or independently empty fields of space-time. There can be no space before there is something to go in it; neither is there time before something happens. Relativity, as Hocking understands it, argues that event is the "elemental real," and the possibility of the event being related to something is given with the event. In other words, content, and the field which provides the "undifferentiated continuum" within which the content exists, go together. On this basis he challenges Hume's assumption that God could eliminate evil from the world without otherwise altering the structure of the world as we know it. (Chapter IV, above.)

Thirdly, Hocking goes on, "Wherever there are plural Facts of the same kind, there is a Field including them and essential to their being. Corollary: No pluralism can be a final metaphysic."[38] The crucial problem here is creativity. Whitehead binds up the pluralism of his universe through the ultimate category of creativity, in which the plural events of space-time become a single occasion which is simply "the universe." For Hocking, however, the unity of the world cannot lie in a separate creativity, but in a creativity within the context of plurality itself. No abstract creative ultimate can solve the problem of nature's arbitrary factuality. For Hocking, creativity is the criterion of reality for any particular self. The freedom on which this creative possibility depends is a freedom of concrete choice. It is precisely the plurality of space and time, as clarified by physical field theory, which makes it possible for him to present the metaphor of possible worlds for the self to choose from, which he had speculated on earlier in *The Self, Its Body and Freedom*.

When we contemplate alternate courses of action, we survey in imagination what the different courses would involve. The contemplated world in the mind is nonexistent. Nevertheless, it is possible, waiting only to be "realized" by a decision.[39] What the active self does is to weave other worlds into the texture of his own present given world. Freedom is concrete because it alters the particulars of the sequence of events in the actual space-time world.[40] The self is thus a "vinculum," "a hinge of transition"[41] between possible worlds and the actual world. As such, the self cannot be said to be a member of either world, although the body does become a member of each contemplated world. The body always remains distinctively that of a unique, individual person, but the body of the self's different worlds is numerically different in keeping with the divergent situations of divergent worlds. In dreams, for example—although body may be curiously absent from many of our dreams— we may discover that we can fly. Body is therefore a function of two independent variables, not of one only; it is in part, with life itself, a gift of "fact," but it is also in part a function of the self, serving that self's decisions and its capacity to create what, apart from the self's thought, "the *world would not contain.*"[42] Human life is therefore a free transaction of what the self conceives through its "prophetic consciousness," its imagination, its dreams, into fact, by way of bodily action.[43]

Anyone who has begun a college essay with a blank sheet of paper and equally blank mind, only to be blessed with a sudden "bright idea," will have wondered where the idea came from. Hocking tells us that it is the result of some "intimate co-operation of thinker and object."[44] He finally rejects the Platonic doctrine of "remembered" ideas, despite an earlier flirtation, along with Whitehead's similar doctrine that the idea is a prehension from some fixed realm of eternal entities. He insists on a radical freedom. It is the self as "vinculum" between the worlds of possibility and actuality which gives birth to the idea, and thus "there is creation in the world of fact. This is concrete freedom."[45]

Hocking was eighty-six in 1959 when he published *The Meaning of Immortality in Human Experience*—the same year in which he completely revised (with Richard Hocking) his *Types of Philosophy*. As he entered his nineties, he began a close cooperation with the young physicist-philosopher, Frederick Werner of Xavier University. Werner had worked with Nils Bohr in Copenhagen, and has been influenced by Hocking's conception of the self as a field of fields. Werner believes that the common ground between contemporary physics and philosophy tends to confirm man's instinctive conviction that the truth about his experienced world has "Integrity."[46] Werner finds both physics and philosophy overcoming the challenge to this integrity posed by the Cartesian bifurcation of nature into *res extensa* and *res cogitans*. In philosophy the challenge is met by a metaphysics such as Hocking's which shows the interdependence of body and mind, nature and selfhood. In physics the challenge is met by quantum theory which overcomes the conflict between the theory-inventing freedom of the scientist, reflected in differential and integral calculus, and the determinism and locally causal necessity of classical physics. In the past the scientist has avoided investigating his own subjectivity. Thus his position as an observing spectator has been a point of freedom in the midst of physical determinism. For Werner this bifurcation in classical physics between the inventive, theoretical freedom of the physicist and the causal determinism of nature is problematical because the freedom of the physicist as spectator is only theoretical. It lacks what Hocking calls the "concrete freedom" to make a real difference in the way things are. The physicist has become alienated from the wholeness or integrity of his world. Today, however, quantum theory rejects locally causal determinism on the basis of experiments where it is impossible to specify or define the position of a particular body at a given moment. What quantum theory can do, however, is to specify patterns of coherence or phase relation between or among particular bodies. These patterns are various, and Werner regards the richness of this variety as a new opportunity for the physicist to express his "concrete freedom" through the generalizations of theory-building.

Contemporary physics still makes use of classical mechanics for description of objective, experimental circumstances and results, but at the same time enlarges the truer aspects of the older theory by this "theory-*inventing* procedure of generalization."[47] Werner comments:

> Building of a generalized theory requires exercise of decision upon one from among a plurality of mathematical generalizations which could be considered. But these mathematical generalizations do not of themselves possess any physical interpretation. Interpretation must be given to the generalization selected. This giving of meaning to the otherwise rather empty mathematical formalism is a decisive part of theoretical physics. It is no mere discovery, or even a mere selection from some pre-established collection. It is a fresh creation.[48]

Further, and perhaps even more significant for Hocking's conception of the self's decision making (and for his religious conception of the prophetic consciousness), the invented theory is an objective account of reality. The fact that more than one theory will produce an adequate explanation of the phenomenon involved does not mean that the theory invented is "subjective." When Hocking announces that "creativity is a genesis of possibilities of quality which, prior to the begetting deed, had not even a positional existence"[49] he is using language which applies with equal validity to physics and philosophy. Werner values Hocking's conception of the self as a "field of fields" because it "takes seriously the role of invention, as distinct from pure imagination or discovery, in the exercise of concrete freedom."[50]

Creativity is the criterion of reality in the self for Hocking, and the home of creativity is the mind of the individual. It would be a mistake, however, to speak of individual creativity as though it could exist in abstract isolation from the community. Creativity *"bears the individual mark,"* but there is much evidence which suggests "that the *telos* has wider origins."[51] The creative work is privately done, but it cannot remain private, for it belongs to our world, and not just to the world of its author. The work of the creative individual has a destiny beyond itself, and this destiny inevitably involves participation in the life of the organized human community.

Chapter VIII

REMAKING HUMAN NATURE

MAN IS THE MOST MALLEABLE OF CREATURES. At birth he is the least finished among mammals and has the largest prospects for development. He is, however, the most difficult animal to deal with. Growth, development, and learning are characteristic of his nature, but so is the reaction against them. Man resists change. He is pugnacious, greedy, sexually impulsive, and fearful; and he is inexhaustibly clever and subtle in expressing these antisocial instincts. Somehow his instincts must be dealt with if the social problems of war, superstition, and political corruption are to be solved. But how? Naturalism counsels liberation, assuming that instinct naturally knows what it wants and can find its way to satisfaction unaided. But how, asks Hocking, can instinct *know?*[1] In the conflict with disciplines of all sorts, he points out that the Nietzsches, the Schlegels, the Walt Whitmans—all those who would have us sing an unbound song of ourselves —have regarded life as a quantity and decreed: "If all other things are equal, always express, never repress." This lusty advice is magnificently alive, and there is a certain egalitarian justice in its democracy of human instinct; but it fails to provide any leadership for conflicting impulses. Instinct, in order to be fulfilled, needs to know what it is looking for. But Hocking wants first to know how instinct works.

A realistic sociology must understand the nature of the problem before it can suggest a viable solution.

Hocking notes that biology as a discipline defines instinct as a group of reflexes which follow a regular order, in sequence, to a significant conclusion—as in wooing, nesting, mating, etc.[2] The mechanism of the serial progression is made possible through a happy economy whereby the conclusion of one stage furnishes the necessary part of the stimulus for the next. Hocking is particularly interested in the push toward a significant end in which the action terminates. Since individual instinct tends to favor the wider interests of the organism as a whole, nervous circuits must, at some point, pass through the highest nervous center which controls the whole organism. Ultimately, the significant end of instinct is the life of the organism. Instinct is thus a matter of consciousness as well as subconsciousness, of mind and memory in man. Therefore, Hocking notes, instinct is legitimate material for remaking.[3] Instinct provides our objects with value, but since we have a good many instinctive values, which often conflict, the questions arise: does the self have a biological integrity in which instincts derive from a central group of instincts, or is there perhaps a single instinct which provides the nucleus for all human values? The challenge of these questions lies in the subtle balance, variety, and coalescence of man's instinctive equipment; but there do seem to be some instincts which are broader than others, holding lesser instincts under their control. There are, Hocking believes, some instincts which are primarily central, i.e. conditions of the center of organization in the organism. He calls these "necessary interests" not because there is any logical necessity involved but rather because they are constitutionally necessary.[4] His empiricism is as strong as his idealism in these matters, and he takes advantage of this honest holiday from logical necessity to play a bit with the idea of rhythm as a necessary interest.

Consider the universal tendency to rhythmic expression, as in dancing, music, design, various forms of play. There are many signs that the appreciation of rhythm is as necessary a consequence of the economy of nervous functions, as rhythmic behavior is of the economy of muscular function, of respiratory function, etc. When we want to gain the full flavor of any sense-impression, we repeat it at intervals, as in tasting, stroking, feeling textures, etc. So, too, with those perceptions in which thought is mingled with sense. In realizing the proportions of a facade, a series of buttresses or a segmented cornice aid the "grasp." . . . The principle may be this: that to appreciate any experience in its totality we must resort to the device of really or mimetically building it up from numerable parts; so that whatever we desire to hold vividly before consciousness we will necessarily tend to divide and recompose by segments or in rhythmic intervals. Rhythm would then be a general character of art forms, i.e. of the forms we choose for heightened perception, because of a necessary condition of the neutral substratum of cognition. In this sense we might speak of rhythm as a necessary interest.[5]

Hocking goes on to suggest a list of necessary interests: our natural sociability, certain elements of ambition, and the family affections. Among the formal interests there are, besides rhythm, our instincts for unity, harmony, differentiation, completeness, and simplicity. Self-preservation is also clearly one of man's necessary interests. But Hocking throws out this list almost casually, and shows no inclination to argue it in opposition to current and conflicting assessments. The question which interests him most, and which he regards as most important, is the question of the integrity of these several instincts, the manner in which they cohere in a self; or, more simply, their relation to the one fundamental instinct of an individual—the will. He is convinced that it is virtually impossible to produce a clearly defensible and exhaustive list of necessary interests because these are not distinct and separate entities with characteristic mechanisms and carefully demarcated areas of operation. They are aspects of the single will of the individual. For Hocking there must be such a unity in the catalog of interests—and here the necessity *is* logical—for the only way two radically different experiences of the same self can be distinguished from two different experiencs of different selves is that in a single self they appear as two examples of common value meaning. The self is the common fortune which integrates all of its interests and experiences. The self is "a permanent principle of selection"[6] which establishes a policy toward the influx of instinctive impulse. Its capacity to effect this policy is what Hocking has in mind when he speaks of the will.

> And thus, if men are alike in nature, we should be able to perceive at the center of all "central instincts" and "necessary interests" and indeed within all instinct whatever, a nucleus of common meaning which we would be justified in calling the fundamental instinct of man, the substance of the human will. No one description of this central instinct is likely to be sufficient; but the phrase "will to power" is capable of conveying a large part of the truth.[7]

The source of his doctrine is, of course, Nietzsche's "Wille zur Macht," and at first blush it seems a very unlikely source indeed. How did the genial idealist, the veritable incarnation of sanity and responsibility, the courtly, well-tailored Hocking, Hocking the Christian gentleman, the Harvard man, the American midwesterner, ever get mixed up with "that scapegrace, Nietzsche"? Clearly this Hocking is worlds away from the wild-eyed existentialist, the God-destroyer who was never far from insanity. But the qualities in Hocking which give him his cutting edge—his passionate concern for creativity, the ingenuity of his logic, his globe-trotting wanderlust, the conviction that nature has been given to man as a challenge to his power to remake it, the adventurousness of his marriage to Agnes Hocking, and his delight in her spontaneous and robust refusal to be conventional— these qualities were already beginning to show during his student year in Germany, and it was this in him which responded to Nietzsche. Recalling that year (1902-1903), he mused:

> And then, oddly enough, I got a good deal from that scapegrace, Nietzsche. It was my landlady, Helena Burckhardt of Krausnickstrasse, Berlin, who gave me *Also Sprach Zarathustra;* and I found this reckless player-with-lightning strangely refreshing. I couldn't digest his condemnation of Die Mitleidigenden but I saw what he meant by saying that "it is the will of all great love, the beloved to *create;* and all creators are *hard.*" So I changed his "Wille zur Macht"—to the "will to suffer in creation"; but I see the validity of his rejection of futility as the opposite of any good which can realize T'ien Ming, the appointment of Heaven.[8]

The emphasis on suffering as an element in the will to power was a later development, one not fully articulated until *Experiment in Education* (1954) which contained Hocking's reflections on American efforts at education in Germany after World War II. His discussion of the will in *Human Nature and Its Remaking* makes little reference to suffering. Hocking's will to power has here caught something of Nietzsche's dynamism, but it has no Nietzschean undercurrent of brooding despair, no sense of tragedy, and none of the strident self-aggrandizement of the Übermensch. It is individualistic and optimistic in the American sense, emphasizing (in sophisticated terms) man's capacity to build a better mousetrap, and thereby exercise his creative power to make a difference in his world. This will to power is at the heart of the will to live, and Hocking finds it operative in the most basic human activities. *Human Nature and Its Remaking* is less tightly written than *The Meaning of God,* and its freer style allows more scope for the intellectual's characteristic gift of brilliance. Consider, for example, Hocking's discovery of the will to power in the simple process of eating:

> Food-getting instincts reach their apparent goal in the satisfying of hunger; yet it would be a bold psychology that would affirm that eating, to the human species, has no more general meaning than quenching this craving. Hunger, I dare say, is felt as a diminished status, a sign of a dependence on material intake, which eating both confesses and temporarily removes. It is perhaps the element of physical humility which makes the taking of food a fit occasion for sociability; for here is the most natural and permanent democracy, that of dependence on material nature for continued life. But the social instinct would hardly make so much of a mutual confession of dependence if there were not also a mutual emancipation. Eating, by itself, is a form of conquest, surrounding what is alien and making it part of ourselves. The satisfaction of food to a thoroughly hungry man is less a matter of the aesthetics of taste than a consciousness of making something his own, a sense of mastery. But beyond this, he is aware of eating as releasing the springs of his rightful attitude toward the world, his control of his own fortune. In both ways, the satisfaction of hunger is at the same time a satisfaction of a "love of power."[9]

He makes the same point in regard to play, which he describes as the practice of mastery over plastic materials in order that the self may be prepared to deal effectively with the more recalcitrant materials of the real world. He deals the same way with fear, which makes us flee from water, or fire, or ghosts, or the yawning chasms of empty space (all of which are representative of an *un*canny world) to a world where we may once again say I *can.* The will to power is a will to live as a man, to fulfill the instinctive demands of a genuinely human existence that we deal effectively with the world around us. One of its clearest illustrations is the will of the artist to impose form and order on the world, to deal with the world not as external mass but as meaning. Hocking finds the Nietzschean doctrine right in bringing this will to light and announcing that it is central to human nature. Nietzsche is wrong, according to Hocking, only in his naturalistic assumptions: first, that merely to express this will is to fulfill it; second, that the will to power is necessarily competitive. Power over nature finds its value in the social good which it provides and is therefore a basic element in all actual commonwealth. And the power that one man has over another may at the same time be a means of conferring power on that person, in the same way that a parent's power over a child leads to the development of the child's own power to deal effectively with his world.[10] These observations, Hocking realizes, are sanguine ones, and there are obviously aspects of man's impulsive life which are problematical and even demonic. One of these is the fact of evil in the human will; another is the difficulty which the best intentioned individual will has in fulfilling itself in society where it conflicts with other wills equally in need of fulfilling themselves.

Much of the change in an individual's will is worked by the individual himself. It is seldom achieved in isolation or without the help of external forces; nevertheless "strictly

speaking, nothing can transform a will but itself."[11] This is
not so much a defense of man's creativity vis-à-vis himself as
it is a touch of realism. Social institutions, Hocking is saying, are severely limited in their capacity to change men.
Law, for example, is the state's attempt to reform human
pugnacity. It applies penalties to the man whose wilfulness
has led him into lawbreaking. But does the state actually
punish him? Can it punish? Obviously it does in an empirical sense, which Hocking tends to accept and use. But
the state's intent is to punish effectively. Punishment is
meted out in order to effect a significant difference in the
individual's willing, and the state has no control over
whether this actually occurs. Whether a penalty becomes an
effective punishment depends almost entirely on the individual's decision in regard to his own will. It is for this
reason that Hocking later insists that "the State can apply
the penalties. But it cannot punish."[12]

Not only is society ineffective without the cooperation of
the individual, but there is also some evidence that one's
own experience is always more productive than formal social
institutions—school, church, law—in remaking the will. Perhaps experience *is* the best teacher. Formal training—in college, for example—may rob the individual's formative years
of such definitive experiences as earning one's own living.
Hocking notes, however, that even the education provided
by the "school of hard knocks" is largely social, and that the
individual's understanding of what he wants for himself
comes mainly from the possibilities which he experiences in
contact with others.

The most general modeling force working on the individual, Hocking says, is social convention. Because society
works largely through imitation and suggestion, its influence
is accepted by its subjects with docility and without much

thought. When reason calls custom into question, integrity demands that reason's questions be answered. There are those respectful of tradition, like Aristotle, who are inclined to feel that if many people have held an idea or practised a custom for a long time there must be something in it.[13] On the other hand, there are revolutionaries, like Plato, deeply convinced that ideas acquired at one's mother's knee or from the man-in-the-street are almost always wrong, and who side with the intelligent Socratic individual who must always fight the conventionalized stupidity of the crowd. Hocking stands with Aristotle largely out of appreciation for the social economy involved. Custom, Hocking asserts, provides us with an incredible amount of accumulated capital.[14] Some things can only be learned through individual experience, and other things require the touch of individual experience to drive them home. But how far would we get if we had to do all our learning on our own? The act of enrolling in school is not one that the first-grader could be counted on to choose for himself. It is years before he realizes the value of having been forcibly introduced to the information and experience which have been made available to him through others' trial and error. If there is to be any real progress, the individual must take advantage of society's already collected wisdom.

Society therefore continues not only the work of the individual will's development through experience, but also the entire process of organic evolution. Hocking notes two aspects of this continuing work. The first is in prolonging what he calls the "vestibule of satisfaction."[15] He has in mind the number of preliminary processes which stand between the initial desire and its fulfillment. Once again, food-getting is his illustration. For the amoeba, contact with edibles and "eating" are identical operations. The sea anemone, however, must make preliminary gestures; tentacles are used to gather particles of food. Higher forms of life, equipped with eyes and ears, discern food at a distance, and use appropriate organs to go and get it. More advanced is the creature whose instinct and experience make him prepare for a rainy day or an entire season by storing food. When society interposes further complex conditions "it is but exceeding Nature at her own game. . . . The general principle holds good, that the farther the stimulus is from the satisfaction, the less its intensity, the more it is negligible, and therefore the inconvenience of delay or even of ignoring it is negligible, in the vital economy."[16] This stretching of the vestibule of satisfaction has little purpose from the purely biological standpoint, but it does equip the organism for life in an increasingly complex environment. Its main value is psychological. Not only are powers of self-control enhanced and techniques of satisfaction varied; the meaning of each process is immensely developed.

The second aspect noted by Hocking is that the lengthening of the vestibule of satisfaction allows for limitation of the objects with which one deals. The organs which make it possible for developed animals to get food and store it are precisely those organs which allow for choice in the kind of food. This is not a restriction; it is the development of the power of selective response. When society further decrees that some foods are acceptable and some not, the resulting custom is "in continuance of the direction of phylogenesis and of experience, as before."[17] These considerations lead Hocking to some general assumptions which figure importantly in his approach to the conflict between the individual will and society. In a collectivistic age, he is not ready to sacrifice the needs of the individual. He believes in a potential harmony between the two. Thus he is not afraid of the inevitable massiveness of the coming world civilization. In his assertion that society continues the processes inherent in natural, individual development, he implicitly rejects any Rousseauistic regard for a primitive, precivilized world of a supposedly noble savage, as well as the element of romantic nostalgia embedded in existentialist individualism. Existentialism's introspective concern with the deepest experience of selfhood inevitably pits the individual against the social mass and expresses a deep disaffection for modern society. Hocking's appreciation of existentialism is genuine, but it is within his concern for the coming world civilization, and he values it for what it can contribute to the requirements of living in a new social context. He is on the side of the individual, but he is free to welcome new social forms, and he is not afraid of new social dilemmas.[18]

The individual still faces two crucial problems. One is to decide what he wants, what it means to be a person, what is a genuinely human existence? The second is to relate oneself to others in such a way that one's individuality is fulfilled without sacrificing the individuality of the other in the process. The two problems are obviously interrelated, but the first is essentially concerned with education in the broadest sense, including not only formal education, but the remaking process of art, and the converting process of religion. The second is essentially concerned with the organizing functions of the state, problems of human rights and law, the "cake of custom" which feeds distinctive human cultures; nationalism, internationalism, and problems of civilization. Even here, however, the determinative reality for Hocking is religion, for he is convinced that the religious motivation of the believer's mission toward his fellow men is the key to mutual, individual fulfillment. In the "Christian ambition" to confer spiritual power *on* another, the will to exercise power *over* others—through the instinctive drives of sex, pugnacity and ambition—is converted and redirected. Thus the individual will finds an outlet which is ideally non-competitive. Hocking believes that it is in the reconceiving and humanizing of this religious imperative that the coming world civilization will find a substantial, common basis. We cannot talk of the individual, however, without talking about the "ism," and Hocking is convinced that there are *Lasting Elements of Individualism*. We have already examined the metaphysics of selfhood. We must now add a word on the social and historical background of Western individualism.[19]

In his quest for the original sources of Western individualism, Hocking works his way backwards, noting that there are differing types and, thus, that no single concept can be determined. John Stuart Mill's *Political Economy* is a landmark in the development of economic individualism, although it is clearly a "belated theoretical statement"[20] of the earlier concern for the "rights of man" which grew out of the eighteenth century's democratic revolutions. Prior to the eighteenth century, Hocking points out, modern individualism clearly had its roots in that series of social, economic, and religious events which marked the breakdown of medievalism. In the dissolution of the feudal system and the rise of the guilds, the traditional caste organization of labor was shaken by the beginnings of mobility on the part of the serf. It became increasingly possible for the serf to consider the question, "Whose man shall I be?"[21] And in this element of choice individualism found a foothold. With the change in the feudal economy came a political shift. The desire of kings to tap private resources of wealth resulted in a system of local representation to aid in the collection of this tax. This open route between king and people, instituted for the convenience of the king, also served to inform the king of the needs and views of the people. Thus, Hocking explains, the individual will began to have its effect on the state.[22] In religion, the Protestant Reformation bestowed on the individual conscience the obligation to think for itself, thus substituting the private conviction of the individual for the collective conscience of the church.

Behind these events of history, Hocking finds the beginnings of concern for the soul—an awareness which was part of Western culture's birthright and the earliest seed of Western individualism. The soul is simply the mental individual: the ego or self. In most primitive speculation, the soul was the distinctive part of man, marking off one individual from another in his communal setting of family or tribe, and also distinguishing the essential self from its body. On the basis of this distinctiveness, the soul was conceived as surviving bodily death. This idea was refined by the Platonic conception of a soul able to leave the empirical world of distorted shadows to find its peace in the realm of pure essences. Greek mythology conceived of the purified soul passing through the plain of forgetfulness, blotting out personal memories and social attachments. The Platonic soul is therefore a "pure mental atom."[23] The Christian understanding of the soul, on the other hand, is not so clear cut. There is a distinction to be made between the soul and the body, but the soul cannot be a genuine self without the body, as the dogma of the resurrection of the body affirms. Similarly, while the individual soul must stand alone at the day of judgment, Christian eschatology looks toward the participation of individual souls in a blessed community— the "Kingdom of God." In Christianity, Hocking notes, the soul is distinct but not self-sufficient, either in relation to the physical body or to the social community.

Western thought has entertained influences from both

these conceptions of the soul—the Platonic and the Christian —and Hocking himself tends to honor both. His emphasis is largely on the Christian side as he deals with societal and with mind-body problems; in his religious thought, however, the pull of the Platonic conception is evident. As a social philosopher, Hocking nevertheless harbors a yearning for the flight of the alone to the alone. The prophetic consciousness which seeks to remake history also longs for the purity and peace of oneness with the Divine.

If these are the seeds of Western individualism, what are its characteristic features? Hocking notes three, beginning with the belief in the equality of all men. This is not an empirical judgment. Men are not equal in actual fact, nor are they born with equal opportunities. Hocking frequently pointed out that men are to be regarded as equal before the law (the place where equality tends to become a serious issue) on the metaphysical ground that the soul or selfhood of one man cannot be judged as inherently more or less valuable than the being of another. But while men are essentially equal, it is only at this *essential* point that equality prevails.[24] Equality has a metaphysical, not an empirical, basis. A second feature of individualism is its belief in essential liberty, available to all men. This individual liberty is not one of the original elements of social organization. As there was a law in human society before there was ever a concept of individual rights, so also the community organization of tribe or caste dominates the early ventures in human social development. But in the serf's question—"Whose man shall I be?"—the logic of economic and political individualism begins to work. The collectivist formula is: "To every group, numerous men and sets of men." The logic of individualism demands a new formula: "To every man, numerous groups, and possible groups."[25] The individual is at liberty to choose.

The third feature, Hocking says, is the conviction that an individual is invested with a set of rights which are his not through his accomplishment, but by his existence as a man. These rights spring from his needs as a man, and these needs are the basis for his choice of the possible groups which are available to serve his development and fulfillment as an individual. But since these groups are groups of equals, and since the rights involved are the common rights of each individual, the chosen group is neither an atomistic collection of individuals, nor a heteronomous framework imposed by some higher authority (as in feudal organization); it is a fraternity of free, equal individuals, sharing common rights. On this basis, liberalism—the ideology of individualism—establishes its credo: liberty, equality, fraternity.

It is part of Hocking's liberal creed and his first postulate for a good society that the societal goals must find common ground with the goals of the individual will.[26] The tendency of society to be repressive—in imposing the ideals and standards of the group on the individual, in limiting the scope of individual development to allow for the development of others, and in prescribing fixed institutional forms of accepted behavior—must be corrected if the individual is to regard social modeling as good. While there is no society which identifies its goals completely with those of the individual, Hocking finds several social arrangements which help to secure the demands of his postulate. The first of these is, of course, the family, that "most altruistic part of the social shell." It is the individual's good fortune, Hocking feels, that his introduction to the impact of social modeling comes through those dedicated to his individual development; "he is born among his well-wishers."[27] After the family there are those "Recommenders" of value to whom society accords a position of immunity from conventional controls so that they may speak as free spirits. Traditionally these were the elders, the priests, prophets, and medicine men. Today they are the scholars, the men of letters and the arts whose essential work is liberal reflection on the authority, and we look to them to articulate what is best in our society and in ourselves. But if the value of the recommender lies in the fact that his perspective transcends the immediate conflicts between *meum* and *tuum,* Hocking points out also the danger involved in the ivory tower which is often the recommender's home. The recommender's advice tends to be too clear, simple, refined, abstract. We might have expected Hocking to turn pragmatist at this point, appealing to the man of experience as an antidote to the overly aesthetic emphasis of pure ideals; but he finds a natural corrective for the "tyranny of abstractions" provided by opposing abstractions which force the individual to select between them or to relate them dialectically.[28] And the role of the recommender is not exhausted by his articulation of what he thinks. The real identity between the desire of the individual and the role which society recommends to him is established in the mechanics of admiration, whereby "what I admire in others I wish for myself." Hence, "what they would admire in me, I must wish for in myself."[29]

Admiration is, of course, dangerous business, and modern realism tends to temper any hero-worship. It is fashionable to be cynical; we rejoice in the flaws of the great. Nevertheless, we continue to chart our course by specific reference to those who symbolize for us the valued energies and graces of manhood. Even the most original and unique spirits admit influences, and these, Hocking insists, do not alienate a man from his own genius, but rather recall him to himself. "What my friend wishes me to be, and what I would appear to him to be, is without doubt what I also demand for myself. In this instance, at least, I am recalled to my own freedom. And this is the natural destiny of all the arrangements by which society foists ideals upon individual lives."[30]

The second of Hocking's postulates for a good society concerns the transformation of competitive interests. "Every competitive interest must be so transformed or interpreted as to be non-competitive, or an ingredient in a non-competitive interest."[31] Hocking admits that the competitive interest in the primary, economic needs of food, shelter, etc., will probably always be competitive in part; but the necessary interests of the self in such things as unity, order, rhythm are not restricted. When one person serves his own necessary interest, he is also serving those of others. The will to live, as the basic, necessary interest, is not essentially competitive or mutually exclusive—it does not demand "my life or yours."[32] The ideal society will therefore not be one which eliminates competition, but one which subordinates the competitive elements to the non-competitive. Hocking's solution, in short, is that ideas are the one thing in society which are both competitive and of unlimited supply. Ideas are power of a mutually rewarding sort. I convince others of my idea, and they are brought under my power. But because I have served them with that idea, they enter into its power consciously and freely. For Hocking, "culture" is simply the accumulation of ideas, and the state is the objective condition of society which makes possible such cultural, non-conflicting satisfaction of individual wills to power. The state is therefore a necessary object for the fulfillment of an individual will to power: not any specific state, but some corporate, mutually responsible, human, political community. The state cannot provide this satisfaction in itself, but such satisfaction is impossible apart from the state.[33] It is the existence of the state, Hocking contends, which allows the competitive form of the will to power (the struggle for economic survival) to assume a non-conflicting form in the market of ideas. Education is the means whereby the state preserves and expands the idea-capital of its culture.

Chapter IX

EDUCATION

THE RANGE AND VARIETY OF HOCKING'S work in education make it one of the most arresting aspects of his philosophy. Before he entered Harvard as an undergraduate, he had already had experience teaching elementary grades in a one-room schoolhouse, Latin in a normal school, and mathematics in a business college. He had served as principal of a public school. His first published philosophical essay was concerned with the method of teaching arithmetic to children.[1] He put his experience of elementary education to work in later years when he and Agnes Hocking founded what became the Shady Hill School in Cambridge, Massachusetts.[2] During World War I, he was called on to lecture to the military on *Morale and Its Enemies*.[3] He has written on the place of religion in state universities[4] and on the values of a college education.[5] He devoted an important but little-read book to an evaluation of one of the largest and most unique educational ventures of recent years—the program of re-educating Germany after World War II.[6] Against this background, his unpublished memoir on "Varieties of Educational Experience"[7] seems modestly titled indeed.

This variety of educational adventures is matched by a variety in style and emotional approach to different problems. There are cool, detached, technical essays dealing with the abstract side of the problem.[8] There are humane discussions, more typical of the man of letters than the technical philosopher, laced with common sense and humor and warmed by his obvious affection for children and the young.[9] But there is also *Experiment in Education: What We Can Learn From Teaching Germany,* the most passionate, personal, prophetic essay Hocking ever wrote. He was not one to lose his head, and the writing is controlled throughout; but nowhere is the cutting edge of his criticism sharper, the urgency of his convictions more apparent.[10] Here he was less concerned to be nice, more willing to be nakedly forthright. As in none of his other writings, he exclaims ("ye gods" punctuates the argument repeatedly); he quotes others' cuss words ("damn" appears in his genteel writing for the first time); he appeals directly to the reader, prodding him, questioning him, asking for his judgment, spurring him to take a stand. He is far from the meditative quiet of the philosopher's study, in fact "out of doors" in the midst of shattered and defeated Germany, a Germany he had learned to love and believe in. He gets his hands dirty in the spiritual and ideological rubble which is the aftermath of war, testing the ideals of meaning against the pragmatic requirements of tragic human experience. He comes away convinced that America lacked the wisdom to see the elemental moral issue involved and the faith to believe that Germany could learn the lesson which tragedy had to teach. Education, he tells us, is a serious venture, drawing on the best of man's faith and wisdom. It is, after all, his own vocation as professor. Education, next to religion, is the closest one gets to the bedrock of human culture, the broadest category for dealing with the dynamic by which society seeks to develop and improve itself and the idea-capital of its culture. *Experiment in Education* is not the irascible outburst of an old man out of love with the younger generation's world. It is a prophetic announcement from one of the few American philosophers of history and civilization, and it is concerned with the binding ingredients of Western culture and the failure of a great nation in the midst of her crucial venture to discern them. Hocking's statements here are especially telling when viewed next to his earlier thinking on education.

Hocking recognized early that society has never been willing simply to let children grow up. Social self-consciousness, he notes, takes the form of history, and the most basic form of education is passed from generation to generation in the form of epic, folklore, and myth—in modern societies no less than in primitive ones.[11] The importance of the state is obvious, for, at the same time that the child learns what it means to be a human being, he is also learning what it means to be a person in this particular social context. To learn to be a man in America is also to learn to be an American. Thus society, through its traditions, communicates a type, even while it introduces the learner to traditions other than his own, preparing for growth beyond his particular type. Hocking feels that the initial emphasis on a particular cultural and even national type is justified, not on parochial or nationalistic grounds, but because "the first task of education is to *bring his full will into existence.* And this can only be done by a process so intimate that in doing it the type is inevitably transmitted."[12]

This means that moral and religious values are somehow to be "taught." Here Hocking must face not only the age-old dilemma of Plato's *Protagoras,* whether virtue is "teachable,"[13] but also the modern secular conviction that the developing will should not be overborne by the advocacy of particular moral and religious values, but, rather, should be exposed to a variety of alternatives and left to choose whatever spiritual bargain it is prepared to pay for. Hocking agrees that the first work of education is exposure—but exposure to that which calls out the best responses of the developing will. He opposes both indoctrination on the one hand, and completely secularized education on the other. An educational vacuum amounts to a negation. The lack of an urgent concern for moral and religious values is an announcement that these are not matters of urgent concern. The child has rights, to be sure; but:

> the first of these rights is not that they be left free to choose their way of life, i.e. to make bricks without either straw or clay. Their first right is that they be offered something positive, the best the group has so far found. Against errors and interested propaganda the growing will has natural protection: it has *no protection against starvation,* nor against the substitution of inferior food for good food.[14]

The crucial element in education, according to Hocking, is the teacher, and the first qualification for a teacher is to be happy.[15] Excellence in education is for most of us a matter of method and content, of range and depth of a teacher's knowledge. We do not inquire after his personal habits and beliefs, unless they are clearly outside an acceptable moral and political range. What he believes or fails to believe is his own affair. No teacher application yet developed asks the applicant if he's happy. But Hocking is not proposing a happiness quotient for teacher-testing, nor is he arguing for conformity or uniformity in teacher's beliefs. By happiness he does not mean a temperamental gaiety, perpetually humming to keep its spirits up. Happiness is "the subconscious and hence serious affirmation of life as a whole by the will as a whole."[16] It is the essential characteristic of maturity. It is crucial because the final test of education is not how much content a child remembers but what kind of a person he becomes. Second only to his parents, the greatest influence on his development is his teacher. And the influence which a teacher has on his pupils is determined by what kind of a person he is. Hocking has a healthy regard for the shrewdness and pragmatic wisdom of children. "They will tend to adopt the beliefs of those whom they instinctively recognize as happy, and no others."[17] On this basis he is prepared to let the chips fall where they may, and here a necessary freedom comes into play. If there are no recommenders of established values in a child's experience, these values will die a natural death. Varieties of religious and ethical experience should have their representatives, and they must be believers and valuers of the beliefs and values they present. The will is the thing to be developed, and it must wrestle with things which matter in the hands of people who care for them. The thorough-going secular ideal of education is too abstract. It touches the speculative fancy, but not the will, and hence fails in its educational responsibility.

The proportion of the will is as important to Hocking's educational view as its dimension, however, and he calls for a balance between the instincts which deal with persons and those which deal with things.[18] Modern education tends to emphasize "interpersonal relationships." A child is evaluated in terms of his ability to "get along with the group." We are beginning to recognize the dangers of "groupism"—dangers evidenced by our lonely crowds and by a rebellious youth which advertizes its yearning for individuality in "freedom" movements of all kinds. The cure for this oversocialization is less clear. Hocking notes the increasing problem of boredom on the part of children who have lost the capacity to "be by themselves" and suggests that education ought to encourage a *companionable interest in nature.*[19] Two values are involved: one is the freedom to follow an uninterrupted train of thought; the other is the encouragement of the poetic and even animistic imagination, as nature becomes a living fabric of one's world.

This advice comes from one whose dialectic insists on the objective character of nature. While to Hocking natural realism is a necessary abstraction for both metaphysical analysis and technological development, it is a phase in the mind's way to truth about the whole. This truth combines the scientific view of nature with the poetic and religious instinct that nature has a meaning. For the farmer a field of wheat is food for hungry bellies; for the child and the poet the beauty of the sight is food for the soul. Both are half-truths. For the farmer to miss what the child sees is to miss part of the joy of his work. For the child to understand the farmer's interest is to begin serious assessment of life in a mature world. But modernity suffers from the busyness of objective concerns; it needs to learn from the Orient that valuing time means *taking* time. Hocking comments:

> What and how much solitude may mean to any child cannot be told in advance: education can only effect the exposure, not at first without guidance, and certainly not without noting results. Let me quote from a letter written by Sir Rabindranath Tagore to Mr. Fredric Rose, Stockton Heath, England. "Mornings and evenings (speaking of his school at Bolpur) fifteen minutes' time is given them to sit in an open space, composing their minds for worship. We never watch them and ask questions about what they think in those times, but leave it entirely to themselves, to the spirit of the place and the time and the suggestion of the practice itself. We rely more upon the subconscious influence of Nature, of the association of the place and the daily life of worship that we live than on any conscious effort to teach them."[20]

This Eastern capacity for meditation, and the stoic calm

which goes with it, may be bought at too great a price, since they often express the conviction that fate has decreed the individual's unchangeable *karma,* and he can only accept it and attempt to purify his soul for the next incarnation. But even a dubious metaphysic does not negate the value of taking time to explore the dimensions of solitude in a natural setting which "teases out essays in interpretation."[21] Americans are at the mercy of their energies. We find patience difficult to come by. But Hocking warns us that important ideas do not burst full-blown from the mind immediately upon conception. Like physical embryos, embryonic ideas require time to mature before they are strong enough to make their way in the world on their own. Much of our current intellectualism is brilliant, but it lacks profundity. This is due, at least in part, to adverse social, cultural and educational conditions, which do not allow adequate gestation for our best thought.

Hocking does not enter into the old debate whether spontaneous interest or disciplined work is the best training for the will—a debate central to the discussion of what was loosely termed "progressive education." Neither pure difficulty (attacking a problem because it is hard) nor pure ease (attacking a problem because of spontaneous desire) are particularly instructive, he thinks, although education must fit children to deal with difficulties, as it must elicit their interest. The right stimulus for the developing will to power, Hocking believes, is the hope of success in the face of difficulty; *"interest accompanies any task in which a mental momentum is established."*[22] Growing effectiveness of the will to power means learning to overcome difficulties; and without difficulty, there can be no lasting interest in a problem. In the educational venture, as in any human vocation, the only work that is fun is hard work.

Hocking, we know, recognized that social modeling attempts do turn the potentially dangerous instincts of sex, pugnacity, and ambition into creative channels. Sex he viewed as particularly problematical, because economic conditions and social custom usually require a delay in sexual satisfaction until formal education is concluded. Even a liberalized sex ethic will continue to require a high degree of sublimation. Hocking notes that "children usually grow up in families" and this is "nature's simple and effective device for imposing on the powerful current of sex-feeling its presumptive meaning: every child starts life with a prejudice to the effect that its affections will lead it sooner or later to found a family resembling (with improvements) the family from which it came."[23] The necessary prolongation of the will's vestibule of sexual satisfaction results in a sublimation of impulse into the imagination. Imagination allows the individual to explore the realm of sexuality without paying the cost which such adventure demands in the real world in relation to real people. Delay thus serves a function which we have already noted in regard to instinctive satisfaction; it increases the capacity of selectivity and allows time to comprehend the significance of impulse on the whole of one's life. Hocking asks how instinct can know what it wants. His answer is that, in itself, it can't and doesn't. Sexual instinct must take its place within the total will to power, and this will borrows sexuality's sublimated energies for the task of "mental world building," which is simply the construction of one's philosophy of life. Hocking contends that the prolonging of sexual fulfillment until it can be fully realized in marriage and a family allows time for a self-conscious will to power to understand and decide what it wants. The energy of sexual impulse is therefore serving its own ultimate fulfillment in lending its sublimated energies to making a philosophy of life.

Hocking feels that we all must take on the metaphysical job of deciding what is real in the world and what is not. Education leads young people to the place where they must forsake the spiritual umbilical cord which has, through the authority of parents and teachers, attached them to the world. They must now find attachments of their own. The old beliefs may be tested and found true, but testing requires at least a hypothetical abandonment, so that the values and beliefs to which one returns are one's own and not another's.[24] At this point the teacher stands aside. The values and beliefs which society seeks to transmit to the young through education cannot be directly transmitted. There is no greater disappointment to a teacher than a student who simply imitates his teacher's views. As Hocking remarks, "Imitation never quite imitates; education never educes the most vital power."[25] Hocking thus sides with Socrates in his debate with Protagoras over whether or not virtue can be taught.[26] Socrates' famous assertion that nobody can really teach anybody else anything—each one has to learn it for himself—is matched by Hocking's assertion that the will cannot be changed by the forces of social modeling or education: it can be changed only by itself. This does not make education negligible—Hocking, like Socrates, gave his life to it. Good teaching can help smooth rough places in the way of a student's path to truth, and it inevitably reveals the teacher's own convictions for what they may prove to be worth. But when a student comes to the place where he must claim his new attachments, he is on his own. Hocking feels that the truth in this most important of all intellectual ventures is something that neither dialectic nor good teaching can command. It is the crown of education, but at the same time it is something which lies just beyond the process of education itself.

> For each man . . . there is a region of consciousness more nearly just and free than others, looking out toward absolute truth, if not seeing it. In all ages men have sought out this region, and have found there a promise of freedom from all residual tyrannies of custom and education; and from this source innovations without number have made their way into social life. What men have called their religion has been the inertia-breaking, bond-breaking power, the mother of much explorative thought. It has at times exercised a tyranny of its own, and this is the most hideous of tyrannies because it invades the region of most intimate freedom. But from it has come the power for breaking these same shackles. There you may find or recover the vision which nullifies all imposture of the Established, the Entrenched, of all the self-satisfied Toryisms, Capitalisms, Obscurantisms of the world. And there you may find what is not less necessary for originality: unity in the midst of distraction, composure in the midst of necessary and unnecessary flux, quiet confidence in your own eyesight in presence of the Newest, the Noisiest, the Scientificalist, the Blatantest, all the brow-beating expositions of pseudo-Originality, pseudo-Progress. Your need is not for novelty for its own sake, but for truth: out of your personal relation to truth comes all the novelty that can serve you, or mankind through you. This personal relation to truth you must win for yourself; but you may be left with good hope to win it, for truth is no dead thing, but is itself a spirit.[27]

Education has not done its job until it has presented the individual with a moral and religious challenge. It was because the American military government in Germany failed to see the importance of this challenge that Hocking found the experiment in teaching Germany a failure. And the significance of this failure is not what it has meant for Germany, but what it means for the ideas and ideals of Western culture as it absorbs secularism and communism and faces the external challenge of the Asian revolution. It is important because the American educational program was more or less consciously responsible *"to the world community, and its opinion*—even if that community was a mere blueprint to be realized in part by their action."[28] The character-type with which American educators were working was intended to be an approximation of the best in Western culture; to have failed in this venture was to bring into question the Western contribution to a growing world culture. The American failure in post-war Germany lent added seriousness to Hocking's work on *The Coming World Civilization,* in which he set forth the permanent values of the Western tradition and the terms in which they might become viable in the new community of nations.

What was the issue? What was it in the German *Wille zur Macht* which needed remaking? Not, we can be sure, the fact of a will to power itself. To those sentimentalists who argued that Germany's desire for national power was the issue, Hocking replied simply that every nation wants and needs power. Was it Nazism which was at fault? Hocking goes back to the first published program of the National Socialist Party in 1920.[29] The program breathes an embittered racist nationalism and contains much potential political folly, but, in Hocking's view, it fell short of criminality. "It was not National Socialism as a political prospectus we were fighting." The issue was seven deadly sins against civilization.

We were fighting the police state together with its tools, the concentration camp and the revived and improved torture chamber, the cancelling of hard-won human rights, the mass slaughter of Jews, the systematic lying for the public mind with the deliberate cultivation of international hatred, the willingness to use aggressive war and thorough-going perfidy as means to national ends.[30]

The issue was the overthrow of the scruple, articulated by Kant and inherited from Christianity, of respect for the individual human being, who is to be regarded as an end in himself, and never as a mere means to anyone's ends. This is the point at which Nazism becomes Hitlerism. "Hitlerism was simply this, that with all other scruples *this Christian-Kantian scruple about humanity must also be subordinated to the national cause.*"[31] In Hocking's view, Hitler was one of the *Terribles simplificateurs* forseen by Burckhardt; and the cure to be administered was therefore also correspondingly simple. Hitler's moral madness was to subvert everything, most particularly the regard for the human individual, to the national dream. The American educating task was to bring people back to sanity. Hitler posed the question whether this Christian-Kantian scruple was a kindly moral sentiment, a relatively useful maxim for bourgeois living; *or* whether it was "*a demand lying like an absolute at the heart of our civilization.*"[32]

Hocking's observation—offered as part of a lecture at the University of Munich in 1948—was that the Americans never undertook to prove Hitler wrong. He points out two reasons for our failure: one, with which he sympathizes, is that "sanity" has to be recognized, and cannot be proved; the second is that "we ourselves had largely ceased to believe in axioms or any other form of absolute, and to this extent our mentality gave Hitler the right of way—he made our philosophy of relativity his own, carried it to the end, and left us only the residue of raging moral resentment devoid of intellectual support."[33] If the German mind was educed from Hitlerism to the values which had originally made German culture the great achievement that it is—and Hocking has no doubt but that Germany has been thus educated—it was largely due to the work of two events, neither of which were solely American or the result of the American educational program. One was the defeat itself, which spoke for itself. The other was the court for the trial of war criminals at Nürnberg. Hocking is convinced that *"to most Germans who had lent a tentative ear to Hitlerism, the defeat alone was sufficient* to reanimate the latent normal selfhood."[34] And while there was some antipathy in Germany to the work of the court, Hocking is convinced—and subsequent German prosecution of war criminals on German initiative seems to confirm—that most Germans agreed with Mr. Justice Jackson that "The Germans—as much as the outside world— have an account to settle with the defendants."[35]

But if the defeat and the court effected the necessary change in the German national will, perhaps the whole American idea of an educational program was misconceived? No; both the defeat and the work of the court were morally ambiguous. In the midst of warfare it was not the Germans alone who destroyed life heedlessly. And the work of the court was an *apologia pro bello nostro* which refused to turn the searchlight of justice on its own war crimes, as well as those of the defeated enemy. In short, the problem of identifying the intellectual root of the moral lapse which was Hitlerism, and of which we ourselves were not totally innocent, still remained; and we failed to resolve it.

The intellectual root of this lapse is the idea of an "absolute," which our prevalent mentality has become too flabby to stomach. We have, as educators, become fascinated with the first initiation of the growing mind, the discovery of relativity—an epoch-making discovery for every adolescent, an emancipation from provincialism, from the dogmatism of sheltered thinking, a new and liberating capacity to think all of one's thoughts as "merely mine," ergo, conditioned by my special circumstances, ergo "relative." . . . And there we stick: unable to take the next step—to discover the *relativity of relativity*; which means the working presence, within the judgment of relativity itself, of an absolute to be recognized and held. With the same mental naïveté that fancies truths of experience to be at sword's points with *a priori* truth, or that induction must be hostile to deduction, we, who have entered the wide liberty of the relative, shudder at the very term "absolute" as the logical incarnation of the totalitarian spirit. It is the precise opposite.[36]

Hocking is convinced that, in spite of our intellectual flabbiness, it was a working absolute which called the West to oppose Hitler; and that "only a moral absolute can hold its own in meeting the claims of absolute political power."[37]

The absolute which the German tragedy required was not an abstract principle, but what a German student correspondent of Hocking's referred to as *die tragende Idee*: literally a "sustaining" or "dominant" idea, which Hocking translates pragmatically not as a goal or ideal that merely sustains other ideas, but as a central idea which helps overcome obstacles, and hence a "load-lifting Idea." Does Western thought provide such an idea? Hocking believes that it does, and he begins his analysis of it by noting existentialism's rediscovery of the "underlying pain of being human."[38] Two elements are involved; one is a "Faustian impulse" striving to know and understand; the other is the *angst* of Kierkegaard, which knows that man is in some sense lost. The paradox of this pain, Hocking feels, is that it is part of the meaning, even the joy, of living.[39] It is the pain of the artist, of the lover, and of all creative workers. In this context Hocking quotes his much-loved line from Nietzsche: "The will of all great love is the beloved to create; and all creators are hard. Thus spake Zarathustra."[40] Here is a solution to part of the mystery of evil in the world; love desires to serve the beloved, and service is always pain-requiring. "Purely for the love of love, we could never endure a world which allowed no occasion for suffering."[41]

> But more than this, the perceptions of love and of beauty, pain-demanding, are at the same time perceptions of the nature of reality. They crack open a corner of the "ontological mystery." For whatever our factual world-picture, the world in which we are entangled is one in which loving and being loved are possible; and in which the object of love—never to be owned, a not-myself inhering in a not-myself—has a *revealing* function: here the nature of the vast and silent "It" discloses itself as a "Thou": the dissembling death mask is momentarily torn aside. And what is momentarily revealed, stays revealed.
>
> To perceive this, as metaphysical foundation-fact, as completer account of our human being-in-the-world, is to rediscover the scope of our own will; it becomes seen as a *will to create through suffering.* . . . And for those who have destroyed cities to rebuild, this principle of the *will to create through suffering* may come as an available Load-lifting Idea—first in the realm of metaphysics; and then in the realm of politics."[42]

Once again, and this time in a venture of world scope and significance, Hocking explains that the task of education draws on an element of belief which is beyond the techniques of education itself. In the task of social modeling to which education lends itself, important beginnings are made and the path to truth is attempted. Education itself cannot remake the instincts of sex, pugnacity, and ambition, any more than it can establish the validity of the underlying basis for Western morality. It can and must analyze the biological and social basis and explore the metaphysical meaning of these problems, but in each case the final conversion of the will is such a remaking as only religion can effect. Before we can deal adequately with the question of religion, we must look closely at Hocking's views on law and the problem of rights.

Chapter X

LAW AND HUMAN RIGHTS

HOCKING WAS AT YALE WHEN *The Meaning of God* was first published. The book had been almost ten years in the making, and it was clearly a major statement of a carefully integrated, comprehensive and original point of view. Hocking's friends in the philosophy department at Harvard saw evidence that his philosophical apprenticeship was over, and they invited him to rejoin them.[1] It was not an easy decision to make. The Hockings always referred to their years at Yale as among their happiest. The department there was strong, even though it could not boast the giants which Harvard had harbored during this golden age of American philosophy. Yale was probably a better place for a younger man to develop—giants tend to be a little forbidding and they are not always skilled in the nurture of the young— and Hocking was clearly developing very well there. And though one's alma mater has an acknowledged special appeal, there was more spirit than sentimentality in Hocking's decision to return to Harvard. James was gone, but Royce, Santayana, Münsterberg, and others were there, and Hocking's growing self-confidence was eager to test itself in their company.

His return to Harvard in 1914, just as America was being drawn into war, also marked the serious development of his interest in law, human rights, the state, and world politics which had been stimulated in his California days by his colleague George Holmes Howison. Hocking became a vigorous spokesman for American entry into the League of Nations,[2] and voted for the Democrat James Cox in the presidential elections of 1920 (even though he was a "habitual Republican voter") on the ground that Cox would assure the United States of a prompt and honest entry into the League. The defeat of this prospect served only to sharpen his sense of America's world responsibility. In the following decade he continued his writing on religious philosophy,[3] but the major emphasis of his work now shifted to legal and political theory. Three substantial essays appeared during this period. The first was a little book on *The Present Status of the Philosophy of Law and of Rights.*[4] In his preface to that book he noted that there was already in the press a larger work on *Man and the State,* and that no philosophy of the state could be considered complete without a philosophy of law. He also noted plans for further writing on "the rights of men and nations." These were partially fulfilled in the final chapter of *The Spirit of World Politics* and in two shorter papers, one on "Ways of Thinking About Rights,"[5] published in 1937, and a paper for the International Congress of Philosophy at Amsterdam in 1949 entitled "On the Present Position of the Theory of Natural Right."[6] The latest statement of this concern, and the work which represented the completion of his plan, is *Strength of Men and Nations.*

The beginnings of Hocking's political interest go back to an essay published in 1910 stating the core of his metaphysics, "How Ideas Reach Reality."[7] Here he made extended use of a political analogy to explore the relationship between idea and sensation in the mind.

The state is an effort of society to become fully self-conscious and self-controlling; its idea is so far identical with that of the individual mind. The state deals with its natural data —namely, its physical and economic status, its customs and traditions—just as the self does with its natural data, its sensations and instincts:—it turns them into ideas. The state calls its own ideas, however, by the name of "laws" (or institutions, which are congeries of laws). But a law is always either an experiment, or a statement of the conditions under which experiments must be carried on. The rigidity and fixity of a law is only such as is necessary for a satisfactory experiment. In order to know how life works we must proceed by assuming that we already know, and holding to the assumption until it is proven wrong. So the ideas which we individuals make are either experiments or conditions of experiment: they are so many ways of assuming that we already know reality.[8]

As the whole is the absolute idea which the mind thinks with as it weaves the middle world ideas which constitute its "understanding" of the real, so the specific, detailed laws of the state are grounded in its apprehension of the law of "how life works" which is implied in the details of the state's legal structure. He introduces this analogy with a footnote expressing some surprise that it is not more popular in current philosophy, arguing that "the state is still, as in the days of Plato, the most perfect visible example of the mind in its dealings with reality."[9]

He has argued that idea is not something other than sensation or instinct; it is their articulate and active form. So with law: it is not something other than custom, it is articulate, codified custom, now ready to become politically effective. Secondly, the original intellect does not invent truth; it is the successful utterer of "the truth of nature" which less original minds confirm as true to their own sensations and feeling. So, too, originality in public life does not invent new material, it clarifies what the people must confirm in their previously dumb feelings of right and wrong. Positive experiments, represented by individual laws, are all subject to error, because their adaptation determines the bearing of truth on political life. But, Hocking says, those laws which are the conditions of positive law experiments—the laws regarding laws, their making and enforcing—are not subject to error in the same sense. "We might say, after the old epistemological formula, the customs and predicaments of national society contain all the subject-matter of law—except the political constitution itself."[10] Constitutions are, in actual fact, subject to amendment. Does this destroy Hocking's argument for an absolute which informs the law, an argument figuring prominently, by implication, in his assessment of the American educational failure in Germany? Why did the political constitution of post-war Germany require such radical alteration? Was it simply an exercise of the conqueror's greater power, imposing his will on the defeated? Perhaps; but had this been the case, what was to prevent a free Germany from reverting to Hitlerism? Hocking's answer is simply that Hitlerism forced an unnatural constitution on the German people. The norm for all positive law—the condition of its experiment—is a *natural* form of authority, illustrated in those principles of administration operative in the family and in such situations as the community response to economic emergencies. These constitute a collective social feeling which the State articulates in the form of positive law. As the mind knows nature as given, so "the customs to which [society] gives political birth are already in their crude form, *administered* customs."

In his small book *The Present Status of the Philosophy of*

Law and Rights Hocking is concerned with human rights as one of the most important conditions of our experiment with positive law. This is perhaps the one point in contemporary life where the question of the absolute can gain a sympathetic hearing. To speak of absolutes in personal ethics is no longer popular even among their traditional guardians, the theologians; but to speak of absolutes in civil rights is commonplace, even with the younger generation. (This is at least interesting for a nation which claims pragmatism as its guiding political philosophy.) This notion of rights influences the entire range of law—positively, in the form of laws designed to clarify and protect these rights, and negatively, as a requirement that no law should infringe on them. Hocking has already observed that all men are obviously not equal by an objective standard. What then is the basis for rights shared by all men? In searching for a criterion he argues that the real question is not what was right in the past, but what will be right in the future. Historical relativism breeds on the diversity of historic custom, and issues its verdict that the mores of a particular era can make anything right. Hocking counters with the thought that man is struggling through history to achieve a state of "wakefulness," and that "a state of half-awakeness can prevent almost anything from seeming wrong."[11] The standard for the establishment of laws, which the corporate mind of a people gropes for, and which it first senses dimly, should not be just an accumulation of past experience, according to Hocking. He does agree, however, that the formulation of law is an inductive process. What the people seek is a concrete *a priori* which is gradually uncovered by a historical movement toward increasing wakefulness.

This is not to be mistaken for the old liberal idea of inevitable progress, to which Hocking specifically refuses to appeal; but it does show that he is not content with the contemporary flux philosophies of history. Toynbee may seem too schematic, too ready with interpretive formulas such as "challenge and response." But Hocking is closer to Toynbee than he is to Karl Löwith on the one hand, or nineteenth-century liberal optimism on the other. Hocking's own view is that some elements, once introduced into human history, are "unlosable."

> There is in history a certain tough cumulativeness at two levels—levels at which mankind cannot forget—the level of technic and the level of insight. At these levels there is set into human nature a *mental ratchet* which prevents total slipping back, a selective holding function which can easily escape notice amid apparently unlimited change . . . . Sciences have been lost, even astronomics and geometrics, but not the multiplication table, nor once devised in India the arithmetical zero, nor once mastered in Greece the science of proof. . . . History, for good reason, finds it hard to identify the cumulative characters. Yet unless they are recognized the total structure of history threatens to be that of a record —on the one hand of perpetual passing, *das Einmalige,* or on the other, of the recurrent and sterile, losing sight of its most significant ingredient, *the unlosable.*[12]

Convictions about human rights belong to those unlosables which occur at the level of insight. Just how tough cumulative insight can be is illustrated by the fact that it reasserted itself in spite of Hitler. But the question remains: what is the basis for our assertion of our right? Hocking's empirical dialectic is looking for a solution to the conflict between an abstract theory of right and the concrete requirements of culture—or between what he calls the "standard of justice" and the "standard of social utility." Culture requires a political state, and the state, in turn, requires that individuals should be ready, if need be, to sacrifice themselves for the state. Such sacrifice is one of the commonplace facts of society. He distinguishes, however, between the sacrifice of oneself or one's goods and the sacrifice of one's rights. It appears that rights are self-transcending. We are prepared to lay down our lives for certain rights and the state must recognize their inviolability. But, as Hocking recognizes, we are once again faced with the conflict between the individual and society. On the one hand, no sacrifice of right is sanctioned by the common welfare. On the other, nothing is just which goes against the total cultural interest. The state does require that I give up some rights—my property rights, for example—when the state claims eminent domain. In this case, we must say that either a certain injustice is necessary, or we must say—as Hocking says—that the overriding of a defined right in such a case is not an injustice.

The residents of any community agitated over proposals for a new highway running through cherished private property will not find much consolation in Hocking's views. They are convinced that their property right is absolute, and that a grave injustice has been done them.[13] Hocking's reply is that they have confused their *rights* with their *interests* by way of a too readily domesticated absolute. He flatly denies that there is any such thing as an inviolable absolute natural right to life, liberty and the pursuit of happiness. He rejects the assumption that individuals have rights by virtue of their citizenship. Once again we find him opposing absolute idealism, this time as it appears in the popular mind. He has no use for static absolutes. The major premise of the absolute must be joined with the minor premise of the self before it can operate dynamically. Rights are not entirely God-given or constitutionally-given independent of individual will and action. Rights can be lost, and men can

and do disqualify themselves from their rights. Hocking outlines this dynamic understanding of rights with four principles. The first of these is that "legal rights are presumptive
rights."[14] Law treats individuals artificially, i.e. *as if* they
were equal in respect to fundamental rights. He suggests
that lawmakers have never been ignorant of the fact that
individuals are obviously not equal. Why then, he muses,
should laws treat them as if they are? The first and most
obvious reason is that the differences among individuals are
largely irrelevant. Whether I should pay my debts or not does
not depend on whether I am white or black, clever or stupid,
fat or thin. What the law does is to substitute relevant for
irrelevant grounds of difference. If I am charged with mur-
der, my economic status is irrelevant, but my age and mental
condition are not. If I am a minor or a lunatic the law
recognizes these conditions as relevant to judgment in my
case.

But Hocking's more important point concerning the pre-
sumptiveness of the law concerns those cases where the law
deliberately ignores differences which are both relevant and
obvious. With an almost brutal realism, surprising in one of
such sanguine temper, he agrees that some people are more
fit to live than others, thus finding himself in the curious
company of Dostoevsky's Raskolnikov. At the same time,
however, he notes that the law properly refuses us the right
to follow Raskolnikov's example of murdering the less fit
pawnbroker woman. It even refuses us the right to pass
judgment on the fitness of our own lives. The reason for this
refusal is stated in his second principle: "The presumptions
of the law are creative presumptions: they are aimed at conditions to be brought about, and only for that reason ignore
conditions which exist."[15] Judged realistically, all men are
not equally fit to live; but it is desirable that all men should

be. This is not a static presumption, but a creative one calculated to establish the condition which it presumes. These presumptions of the law cannot be too far removed from the real situation or they lose their creative tension. These legal "ideals," if we wish to call them that, must represent a real social potential. Hocking raises the question, for example, of the equality of the vote in a democracy. He muses on the possibility that the right to vote may be too wide of the mark to be a valid presumption. But his main point is clear. The law is future-oriented. This contention is the basis of his argument with Aristotle—who was quite right in arguing that some are born to command and some to obey, but wrong in accepting this condition as static and permanent.[16]

If law is to act creatively on plastic human material it must know what it intends to make of it. It cannot simply look to the past, passively accepting what is relative to any given situation. It must "realise its own future" on the basis of a "valid insight into what human nature is capable of becoming."[17] Good government seeks men of competence who practice politics as the art of the possible. But we have seen enough in our day of skilled political mechanics who lack basic convictions (or have the wrong ones) to know that the crucial thing about any politician is what he believes in. Hocking puts it this way:

> The state-builder must give himself to the democracy of the future. He must dedicate himself to the social contract,—not the contract signed and sealed in a mythical antiquity, but the contract in which the individual and the free spirits of future men will be able to join, and in joining sanction the restraints, the efforts, the dreams of all past history.[18]

Lest this talk of vision seem too idealistic, we must look at Hocking's third principle—a practical one: "Presumptive rights are the conditions under which individual powers normally develop."[19] Individual goals must be related to social goals, and the individual must fulfill a social "function." But having insisted that the individual's normal rights are not absolute, Hocking likewise insists that they are not granted as a reward for fulfilling a social function. Society has an interest in the functions which an individual presently performs, but it has an equal interest in functions which are not yet known, either to the individual or to society. Society, for example, needs men to function as scientists. But science requires a certain talent which can neither be compelled nor predicted. Rights are therefore not a set of conditions which promote the performance of functions, but "a set of conditions which *promote the development of powers*."[20] Law and education are both geared to the development of the individual will to power, for it is as certain that society will gain from the development of unknown and unknowable individual powers as it is that it will suffer from the suppression or stunting of that development. This consideration leads to Hocking's fourth and culminating principle, that "there is one natural right and one only,"[21] and that is the right to develop individual human powers. A man has a right to his own creativity, provided he does not destroy that right by his free choice not to become what he is capable of becoming. "It is not the free will as such that is the subject of the inalienable right; it is the will to be oneself that is the subject. Wherever moral ambition exists, there right exists."[22]

This formula must be handled delicately; "moral ambition" has content only in Hocking's views on human nature and on the processes of education. What we have here is a dialectic between what was defined earlier as the "standard of justice" and the "standard of social utility." There is a natural right which is absolute, but we must not, Hocking says, claim it too quickly, nor apply it indiscriminately, confusing it with our interests, as the popular mind tends to do. There are valid claims of social utility, but we must not let them subvert the rights of the individual. Hocking accepts the thesis of the natural rights school that there must be a standard for lawmaking, the standard of "no injustice." He denies, however, that it can be an abstract standard, "a pure form without content." He accepts the antithetical view that social utility must be served, but not at the cost of pure historical relativism. Both the individual and society are served "in the character of the individual human will, the concrete good which that will seeks, and the claim which that seeking (which we have described as 'moral ambition') makes upon every agent that can affect it, whether that agent be another individual or the organized community as maker of laws."[23]

This last comment is thoughtful and reasonable. It is also more or less irrelevant, since today the problem of human rights in America centers on the problem of achieving rights for those whose rights have been denied, and Hocking has virtually nothing to say about the rights of the Negro or the ghetto slum dweller. Theoretically it is hard to fault him. He draws a delicate balance between the inherent right of equal opportunity for all men, and the pragmatic test of an individual's "moral ambition." But his discussion is curiously lacking in either psychological or sociological subtlety. He seems unaware that there are certain conditions which are prerequisite for the creative adventure. As the American civil rights movement moves into a full scale social revolution, one thing is clear, and that is that genteel white liberals simply have not comprehended the despair and resentment of those whose opportunity may have been technically equal (as in "separate but equal" schooling) but psychologically and sociologically destructive of their morale. Hocking has missed this issue completely—a failure which also qualifies the success of his evaluation of "the Asian revolution." Here is a comparable psychological and spiritual situation which is communally oriented (toward "the poor," "the colonised," "the colored peoples," "the peasant," etc.) and historically obsessed with the righting of past wrongs. Hocking's views are individualistic to a fault. He assumes that the individual's concern for "destiny" is an entirely personal concern. He also assumes that the issue begins with the launching of the individual's career rather than with those historic roots of an individual's community which often determine his own understanding of his individual destiny.

I must not imply that Hocking was either unconcerned or unaware of the problems of American Negroes in the midst of a white culture. In at least one extended essay he tried to set forth an evaluation of the problem in terms of the theoretical structure of rights which he had already detailed. To his credit, he never published this statement. There are times for speaking and times for keeping silent, and Hocking's muse wisely instructed him that this was not an issue on which he had been granted a genuinely prophetic consciousness.

Hocking was more comfortable when dealing with the historical bases of modern legal philosophy. Law, to Hocking, is the distinguishing feature of the state; in fact he concludes: "where the law is, there is the state."[24] But law presupposes a state which legislates, and *Man and the State* deals with this prior question of the source and nature of the state.

Chapter XI

THE STATE AND DEMOCRACY

THE LIFE OF THE STATE IS A manifestation of that group-forming process which provides the basis for human society in the family and reaches back into animal life in the primitive forms of flock, pride, swarm, school, and herd. There ought to be a name for this general process, but most of our familiar names specify particular instances of group-making, such as the gathering of a crowd, the courtship of lovers, the mustering of troops, and the growth of political parties. Hocking is not one to splash about with esoteric verbal inventions of his own. Marcel notes that the use of such terminology helps popularize a philosopher's work—he has Heidegger in mind; but he calls it arrogance and finds it a mark of Hocking's wholeness and health as a thinker that he is never intentionally obscure.[1] But the group-making process needs a name, and Hocking suggests:

> Why not simply call it the *com-motive* process, the process which moves together? The fact is that among all the *motive* impulses that affect individual behavior, some are naturally *com-motive* impulses, inasmuch as they appear to the mind as sharable or needing to be shared.[2]

This immediately raises the possibility of a group mind. Hocking is working with an individual psychology. Is this adequate to an examination of large groups, particularly the state? Put an individual in a mob and he behaves in ways which a purely individual psychology does not expect. Definitive national characteristics lead us to speak of "the American mind," and cultural characteristics lend credence to the idea of "the Asian mentality," etc. Our experience tells us that groups are agents of action which does not emanate from any particular person. Our philosophical and judicial theorizing about nations, trade unions, and partnerships deals with these groups as having identities and responsibilities not equally shared by the individuals which constitute them. Royce had argued for the reality of a group mind on the ground that whatever produced a real effect is a real author, using language as an example: "The creator of the English speech is the English people. Hence the English people is itself some sort of mental unit with a mind of its own."[3] Even William James, individualistic condemner of the absolute though he was, finally came to the view that since "the self-compounding of mind in its smaller and more accessible portions seems a certain fact . . . the speculative assumption of a similar but wider compounding . . . must be reckoned with as a legitimate hypothesis. The absolute is not the impossible being I once thought it."[4]

Hocking agrees that "the national mind" is a useful metaphor, neither fanciful nor groundless, but he cannot see that it is ever *"the sole author of any deed."*[5] It is an influence operative in the thought and action of national leaders and citizenry, but not numerically distinct from the minds of individuals. If a corporation is accused of price-rigging, its responsible executives must stand trial; so, too, war crimes are not charged to the nation per se, but to those individuals who are most deeply and specifically involved. Group minds, Hocking thinks, do not exist, but the vitality of the metaphor indicates that the state does provide something of crucial importance to the life of its citizenry. For consider: as an individual mind requires the world of objects before it can qualify as a will-expressing self, the self's familiar habitat —the tools of his trade, his physical routine, etc.—all are part of his enlarged self. Clothes may not make the man, but they reflect who he is and are therefore part of himself. Isn't there a sense in which one can say that Hocking *is* the big stone house in Madison which he designed and whose building he oversaw? These things are beyond the original reaches of self, yet they belong to the full dimensions of selfhood. These extensions of the self to include physical objects and surroundings he calls "vital circuits" or "will circuits"[6] and they become particularly important when they include our social commitments as well. In social undertakings the individual will is both bounded and enhanced by the presence of other wills flowing through the same circuit, and the state is the incorporation of these will circuits in a particular national community. The state is not a self, but as the aggregate of individual will circuits it establishes a will to power of its own, dependent upon but not entirely identifiable with its individual constituent wills. Encompassing the common physical objects of a common territory (the Californian returning from a European holiday is "home" when he lands in New York) Hocking defines the state as *"the circuit required by the will to power of each member, coincident for all the people of a defined territory, and including them."*[7] The physical conditions of a nation's geography, climate, natural resources, access to the sea, etc., are only accidentally related to the national will which uses them, yet they are necessary to the functioning of that will, and they help to explain why the universal need does not create a universal state, but nation-states. Even *The Coming World Civilization*, which makes so much of a world faith, does not foresee a world state. As early as 1912 Hocking had made it clear that "By such super-nationalism in religion, national individuality is not obscured, but rather promoted. We require a world-religion just because we do not require, nor wish, a world state."[8]

The particularity of a nation's involvement with a limited group in a limited geographical area also explains why the state is not to be thought of as a contract struck by men-in-general, or by those in a particular area who are agreeable, leaving the rest outside. The state is an all or nothing affair involving "these men . . . who are now on the ground."[9] The state is not, as the idealists would have it, an idea or principle which permeates the thinking of its citizenry. The state is an expression of man's will to power. It is an artificial construct, but man is by nature an artificer, and to this extent the state is natural. Hocking's metaphysics makes it clear that no human society is possible apart from the prior presence of a super-self who provides the terms of communication among men, making it possible for individual will circuits to coincide. By the same token, the religious unity of men is deeper than any political association, and the growing world community will be viable only on the basis of the religious bond—a thesis which we shall explore later. But the state is not God, and he is at great pains to distinguish between the social realism of his political philosophy and the absolute idealism of his religious thought.

> It is as important to distinguish them as it is to see their connection, and particularly important at present. For men are always more widely conscious of the fact of underlying unity than they are of its nature: and in proportion as they lose their grasp of metaphysical reality, they incline to recover their loss by making gods of social groups, of 'society,'

or 'state,' or 'humanity,' to the boundless confusion of political theory, and to vast practical losses in terms of liberty . . .[10]

The state is power, but realists who follow Kant's dictum that the work of the state is primarily in the external or physical sphere have failed to analyze power with sufficient care. Hocking finds three forms: physical force, bargain power, and the power of prestige. Physical force speaks for itself, but the other two merit a word of comment.[11] Much of the state's power derives from its bargaining position in supplying the necessities of protection and peace, and this characteristic of the state figures prominently in contract theories, especially that of Hobbes. But Hocking finds Hobbes' view of Leviathan too commercial, and unduly informed by fear. In authorizing the state to exact all that the traffic will bear in return for the blessings of peace, Hobbes' logic requires a dissolution of the bargain at the point where the state is unable to deliver the goods, e.g., in time of war. In actual fact, however, the bargain does not usually collapse under these conditions, and this leads Hocking to suspect that the primary source of the state's power lies neither in its physical force nor its bargain power, but in its prestige. Bargain power depends upon "desires to have," while the power of prestige is dependent upon what Hocking calls "desires to be."

Take marriage. It is, indeed, a contract, and there is a certain bargain power which each has over the other. But the desire to be, i.e. the desire to attain certain qualities, based on the mutual need for personal growth, is the value which cements the association. So also with the state. The weakness of the contract theory of the state lies in the fact that a contract assumes that the contracting parties remain essentially the same during the exchange of goods or services. Contracts are conservative; they seek to maintain what is already known, and are thus far static. Hocking's view of the state, on the other hand, is dynamic. States have destinies, and the state requires growth of itself and its citizenry toward those values which give the state its prestige. On the contract basis it is difficult to explain why the state should be adorned with dignity, ceremony, and wealth. What contract theories miss (and Hocking includes here the economic interpretation of the state which is a special form of the contract theory), is what the common citizen sees in the state: a means of becoming what he desires to become, and not simply a means of having what he desires to have.[12] In order to function at all the state must inspire in its citizenry the conviction that it is at least attempting justice, even though citizens may be critical of certain existing laws. Americans for whom certain Supreme Court rulings are anathema attack them precisely on the ground that they are un-American. The state which legislates what to him is injustice nevertheless maintains its prestige. America has disappointed him, yet he would attack any man who questions his own "Americanism."

The normal bargain power of the state is dependent upon the force of its prestige. This is not its only power, to be sure. It may use physical force because the state exists to do things, and not simply to keep order while its citizens do things. Whatever moral power the state has requires the effective instrument of physical force. The state's monopoly on physical force, says Hocking, not only prevents anarchy and promotes reason in settling social disputes; it also displays the state's prestige and uniqueness vis-à-vis all other social groups.

The state promotes the making of men by promoting the free and natural development of those bargain and prestige powers which they exercise and amid which they live. Standing outside the area of these powers and maintaining their free play, it receives the grant of force and the confirmation of its uniqueness, its embodiment of the reflective capacity of human nature.[13]

This elusive matter of prestige is important for any state, but it leads into the heart of the matter for a democracy. Hocking notes that all government is *of* the people—"what else is there to be governed?"[14]—and all government professes to be *for* the people, even Czarist autocracies and Nazi dictatorships. The rub comes with government *by* the people, which is literally impossible but morally feasible if "there is an *esprit de corps* which rulers can feel, interpret, and obey."[15] Democracy is that method of governing whereby doubts and conflicts are brought into open contest and decided in favor of the majority. Hocking points out that winner and loser alike accept the result as their own because all have participated in good faith, trusting that each acted honestly, as he saw it, for the good of all. Unless this confidence is justified, "Government 'by the people' is moonshine," and he adds: "The premise [of democracy] is simply false unless there is indeed something universal in the value sense of each member."[16] Americans tend to let gut reactions substitute for metaphysical analysis in their view of democracy, but Hocking bears down on the inescapable metaphysical implications of human brotherhood. Rousseau catches something of it in his talk of "the general will," but each nation gives it an interpretation which is prior to its specific acts of will. Hocking calls it " the national premise" and finds that "the degree of effective democracy is proportionate to the firmness of the national premise."[17] In *Strength of Men and Nations* he examines the American national premise—incorporating, as it does, elements of what is popularly referred to as "the American dream"—as it conflicts with the national premise of the USSR.

The American adventure, contemporaneous with the opening of the modern period in philosophy (beginning on the continent with Descartes, Locke and Grotius), struggled on the practical level with the same issue which Europe was dealing with on the theoretical plane. That issue was the relationship between science and its technology on the one hand, and between religion and morality on the other. Colonial America needed both applied science and applied faith in its wilderness-taming venture. Private property and the individual enterprise which won it loomed large in the thinking of the growing nation, as did the individualistic Protestantism of Pastor John Robinson, Roger Williams and Jonathan Edwards. The national premise developed, as such premises always do, as a two-way process, "from Idea into the changing facts; from the facts into the idea."[18] Crucial to the constitution of the new nation, and specified in a separate document, was its Bill of Rights. Liberty was the cornerstone of the republic, and liberty, says Hocking, is simply the summary of a man's rights. Taken as absolute, and so stated, experience made it clear that "plural rights, taken as absolute, conflict with one another,"[19] as when the public figure's right to privacy runs counter to the newspaper editor's right to know.

> In sum, what our experience has brought us to see is (i) that there are no unconditional legal rights, and (ii) that there is one and only one absolute moral right, the right to

become a whole man, or, in other words, to find one's task in the world and do it.[20]

He honors democracy because its methods—free public discussion and participation in choosing the structure and officers of government—serve this unfolding of human powers. In broad terms, the purpose of the state is to educate, to aid in the remaking of human nature into something which the state does not preconceive as a blueprint, but which it holds as an item of faith. He admits that democracy is an inefficient form of government, and he takes seriously Carlyle's observation that Bobus will elect Bobissimus. He acknowledges that democracy trusts the judgment and intelligence of man beyond the fact, and relies on a political honor to seek the public good which is not always conspicuous in the halls of government. Political cynicism announces that men are not thus trustworthy, but by the withdrawal of trust removes the only condition which could breed trustworthiness. Democracy ventures trust, knowing that if it is not ventured it cannot be gained. "It learns its perils, and through defining them and being compelled to wash its linen in public, consciously raises the level of public integrity."[21] Hocking's comment that "Democracy alone can cure the evils of democracy" echoes Reinhold Niebuhr's famous statement that the good in men makes democracy possible, while the evil in men makes democracy necessary.

Democracy is geared to this one inalienable human right, the right to learn, to grow, to wake up, to become someone worth being, and the strength of democracy is the "lifting power"[22] which is available to the individual through the gift of responsibility. But democracy faces the constant temptation of confusing rights with interests, of using the moment of responsibility for the whole as an opportunity

for personal gain. Mere size accentuates the problem for
America. Hawaii is as much a state of the union as Maine,
but can the conservative New Englander be counted on to
consider seriously the problems and prospects of a place
which he knows only through travel posters? Hocking calls
the failure to accept democratic responsibility an aspect of
democracy's primitive stage, and he finds much in American
life which indicates that we have not yet passed entirely beyond this stage. He feels that "this nation exhibits, in a moment of crisis, a radical weakness, an incapacity for sacrifice
and self-restraint in the pursuit of that good-of-the-whole
which, through defect of habit, has lost its place as the first
premise of our action."[23] By contrast, he notes a "seriousness" which characterizes the energetic nation-building of
the USSR. From the contrast America has learned an important lesson: democracy is vulnerable to a "supine psychology" (what can America do for me?) as dictatorships are not.
Having gained new respect for a nation being built along
different lines than our own, we find ourselves forced to re-
think the basic issues which divide us.

Strength of Men and Nations was a tract for the times
(1959), and much of it is already out of date. It is now a
truism—as it was not a few short years ago—to admit that
"communism verus capitalism" is not a valid label for the
basic issues between the United States and the Soviet Union.
Neither the communist world nor the free world are the
economic, political and military monoliths they once were.
The welfare state has tempered Western capitalism, and
profit motives and demands for consumer goods have
changed the face of European and Eurasian communism.
China rightly sees that Russian communism is "revisionist,"
and the John Birch society is not entirely wrong in sus-
pecting America of "socialism." These developments figure
in Hocking's philosophy of history which we will examine

in Part Three under the heading, "The Coming World Civilization." There is one further basic issue in his philosophy of the state which looms large in the conflict between capitalist America and communist Russia, however, and that is the economic interpretation of the state.

Property is, after all, a matter of life and death, especially as it touches on the essentials of food, clothing, and shelter. It follows that property systems will be matters of equal seriousness. A social group is necessarily committed to one such system, and survival demands the protection of that system. The key to the economic theory is not simply the emphasis it puts on the enormous political influence of property interests. Hocking credits it with having opened our eyes to the manifold ways in which economic motives have influenced laws, constitutions, manners, and beliefs; but this awareness only expands an insight which goes back to Plato and Aristotle, who recognized property as a source of strife which influences policy, breeds classes and parties, and sparks revolutions. Machiavelli noted the incompatibility between the interests of the idle rich and republican government; Hobbes wrote of the conflict between economic classes; Montesquieu and Hegel argued that means of livelihood affect the spirit of a people and its laws.[24] The real substance of the economic theory is the proposition that "political power is in substance economic power." We know already that Ernest Hocking doesn't believe this, but he never rejects anything out of hand, convinced that you can learn something from any serious advocate of a point of view. Hocking agrees with the Oxford don who suggested that three questions should be asked of any philosopher: "What does he mean by what he says? Why do I disagree? And finally: How could a man who is so much more intelligent than I am believe such rubbish?"[25]

The issue is whether or not economic interest is the force

which binds people together in a political unit. Hocking
finds that economic interest does have some binding power.
Not, to be sure, at the most primitive level—simple hunger,
for example. "Hunger contends against its neighbor for its
bone and drags it into hiding."[26] But the beginnings of social
organization do use the binding power of economic cement.
The group is better than the individual for hunting, barn-
raising, and so forth. Arrangements for mutual back-scratch-
ing bring economic benefit to all concerned. The primitive
economy of the forest gives way to the cooperative economy
of the village. But what happens when the town and city
begin to involve a wider society in the economic enterprise?
The primitive divisive nature of economy begins to reassert
itself. Corporations, industries, unions—all are fundamentally concerned for their own benefit, and a rivalry of com-
peting groups is inevitable. What is good for General Motors
may well be good for the country, but the country always
takes second place. Hocking points out that the basic commitment of the corporation is first and foremost to its own
economic enterprise. The business of business is business.
Further, economic considerations, pure and simple, regard
men not as human beings but as an economic item called
"labor."

> But human beings, while they can endure sometimes to re-
> duce others to items in their own calculations, cannot endure
> to be so reduced by them: each one fundamentally resents
> being treated "as a means only." Hence the general habit of
> considering the other man so far as he is useful to me and
> no farther is a trait which, given sole sway in any com-
> munity, would reduce it in time to its elemental dust.
> Economy alone could destroy, it could not create the na-
> tion.[27]

And, of course, it is precisely this moral resentment against the exploitation of the workers which gave birth to communism and its immensely influential version of the economic theory of the state. Hocking sees this, and points out the incompatibility of economic realism and revolutionary resentment.

> Socialists have always relied, not upon their economy alone, but upon moral resentment of wrong and moral enthusiasm for a better order, to build their community. They have announced an economic interpretation only to abandon it.[28]

To the question—how can the economic determinists "believe such rubbish"—Hocking replies that they don't. He picks apart the logic of economic determinism—if all ideology is economically determined and therefore false, what is to save Marxism itself from the same criticism, etc.—until he finally becomes convinced that the "realism" of the economic theory is largely fictitious. He then goes on to detail the view with which we are now familiar, that it is the nation which makes the economy, and not the economy which makes the nation.

Based as it is on the will to power, and rejecting the metaphysical mystique of a group mind, Hocking's philosophy of the state falls more on the realistic than the idealistic side. But as it stands it is obviously incomplete. We cannot know what the state is about until we know where it derives its understanding of man. The prestige and purpose of the state, as well as its "commotive" power, are tied up in something which is beyond the state. Having rejected humanism Hocking goes beyond humanism for that crucial source of insight into the nature of man and society.

Part Three

RELIGION AND A
WORLD CIVILIZATION

Chapter XII

ART AND DESTINY

HOCKING NEVER DEVELOPED AN INDEPENDENT theory of aesthetics, in the manner of Suzanne Langer or Dewey, but his scattered comments about art are important nonetheless. He was a painter and musician of moderate merit and held firm convictions about the truth inherent in creativity:

> The highest good of the individual life is not in the acceptance, nor in the criticism, but in the remaking of ideas and thereby of institutional life; affecting a change in the world which will last because it deserves to last; revising a law, painting a picture, building an arch, educating a child, —acting in such wise that your deposit of truth finds its way into the universal current of life.[1]

In other words, as he says so often in so many different ways, "the criterion of reality is creativity, both for the world and for the individual."[2] It is this concern for creativity which characterizes his individualism, draws him to Nietzsche, makes him value Democracy. The development of creativity is what education is all about, and creativity is the secret of the Christian mission to convert the world into the "kingdom."[3] Hocking's understanding of it deepened as he grew older. Even in the enthusiasm of youth he never thought creativity was easy. There was always an ultimate to be strived for, and always the danger that we would fall away from its disciplined demand. *The Meaning of God* had not entirely forgotten the youthful experience of conversion in a Methodist experience meeting, and the fear of Hell which accompanied it.[4] But Hocking's early theology was scarcely of the Hell-fire sort. If a man failed to respond to the creative possibilities to which life called him, he was missing its meaning and would be consigned to dullness, sloth, ignorance—a less than truly human existence, but not to the flames of Hell. The creative adventure, as the young Hocking saw it, was strenuous, hard, demanding work; but thoroughly rewarding, hopeful and glad. He spoke of suffering in *Human Nature and Its Remaking*,[5] but it was not enough of a category of his thinking to find its way into the index of the book.[6] When he saw what had happened to his beloved Germany during World War II, however, and the immensity of the tragic load which had to be lifted by German youth in making a new world for themselves, his theology found new significance in the suffering of Jesus Christ, and his philosophy of life took a new look at the experience of the artist.

This was Hocking's introduction to Existentialism as a point of view. He had always honored Marcel, but more for his metaphysics than his traces of *angst*. As a systematician who had been bothered years before by William James' lack of method, he found it hard to feel much sympathy for the existentialist's delight in anti-system.[7] But he read Camus with increasing respect for the authenticity of his dealing with the Absurd; and Camus' relative calmness, along with his French gift of clarity, got through to him. At the same time that his view on world religions was welcoming a humanizing of the older doctrines of Hell-fire, his philosophy of art was beginning to talk about the importance of a "descent into Hell," which was necessary for artistic integrity because only here could one understand the crisis of modernity. So *Strength of Men and Nations* makes a frontispiece of a line from Camus' *The Rebel*—"To create today, is to create dangerously." Now danger has a touch of tragedy in it. Art plays a serious role in man's quest for life's meaning. And it first expresses itself, according to Hocking, simply as an overflow of physical energy.

> Art begins in something less than art, perhaps simply in the animal caper that proclaims caprice, the flourish of limb or voice that turns into dance or song—but always the more-than-necessary, and always with a subconscious tribute to life running deeper than the play.[8]

Economy and statecraft deal with the necessities of life, but culture also includes unnecessary embellishments in the form of painted walls in the sheltering cave, and carved handles on useful tools. Perhaps even more than economy and polity, the art of a people indicates who they are and what they value. "Hence it is that the most open book to the soul of a people is the element of style in its living quarters, its settlement-planning, its architecture."[9] Art is closer than any other aspect of culture to the instinctive life of man, and it provides the freest and most imaginative expression of his otherwise inarticulate desires. Unsatisfied wish can play unencumbered in the realm of dreams, but imagination establishes nothing by itself because it has nothing to overcome, no medium in which to work. The pure vitality of the imagination needs to submit itself to the formal demands of sound, color, movement or speech in the physical world. Then the dream is given substance and consistency. "The work of art is the dream made *objective, permanent, self-conscious, mutual.*"[10] Hocking therefore agrees with the Freudian view that art represents repressed wish, although this strikes him as axiomatic, "For if man makes anything at all, how should he make except in such wise as to satisfy himself? The work of his hand will necessarily reveal any craving analysed or not which is given liberty to assert itself in that work."[11] However, he continues to reject Freudian reductionism. It is not any one particular wish which art expresses, but the total wish of man—his essential will to power.

The place of mutuality in art needs a special word in view of the contemporary conviction that the work of art expresses the unique subjective insight of the individual artist, and that we must not impose any conventional social criteria in evaluating it. This is aesthetic solipsism. We know his view that solipsism, while often proclaimed, has never been genuinely believed. And when this lack of logical seriousness is compounded with self-seriousness Hocking can be blunt. A young painter once showed Hocking an abstract painting of "the Spirit" emanating forth in clusters of curving offshoots from a central blob, presumably the young man's soul. Asked earnestly by the artist: "What do you think of it?" Hocking replied "It looks like a potato, sprouting."[12] In general, his views on modern art tended to be a trifle testy.

Hocking is convinced that art speaks of a reality that is common to all men. It therefore follows that "good" art, however one defines it, can be recognized as such by others. This does not mean, however, that popularity is the final test for any artist.

> [The artist's] art is "beyond society" inasmuch as its source is in his private dream of precisely that good which society so far fails to supply.

To this extent art must necessarily be private, inner, uniquely individual. Hocking goes on:

But he intends none the less through his art to speak across to the similarly unsatisfied wishes of his kind. In displaying his work, it is as if he said, "This is my wish,— Is it yours also?—Has it *man* in it?[13]

To this extent, art is communal. And it is a mark of a culture's health that the community has the courage of its instinctive appreciation of what is good and what isn't. Here Hocking is applying his conviction that there is a universality of private experience. Descartes bears witness to it when he *publishes* his private meditations; and the artist bears witness to it when he hangs his painting, plays his music, reads and publishes his poetry and novel. This is his answer both to metaphysical communism and a morally solipsistic abstract individualism in the arts as well as in philosophy and politics. In its politics of anti-individualism, Russian communism came close to destroying its cultural heritage in the arts.

It is a radical weakness of revolution on Marxian lines that the "exploiting classes" in regions dominantly agricultural rather than industrial—that means China as well as Russia —are likely, as landed aristocracy, to be the bearers of the *historic culture* of the nation; and with their liquidation— not the national spirit itself, but the voice of that spirit, is muted.[14]

But if Russia has been too hostile to its creative individuals, America's "faith in the ever-fertile leadings of experience, in exploration, flexibility, in the sacred liberty to challenge all fixed standards" and the fact that "we make it a principle to sit loose on 'principles' " has led to a crisis in the arts of a different sort.[15] The situation calls for a reevaluation of the role of art in our time, and Hocking finds in Camus a prophetic voice. Standing in the shadow of the

cruelty and meaninglessness of human life, Camus encounters a "blank factuality" which he labels, "The Absurd."
Hocking had already established irrational fact as a category
of his own thought. In and of itself it has no meaning; it is
only when the mind moves to the context from which fact
has been abstracted that one discovers the infinite shadow
tying fact to the source of all our meanings.[16] The natural
realism of his dialectic insists that "I am in the world" and
that the world of fact is "non-impulsive," purposeless. Beginning with Whitehead's "here we are," it is only later that
one moves to the complementing insight that there is a sense
in which "the world is in me," making it possible for recalcitrant fact to serve that field of fields which is the self in
the working out of its destiny. But what Hocking learns
from Camus, and as a result of his German experience, is
that he has moved too quickly from the meaninglessness of
fact to its metaphysically redeeming shadow. Camus recalls
him to his own words:

> There is everything in human experience to give us, as we
> look at the facts of nature and at the facts of history, a
> sense of loneliness in the presence of the great unknown.
> There it is in its immensity, operating according to natural
> laws, opaque, silent, inscrutable, frequently cruel, and ap-
> parently uninterested in the lot of us poor human beings.[17]

Camus confronts this immensity, laying himself open to
its absurdity, refusing to fend off the threat of fact's meaninglessness by a too-easy belief in the gods; refusing also
either to exploit other men, or to put his hopes in a social
revolution which can only replace one tyranny by another.
Here is solipsism again, but Hocking now appreciates the
deeper significance of his own dialectic, that only "through
carrying the logic of solipsism to the end" can a cure be

found.[18] Camus' power lies in his courage to suffer through
the soul's solitude, and at the end of that solitude find the
basis for a personal revolt which proclaims a new mutuality
and solidarity. Hocking has no sympathy with the charla-
tanism which has captured much modern art, but he honors
the magnificent achievement of those who have taken the
crisis of modernity seriously.

> To generalize [Camus'] meaning, let us say that the mission
> of art is the *Redemption of the Absurd,* overcoming the ir-
> rational brute-fact-aspect of existence, not by legality nor by
> other-worldly hopes, but by the immediate attraction of a
> vision of human nobility in creating solidarity. The mission
> of art is to evoke images that universally persuade, and thus
> create the will to unite.[19]

For his own part, of course, Hocking has always been convinced of God's presence in the midst of solitude. Might he
not be tempted to say—as so many Christians said when they
read Camus' *The Fall*—that Camus was just seeing the light
which they had already seen. He says, rather, that Camus
has done something new for him, and for the times in which
they both live. He states the relationship between himself
("religion") and Camus ("Modernity") this way:

> What religion may say, and truly say, is that this inter-
> subjective reality is nothing other than its own eternal and
> unswerving doctrine of God, whose meaning in human ex-
> perience is now belatedly discerned. To which Modernity
> might be conceived to reply, "That is true; and religion's
> honor also is to hold to its own certitude. But that certitude
> has not hitherto been held, nor could it be held, as an answer
> to the question which I, Modernity, alone have raised. It is
> I who have descended deepest into the Hell of the soul's
> solitude. And having through the agony of my own loyalty
> to truth at last been able to say, 'Behold Thou art there,'

I add for all future time that dimension to the meaning of religion."[20]

Hocking looks to Friedrich Schiller's *Letters on Aesthetic Education* for a clear view of the historic function of art. It must be free, owned by no group or individual, responsible only to the insight of the artist himself. It cannot "subordinate the senses"—Kant's prescription for culture's control over impulse. Civilization is the harmonizing of impulse and reason, and Schiller sees that "art alone can educate mankind, for only art can act on feelings directly."[21] Camus agrees here with Schiller, and Hocking applauds them both; but then points out that "for both, the question arises, who or what will educate the artists?" Or, to put the question differently, "What is the source of the artist's inspiration, the initial push which sends him on his creative way?" The question has come up once before, in dealing with Hocking's view of the self, and it is time to do it justice.

Hocking's views on art—synonymous, in the broad sense, with creativity—lead us to the third major category of his metaphysics, that of destiny. Here he parts company with Schiller and Camus, for whom the creative act is self-originating. For Hocking, creativity is the result of a process which he sums up in a metaphor taken from family life—it is "parented" by the individual's relationship to the absolute, which is, in the broadest possible sense, a man's "religion."[22] In *The Meaning of God* he expressed the historical view that "all the arts of common life owe their present status and vitality to some sojourn within the historic body of religion" and that religion could therefore be referred to (in what he admitted was "a vague figure") as "the mother of the Arts."[23] In that book he had also included a carefully worked out theory of inspiration, countering both theories of self-origination and theologies which failed to draw lines of connection between the mystic's worship, and the prophet's work in the world.[24]

The creative imagination works on stuff. Art is a relation between idea and this material. Or, one might say, art is the mastery of stuff by idea. But lest we think too readily of the artist as master, Hocking reminds us that creativity requires apprenticeship: we have to learn how to create. Apprenticeship to what? To the nature of one's materials and the range of techniques applicable to them. Hocking says man must obey nature in order to master her; but more than that: "Creation in art . . . presupposes a virtuosity of realism in experience, whose finding is issued with the personal hallmark of the artist."[25] Here, interestingly enough, Hocking finds himself in company with the modernists, many of whom deny his insistence that beauty must be characteristic of the work of art,[26] but most of whom would agree that art must deal with "what's really real." The creative venture of the original mind gives us an account of the nature of the real. Creativity is always a celebration of being. But Hocking wants us to see that nothing, however artful, can be creative if it lies. It is possible to speak of the element of truth as speculative, or poetic, or concerned with the artist's belief, and Hocking clearly has precise content ready for any of these terms; but by themselves they smack too much of daydreaming, of the little world of one's own, of poignant irrelevance, of sentimentality. For Hocking, to stop with simple "realism" is to be "wise-dog-mindful-of-his-bacon," fearful of the dangerous living which is metaphysics. But to begin with fantasy or irrelevance is to pass too quickly by the chastening world of hard fact. The first movement of creative integrity is the "empirical plunge." Creativity depends upon a prior realism.

Hocking recognizes, however, that the new idea "often arrives without our intent or plan."[27] It cannot be forced; it does not live in the bowels of the typewriter, in the blood stream of the pen, or in some undiscovered country of the mind. We must struggle for it—it is not bought cheaply— but we must also wait. As the adage of Ptah Hotep has it, "The boatsman reaches the landing partly by pulling and partly by letting go!"[28] And yet, when it comes, it is the result of both effort and grace, a "maternal brooding" in cooperation with nature. That which results did not previously exist, embedded in the fore-ordained structure of things. As Hocking puts it: "God would never have thought of [Tschaikowski's music] without Tschaikowski."[29] Hocking joins with Charles Hartshorne when he says that the work of the creative mind "enriches the life of God." But then, where does the music come from? The crucial question, to be sure. But Hocking suggests that we move first in the other direction and speak of what we know for sure: Where does the music go?

> It is of the essence of human creation that its product, like its gestation, belongs not alone to the author's world but to *our* world. . . . Each such decision, and each such output of idea, is attended by the simple certitude that one's private thought is in its nature universal—the natural, unquestioned *intersubjectivity of experience.* To say this is to recognize an ultimate factor of kinship, perhaps of collaboration, in the objective source of things. It is also to say that the creative self perceives his product as having a destiny beyond himself. This, its destiny, is part of its being; and also a part of his. The idea of destiny becomes part of our empirical outlook.[30]

Empirical in what sense? Natural science takes its experienced facts in order, one by one; it counts, names, identifies, categorizes. The meat of experience is butchered, sorted, cellophane wrapped, labeled according to cut—and only then displayed under the cool, analytic fluorescence of the scientific supermarket. Admittedly, this is an ideal way to take experience for the purposes of science. But does reality *come* that way, pre-packaged? The supermarket meat counter provides an ideal arrangement for the housewife whose purposes are directed toward steak-for-dinner. But the reality of the steak is bound up in the prior reality of the steer; and the scientific fact depends, in turn, on its own larger context. If one's purpose is to understand the larger whole, the perspective of the supermarket is too narrow. The field-concept, underlying all the discontinuities of empirical scientific fact-finding and its abstracted "experience," accounts for the wholeness which we feel in our world. "Within this felt unity, there is a richness of experience which is at a disadvantage for recognition, partly because it is too near us, beneath the level of specific language, and partly because its aspects are mutually involved."[31] Hocking is concerned that we recognize a region of "nuclear awareness" of the world, and its three basic constituents. There is selfhood, so immediate that Hume, concentrating on separate impressions, failed to find it and concluded it must be a myth. There is the intersubjective experience of community with the Thou, the other minds of our social world. And there is the physical, bodily sense of our own well-being (or illness), progressing in time, involving us in a sense of *telos*, of meaning, of work-to-be-done and done well—in short, a sense of destiny. Here, in summary, is the metaphysical fruit of Hocking's social realism in which I, Thou, and It are bound together, interdependent, instinctively known as such in a feeling both cognitive and emotional.

This nuclear awareness is not just a sense of relationships, a grasp of one's metaphysical status. It is also, perhaps even primarily, a sense of power, an intimation of that capacity which Eddington notes when he argues that the process of existing is guided by an awareness of what I can or cannot do. Hocking suggests that the most native of all powers, the one dimension of the will to power which is basic to all the rest, is simply the conviction that I *can* meet all that is over-against-me, not only in the immensities of nature and society which Camus has faced so courageously, but also the hidden inner depths of selfhood. For he reminds us that the will-to-live is something much more than a simple will-to-exist. Even the embryo knows a will-to-grow. (There is considerable medical evidence that a patient who lacks the will to get better does not get better. It is at least conceivable that many of the natural processes of the body are dependent upon the cooperating thrust of the healthy will to power.) The developing individual knows a will-to-live-as-human-being. Included in this will is the requirement of thinking; Hocking is convinced that there is nothing biologically necessary about rational thought. Why, he asks, should we think a world? Why not just sit back and enjoy sense-aesthesis? Is it just because we are afraid that others will think us lazy? But there are those who defy almost every other social convention. Is it just our own inner conscience that prevents us? If we really wanted to, would it not be possible? Perhaps it is not what we really want.

Hocking pushes on. He is not constructing a theory or presenting a proof for a point of view. He is trying to describe an experience which may be universal and is largely hidden because no one can quite remember what it is like first to think a world. This is why so much of Hocking's writing is impressionistic. It sounds oracular but he is appealing more than announcing. He is asking whether we recognize his experience as our own, and therefore possibly as human experience. In order to do so, we must strain to catch elements of thought and feeling which are well below the mind's surface and often rooted far back in one's personal history. Vague impressions are all one can hope for, but Hocking believes that—at this profound level—vague impressions and the commitments which grow out of them determine the unique quality of an individual's life.

He suggests that the reason we don't just sit and enjoy the world is that we wouldn't be happy. To be human is to have certain powers, and to be happy is to exercise them. But life is a movement of events streaming around the individual. It is not enough for Hocking to toss a creative act into this stream, like those ancient Chinese poets who sat on the river bank writing their verses on pieces of rice paper and then floated them away on the stream. Hocking senses a direction to the movement of life. Life is not the patternless fluctuation which Heracleitus believed in, or the cyclical ebb and flow on which both the classical Greek and the classical Hindu philosophies of life are based. Hocking's experience is in line with the Christian and liberal view that life has a *telos,* that for each individual there is both a sense of obligation that he has a task to accomplish, and an assurance that success is a real possibility. Calvinism made this sense of destiny specific. Prayerful recourse to the scriptures would reveal one's particular pre-destined role in the economy of God. For Hocking, however, the individual's vocation is not a secret hidden in the mind of God. It is a potentiality within the mind and will of the individual which a hospitable world elicits. Neither pre-ordained or foreknown by anyone, it is a novel, genuinely creative contribution to the human community and to the life of God himself. He writes:

> What I am now suggesting is that we corroborate in ourselves a Destiny-sense, as an empirical element of our nuclear

world-awareness. We cannot be unaware of our own *telos,*
as a total directive integrating all partial ends. Nor can we
be unaware of our immediate and continuing dependence
on a creative real, somehow akin. Our time-vista toward the
future must contain the natural synthesis of this summons
and this assurance.[32]

Remembering the formal discussion of Hocking's metaphysics, in which he argued that God is the creative ground
which makes possible this interrelationship between I, Thou
and It, it is now possible to find metaphysical content with
which to replace the self-origination theory of artistic inspiration. The question is as puzzling to the college undergraduate laboring on a term paper as it is to the genius
struggling with paints or poetry. Where does the "bright
idea," the "insight," the "inspiration" come from? In one
of the concluding chapters of *The Meaning of God* Hocking
had early set forth a defense of his suggestion that religion
is the mother of the arts, and that it is a man's relation to
the absolute which sparks his novel idea.

He begins by noting that moral and cognitive ideas tend
to form systems which are self-perpetuating. In Aristotle's
Ethics, for example, we look for a definition of virtue and
find that virtue is the characteristic of the virtuous man,
who is able to practice virtue because he is virtuous. Only
the virtuous man can become virtuous; only the wise can
gain wisdom. Clearly, to him that hath it shall be given. But
then where does originality come from? Hocking argues that
the enclosedness of this circle is broken by a touch from
outside strong enough to be disorganizing. Something happens in our experience which causes us to realize an old idea
with sharpened consciousness, for the new is always defined
and distinguished in relation to the old. This realization is
a fresh connection with reality, and particularly "with the

reality which the thinker is conscious of in *himself*—that which is realized is 'brought home,' made a conscious part of his own vivid and literal present world."[33] The birth of the new idea is preceded by sharpening realization and repudiation of the old. In the moment of self-consciousness the old idea penetrates to the depths of the self for the first time, and in the resulting reflection on it, the new idea is born. "I wish, then, in the first place, to connect the event of creation with the event of *reflexion*,—that is, with the emergence of a *self*-consciousness out of a consciousness that is pursuing in all smoothness the lines of the empirical object-world."[34]

Now what causes reflection? Generally speaking, Hocking feels that it results from some defeat, a certain inertia in the workings of the mind. In the regular flow of conversation we become aware of our mispronunciation of a word, or soreness in the throat. The empty-handed hunter returns home reflecting that he wanted a tramp in the woods as much as a deer. The workman at the end of an engrossing job suddenly finds it finished and, for a moment, is at a loss for something to do. In all these instances the usual habits of attention and occupation have been defeated. Reflection is simply the result of our situation's demand for something new, and the self supplies that new thing because the self stands outside each and every one of these closed groups of mental and moral habit. This is the source of our freedom from all convention and habit; we are able to transcend it. The self is a vantage point for perspective on the world. But then the critical question: How is reflection possible? Hocking answers:

Now my proposition is that *the power to reflect depends upon the power to find your Absolute,* in the last resort upon practical religion. It is through alliance with the Absolute that man is able to reflect: it is through his reflexion that he becomes creative of novelty, system-destroying novelty.[35]

Self-knowledge is, of course, the most difficult kind of knowledge. It cannot be entirely controlled by the will. It calls for a certain gift for which there are no technical rules. But Hocking's principle is that no self or system can be criticized except in the light of positive content from beyond them. The source of our ability to reflect is therefore simply that which is beyond every finite system, "the Not of all that man can think or say," which is the absolute.[36] This general process of reflection is not unlike the process of induction, whereby the mind moves from parts to the whole. In spite of all that has been written about the science of inductive logic, Hocking is not convinced that "inductive method" is more than a preparation for discovery. "The problem 'To find the common element in a given group of objects' has no solution; there is no general formula for discovering integrals."[37] The success of any induction depends in part upon simple observation and the ability to conceive of things being other than they are. This awareness that the thing observed might be different breeds the capacity to ask questions of things as they are. A background of wide experience helps, as does training, imagination, acquaintance with the facts, etc. The perception of relationships in a group of objects—which may be as good a definition as any of that mystery we call intelligence—is a result of combining external observation and internal reflexion. Hocking concludes:

The inventive artist, poet, musician, has his moments of prelude to idea-making in which *musing* he can hardly tell

whether he is scrutinizing his objects or the stirrings in himself. Reflexion and induction are of the same fabric, and
have the same conditions for success. Every induction is
induced by a prior induction, ultimately a *total induction,*
or judgment about the whole of things,—none other than
my whole-idea, derived from whatever knowledge of the
whole and of God my experience has built up for me. Every
induction is at the same time a deduction, then,—an "It
must be so," parented, though from the background of my
consciousness, by an insight which in its origins is religious.[38]

But thus far one's relation to this whole, while partly
immediate, has also been partly that of a man afar off,
glimpsing a *telos* of perfection which calls him onward, but
remains a vision. For Hocking, however, anything which is
real must, in the end, be literal; he will not talk of a far-off
good unless our destiny will one day unite us with it. In
short, he believes in immortality and has argued for it at
length over a period of years, notably in two books—
Thoughts on Death and Life,[39] and—most recently—*The
Meaning of Immortality in Human Experience.*[40] This interest is one of the distinctive features of Hocking's philosophy. The Christian faithful in the pews still hold to a
vague sense that there is somehow "something beyond," but
there has been remarkably little said by theologians about
the destiny of individuals beyond death.[41] And among philosophers, there has been even less interest in what used to
be a major topic of speculation. Corliss Lamont is a notable
exception.[42]

Hocking begins his philosophical analysis of the possibility
of immortality by rejecting the spatial idea that we move,
in death, from "here" to "there."[43] We do not travel, as
Giordano Bruno thought, to some congenial planet. If there
is rational life elsewhere in the universe, we have reason to

hope that it will prove friendly, but no reason to expect that its populace will be ancestrally familiar. Hocking returns, rather, to the concept of selfhood and world as both having a double boundary, which he first suggested in his "Theses Establishing an Idealistic Metaphysics by a New Route."[44] There, (as we have seen in Chapter VIII), he challenged the space-time monism of Newton and Kant on the basis of modern developments in mathematics and quantum physics. The resulting infinitude of space-time worlds available to the self as "vinculum" relating them, is the philosophical basis for the possibility of immortality. The concrete freedom in which the self realizes an idea "opens an avenue of insight into the possibility of survival" because:

> Whoever is concretely free is co-creator in an actual world: as such he is not *in toto* passive to the integral processes of that world. In the devising of free deeds within the context of particular fact, there is a literal sense in which the self is in the presence of at least one other space world all the time. And to recognize this self as the vinculum, or hinge of transition, between these two space worlds, and as such not a member item in either of them, separates the destiny of that self from the total operation of causes playing within the world of nature.[45]

This philosophical analysis suggests only that physical death may be relative and not absolute. If immortality has real meaning for human experience, analysis must find its organic unity with feeling, without which it is barren, chiefly in the experiences of love and death itself, and their relation to creativity. The impulse of specific love, including the artistic response of the mind to beauty as well as love between persons, appears at first to be the desire to possess. But love cannot be maintained without the continuing freedom of the beloved. Love therefore involves the being of the beloved as a value—a permanent value. "The impulse of caring is to hold that being forever above the accidents of time and death."[46] Is this only the tragic folly of human affection? Hocking finds love always creative, always serving the yet-unborn possibility of the beloved's life. As a result, the *"mission of love in time is never done,"* and the conviction that this mission can be fulfilled in permanently establishing the selfhood of the beloved is part of the meaning of the experience of love.[47]

The experience of death cannot be followed to the end, but those who attend the dying regularly report a normal reversal of the will-to-live, a complicity with nature which is more than simple resignation. It is Hocking's conviction—and these lines were written in his late eighties—that "The peace that comes to the dying is not that of terminus: it is—as I interpret it—the peace of *handing-on,* and of reverting to origins, with the felt opening of a perspective more profoundly valid."[48] The death of which he speaks here is, of course, the natural death of old people, not the tragic destruction of life in its prime with which we are so familiar today. But from the perspective of love, the tragic death of the young only sharpens the conviction that this unfulfilled selfhood deserves a fulfillment which life has not granted. Hocking is not arguing that philosophy can prove immortality. He is logically examining a serious human belief against the background of experience in order to determine whether such a belief is, in fact, believable. This takes us to the cornerstone of Hocking's thought, his philosophy of religion. We located the central problem of the individual in his creative will to power. It is this will which education directs and helps him to remake. In organizing his relations in society, the individual will is given its legal rights which the democratic state encourages him to fulfill in shaping its destiny and his own. But society, in relying on the creativity of its individuals, looks beyond itself for the source of creative power. The arts—whether the common arts of government, child-raising, and home-making, or the more specialized fine arts—reach out and touch this source, whether consciously or instinctively. It is religion, however, which announces most clearly the ultimate meaning of the human adventure. In turning to the role of religion in fulfilling man's instinctive will to power, we have come full circle. Epistemology and metaphysics sent us out into the world to test theory against fact; and the world of fact, demanding its rightful interpretation, sends us back again—this time to enquire after the practical and historical meaning of God in human experience.

Chapter XIII

RELIGION, MYSTICISM, AND THE
PROPHETIC CONSCIOUSNESS

ANYONE WHO TALKS SERIOUSLY ABOUT RELIGION these days is asking for trouble. Even the theologians seem to be against it. Secularism, increasing in the West, means for many people that religious ideas and institutions are not anathema, they are anachronisms—psychological and sociological throwbacks to an outgrown era. Secularism has largely ceased to be an "ism." It is simply the unremarkable way things are. But if the secular man is no longer interested in his own secularism, the theologian is less blasé. After a brief period of lamentation over the Godlessness of the modern world, theology now discovers a secular meaning of the gospel, and Christian sociology celebrates the secular city. Dietrich Bonhoeffer's scattered comments about "religionless Christianity" have spearheaded a radical theological attack on "religion" and all its ways; even the "death of God" is affirmed as a Christian doctrine.[1]

This attack has firm theological grounding in a critical analysis of religion, notably set forth in Hendrik Kraemer's *Religion and the Christian Faith*.[2] And the attack has firm historical grounding in considerations which Wilfred Cantwell Smith has recently spelled out in his *The Meaning and End of Religion*.[3] Kraemer recognizes a religious consciousness in man, and his broad experience and careful scholarship give him a deep appreciation of its value. But religion is a mixed bag. It is an expression of man's noblest spiritual yearnings, and, at the same time, witnesses to man's fantasy, self-aggrandizement, and moral perversity. All particular religions are subject to this ambivalence, Christianity as much as any other. Kraemer therefore distinguishes between the values of man's universal religious consciousness and the crucial element of religious truth, which cannot be universal, but is available only to a particular faith. Christianity as a religion is one among many; he rejects the idea that it is a superior religion. Christian faith, on the other hand, is not the product of any universal religious consciousness, it is the product of God's divine activity, and is simply the sole saving Truth about God. Kraemer is less extreme than Karl Barth, who states flatly that religion is unbelief, and therefore the affair of the godless man. Admitting that this is a valid thesis, Kraemer nevertheless finds Barth's rejection of religion "convulsive" and prefers the "serenity" of Calvin's confession of the greatness of human religion. Kraemer's own greatness is evident in his willingness to suffer this finally unresolved tension between man's god-creating religions, and God's religion-destroying gift of faith. For our purposes, however, the important feature of Kraemer's work is the distinction which he makes between religion—man's consciousness of divinity and the cult life in which he celebrates that consciousness—and faith—that knowledge of God which cannot be conceived or striven for, but only received as a mystery of God's mercy.[4]

Smith, opposing the idea that religion has any definable conceptual essence, notes that the term (from the Latin *religio*) was used rarely, and then only imprecisely, in the early years of the Christian era—referring usually to cultic practice or personal attitude rather than to any specific body of belief. Augustine's *De Vera Religione,* for example, was not an argument for the superiority of the Christian religion. It was an emphasis on the true worship of a transcendent God in a personal relationship which it was the business of the Church to foster. For both the medieval Church and the Reformation, the issue was one of "faith," and it was only in the beginnings of the modern period that "religion" became a systematic entity with a specific intellectual content. With Grotius' *De Veritate Religionis Christianae,* and in the writings of Lord Herbert of Cherbury, religion becomes a matter of doctrine, supposedly with a conceivable and distinguishable "essence." Feuerbach's *The Essence of Christianity* and *The Essence of Religion* popularized the idea that religion has a fixed form which can be distilled by careful analysis. But because of the "inebriating variety of man's religious life" (including the variety *within* each religious tradition) Smith is convinced that this concept, religion, is a mythical beast. We should talk, rather, about "cumulative tradition" and the personal "faith" of individuals.[5]

For Kraemer, religion is spiritually defective, distracting from the centrality of faith. For Smith, religion is intellectually defective, assuming an analyzable essence and therefore distracting from an understanding of the diversity, complexity, and dynamism of the individual believer's faith and practice. To these two criticisms of the idea of religion the Christian West has added practical criticisms of Christian religious cult life: its suburban captivity, liturgical shortcomings, social irrelevance, political irresponsibility, and theological illiteracy. As a result, whether the approach to matters of religion has been theological, historical, or practical, it has been increasingly negative. But while the attacks are sharp, they stop short of total destruction. Kraemer is not out to negate religion, but only to put it in its place. The social critics of the Christian parish church do not, as a rule, advocate its abolition, but rather its reform. And even Smith, whose argument is fairly radical, substitutes for religion those broad components (historical tradition and personal faith) which, to many, seem best to define what religion is.[6] These attacks, coming largely from Western Protestant Christians, have produced practical reforms, theological clarification, and a growing realization of the difficulties inherent in any comparative study of religions. They have not, however, produced the radical new concepts which they seemed to call for: is there, after all, a better word than "religion"? And the new experimental forms of Church life have often reformed, but seldom radically broken away from traditional patterns.

For Hocking's world perspective, it is important to note that this debate is only peripherally relevant to Asia, where religion and culture are still inextricably intertwined. Hocking has his own program for intellectual and practical reform, centering in a "re-conception" of every positive religion, and a "de-Westernization" of Christian theology and cult life. He has himself pointed out the difficulty of defining religion, and when he speaks, as indeed he does, of the essence of religion, he does not have in mind the rational conceptual essence of Ludwig Feuerbach. In *Living Religions and a World Faith* Hocking measured the problem of definition, noting that Oriental religions are relatively formless and lacking the institutionalization characteristic of the Christian church. These religions are not exclusive in their claims; many a Chinese householder is a Confucian in life but is buried with Taoist or Buddhist ceremonies. They have large varieties of authoritative personnel (scholars, monks, priests, *saddhus,* lay mystics of all kinds, etc.). Their reliance on various philosophies (as opposed to the more historical, dogmatic, prophetic religions of the Semitic Near East) makes it almost impossible to condense their intellectual variety into a normative set of dogmatic ideas.[7] (Hinduism, for example—despite all the weighty attempts at definition in the scholarly texts—is simply the religion of the Hindus, and "Hindu" is a geographical, not a religious term. The Hindus are simply the people of "Hind," the areas adjacent to the Indus river.[8]) Hocking would admit, therefore, that "religion" is an increasingly difficult term to employ usefully. He feels, however, that it connotes one of those basic categories of human experience which we can scarcely do without. He is not far from Tillich's psychological definition of religion as a man's "ultimate concern"; but his most characteristic early emphasis was teleological. In this world of becoming, full of beginnings which are never brought to the final fulfillment of which we feel them capable, religion is "anticipated attainment" of that fulfillment.[9] It is for this fulfillment, which lies out beyond the rim of history, that the artist suffers; hence, the pragmatic place of religion in culture is that of "the mother of the Arts."[10] The worshipper, sensing the nearness of God and the promise of his destiny's fulfillment, has a sense of "vicarious attainment" in that moment.[11] Religion, as Hocking sees it, is therefore the conviction that man's individual vocation has permanent significance.

These definitions, all taken from *The Meaning of God,* date from 1912. They are centered in the individual's sense of his own particular destiny. But in 1940, when Hocking published *Living Religions and a World Faith,* he struck a different note, and defined religion as "passion for righteousness, and for the spread of righteousness, conceived as a cosmic demand."[12] Here the emphasis shifts from personal spiritual fulfillment which is sensed now, but finally bestowed only at the *telos,* to the moral work of religion in the human community here and now. Individualism and teleology thus give way to the community and immediacy. Hocking hastens to point out that the factor of "cosmic demand" distinguishes religion from morality, and in so doing he emphasizes the community by insisting that religion is "not solely my own concern."[13] This emphasis is not a departure from the perspective of *The Meaning of God.* There he had set up a dialectical tension between the intense personal experience of the individual worshipper (the mystic) and the social and historical task of religion's work in the world, performed by the believer in his role as prophet. But the emphasis on the spread of righteousness is significant. Here religion is essentially a mission.

In the years following his work on *The Meaning of God,* Hocking was drawn more and more to the problem of religion's historical role. He was particularly fascinated, and not a little frustrated, by the Christian missionary enterprise. Theoretically it seemed to him that this passion for the spread of righteousness was much more important to man's development in culture and history than even its advocates recognized. In actual fact, however, he found missionaries as a whole an unimpressive lot and their entire venture in need of radical rethinking. His work as chairman of the Laymen's Commission investigating foreign missions was his most important and notorious venture into practical affairs, and the commission's report, *Rethinking Missions,* made Hocking a popular and controversial figure. It was one of the most widely read of Hocking's books, and Hocking became embroiled in a series of spirited debates and lectures in defense of his views.

His later writing on religious philosophy—notably *Living*

Religions and a World Faith and *The Coming World Civilization*—takes this practical and historical concern for the spread of righteousness and relates it to the structure of his metaphysics. As a result his philosophy of religion is transformed into a philosophy of history. The "nuclear awareness" of the presence of an "other" who is God—an awareness which integrates the individual's relationship to his neighbor and the natural world—is witnessed to in every positive religion. It is a recognition of this experience by "the true mystics" of differing faiths which constitutes, for Hocking, an embryonic "world faith" in the midst of religious pluralism. This experience of nuclear awareness demands of philosophy that it widen its understanding of the empirical to include the context of meaning from which facts are abstracted. Of religion it demands that men of different faiths enter into dialogue, not simply in the hope of building bridges of cooperation and mutual respect, but in order to recognize that an important bond already exists among them. This bond is not simply a shared experience of religious piety; it is an item of common knowledge of God. The hope of a world civilization is based on religion as a common binding cultural ingredient. Hence the importance of the "true mystics" of every religion who sense their common bond with one another.

The importance of the nuclear awareness of the true mystics again raises the question of Hocking's own mysticism. He regards the mystic vision as the highest experience of worship. The mystic is a key figure in the dramatis personae of his religious dialectic—along with the prophet. The mystic is, if anything, even more important to his philosophy of history, for it is the mystic who best apprehends the emerging elements of world faith. Hocking himself had one or two experiences of extrasensory perception, and he did indeed have a good old-fashioned conversion experience when he was a boy. But the experience of the classical mystics of whatever religion is extraordinary, and the whole point of Hocking's "mysticism" is precisely its ordinariness. It is the basic, common experience of everyman to which he appeals.

Despite the fact that Hocking has written a great deal *about* mysticism there is no developed mysticism in his own philosophy. I think Hocking had moments when he would like to have been a mystic; those times in his own experience when insight became a "searing flame" helped him to appreciate mysticism as "a momentous thing."[14] But he remains an outsider to the mystic vision. The experience of the true mystic is "sufficient to command respect for the tradition of mysticism, sufficient to justify the attention which through religious history has been focussed upon these individuals."[15] And that is exactly what he does. He respects them, and focusses on them. Like James, he is sensitive to their particular variety of religious experience, and he feels that it justifies his attention to the tradition. Further, he is convinced that the mystic vision is a refined and purified form of something available to us all.

Hocking is a Methodist, not a mystic. One can take as a text for his religious philosophy the psalmist's affirmation, "I will lift up mine eyes unto the hills, from whence cometh my help. My help cometh from the Lord which made heaven and earth." How is it that the hills can transmit the assurance that God is? This is a question which Hocking's religious philosophy sets out to answer. But there is nothing esoteric about this kind of natural experience. The piety which finds solace in nature is not even distinctively religious. The secularist and the monk both find comfort, a little peace, and a measure of renewal from a walk in the woods; and even the inveterate city dweller finds his step a little lighter on a warm spring day. This natural piety, breeding an animal faith about our relation to the world is a point of departure. This is the corner of experience which Hocking's dialectic catches and penetrates. And if it is the mystic who goes deepest into this corner, Hocking is convinced that the valid elements of his experience are different from ours only in degree, not in kind—a conviction which he inherited from James' assumptions in dealing with the *Varieties*.[16]

Mysticism, then, remains an illustration of Hocking's point, not the substance. What is crucial for his philosophy is a widening of the concept of the empirical to include both the sense perception of the positivist, and the feel for the depth of experience so prominent in existentialism. Hocking's appeal is not to some esoteric, specialized, mystic vision. His appeal is simply to what we really see in our first wide open look, before we start narrowing down to our own specialized corner of the field. His is a difficult focus to establish; but it is the non-specialized perspective which we all share, and the only focus which can yield a common view of the human situation.

Hocking's religious philosophy is in line with liberal Christianity's emphasis on the immanence of God in the world.[17] This whole tradition shares in the vocabulary problem concerning the dimensions of experience and the meaning of mystery; but its adherents have had a hard time convincing religious philosophers of the East that they were "mystics." C. T. K. Chari puts it nicely, referring to M. Cunliffe's view[18] that "the would-be American mystic never goes far with his mysticism; the telephone is always ringing; he has to go and shake hands with some delegation or other."[19] Hocking wants a religious sensitivity which feeds its vitality into the workings of the world. He wants men

like Dag Hammarskjold who work all day in the frenzy of
the U. N. and chart their *Markings* in the still of the night.
But when Hocking's own telephone was stilled and the visiting delegation departed, he was usually not to be found in
his closet at prayer, or recording an intensely inward spiritual journey. One might have found him listening to
Tchaikovsky, or watching the last touch of sun on the peak
of Mt. Washington; but he was usually in his study philosophizing on what it all *meant*. It is misleading to call this
"mysticism." We owe it to Hocking, however, to stick to his
own vocabulary, and, thus forewarned, we come to the dialectical relation between the mystic and the prophet.

Hocking does not endorse the "negative metaphysics"
which finds God ineffable (i.e., without predicates), and
which often summarizes mystical knowledge. He feels that
the advocates of such metaphysics have confused their experience of God with the true knowledge of God himself.[20]
He begins with the mystic as willer and worshipper, rather
than with the mystic as knower. An important reason for
this is that mysticism, for Hocking, has a reforming and
prophetic role in the present-day practice of worship. He
feels that conventional worship suffers from over-practice
and dilution, and that mysticism can "reanimate in some
vital fashion our historic system of mediation."[21] By this he
means public worship as well as private—all that we mean
by "church, and all that goes with church."[22]

Ontological mysticism is a venture in detachment which
necessarily follows the path of negation. The mystic is seeking not the whole of reality, but the heart of God. For Hocking a negative method produces a negative result; what the
mystic finds is zero. But the true mystic keeps going. "This
zero is not a place to stay in; but it may be pre-eminently a
place to return to, and *to depart from*."[23] Worship is the

place where the mystic finds the point again—that still point which is at the center of existence. The disinctive note here is that of ambition. As the idealist is one who is satisfied intellectually with nothing less than knowledge of the whole, so the ontological mystic finds that nothing in the world is quite good enough for him. But the venture amounts to zero apart from the dialectical movement of departure, of return to the world. We worship in order to find the meaning of our work. And the meaning of work is worship. Worship as preparation is essentially negative. It is a purgation of one's love of the world, but not, at best, a genuine denial. It is an attempt to put first things first. But the mystic cannot conjure up God. In the end he finds himself empty, silent, waiting. Hocking finds this is as true of Luther's "mystical" reliance on grace and of Schleiermacher's mystical "feeling of absolute dependence" as it is of more extreme forms of mystical quietism.

The thorough-going man of the world, as Hocking sees him, has universalized himself, and lost sight of both that individual self who is within, and the absolute self who is at the heart of his world. His world has become totally known, devoid of mystery. He has, in fact, committed himself totally to an artificial self, a humanly made self, in total rejection of the natural self.[24] Hocking feels that the commitment is entirely right; but spiritual health requires a dialectic of work and worship. Thus the true meaning of the mystical experience is prophetic; i.e. it concerns something yet to be won, some creative work yet to be accomplished, some historical action still waiting to be entered upon. Hocking recognizes that mysticism sought to recover the essential motivation of "all that we mean by Church;" and he is re-examining and re-establishing the traditional religious categories of revelation, inspiration, and the prophetic

consciousness. The concern of the mystic is not to find
something new, "but only to find the Ancient of Days as a
God revealed personally to him."[25] And God, Hocking believes, is not ineffable subject. The history of religion rightly
evolves traditional predicates which are its dogmatic affirmations; Hocking has no patience with that modern humility
which rejects things dogmatic.[26] Religious men will not be
able to find common ground in terms of common *feeling*, or
even common concern. Religion, to Hocking, is a matter of
knowledge, and one does not have a full religious life without dogma stemming from a revelation of the true God.
Dogma will be arrived at inductively, as one tests one's revelation in the world, seeking those things which God loves,
and those which he hates.

Hocking submits first the certainty that there is a God and
a proper praise of Him which goes with that certainty. But
there must be also each man's positive contribution to the
"concrete spiritual wealth of mankind."[27] We cannot, Hocking points out, separate our own reality from that of our
objects, and in the prophetic acting upon these objects in
history we become genuinely real for the first time. It is
necessary for human happiness that man should live not
simply in a realm of chance (accepted by Hegel, Royce, and
James) but in a real world in which he has real power, and
in which he measures his own scope by his power to *make
history*. And, Hocking asks, is this not in fact a power which
we all have? We become conscious of our historic validity:

> and as personality acquires this more perfect poise, the
> exercise of prophetic power may become continuous, not
> simply concentrated in climactic performances. The effect
> of such silent and continuous command may be nothing
> more than this, that things grow in its presence. But this,
> if we have not been mistaken, is what chiefly happens in
> the presence of God. This also is historical action.[28]

Prophecy is a temper of the spirit, a recognition that one's personal destiny is radically affected by will, and that will is a factor of our life in history. This temper combines both the self-sufficiency of the stoic and the universality of the altruist, with a righteous love of power which Hocking finds characteristic of the present age. He implies a natural religion, which all men share. As this natural religion grows into different forms of positive religion it carries with it traces of its origin, which remain common elements of all the positive religions. To this extent, then, one can speak of religion as something which all men share in both their experience of nature, and in the context of their positive religious life. It is significant, however, that Hocking ties in the historical consciousness of the mystic-become-prophet with Christianity.

The concept of religion does not *become* true religion until it develops a historical consciousness, becomes institutionalized and active in the human community. Therefore, "religion" is a theoretical thing, something less than real; it is not a concrete universal until it becomes embodied in a positive institution. Hocking thus rejects John Dewey's suggestion, in *A Common Faith,* that religion be stripped of its institutional trappings and made a general force for unity among men.

What some readers of *Living Religions and a World Faith* have not understood is that the world "faith" which Hocking speaks of is not a world "religion." World faith is a common element to be found in all the world's positive religions, deriving from the natural knowledge of God which all men hold in common. This world faith is an element of world unity in the contemporary religious picture. Further, it is raw material for one of the present living positive religions to take into itself, thus making itself a potential world religion. Whether this is achieved will depend upon the maturity of the particular religion, and also upon the extent to which it carries to a natural and logical conclusion those instincts and insights which all men share in their common knowledge of God. Because Christianity has provided religion with its historical virtues it is best fitted for this historic role. There is thus a dialectical tension between "religion" and Christianity.

If the prophetic ambition is to have any meaning in the world, the world must be conservative of values, and thus unitary and eternal. In the same way that we discover reliability and identity in nature, Hocking says, the historical world must provide the mystic with such a persistent principle or else he must make it for himself. This is the prophetic task, the building of the kingdom, and this task "is the essential purpose of the *religious institution*." Religion has been, from primitive times, the forerunner of international law, and "it alone can create the international spirit, the international obligation; it alone can permanently sustain and ensure that spirit." Thus we are led to the realization that "we require a world religion."[29] If a true human community is possible, it will only be possible on the basis of a religion which encompasses history. This is not only required by the pressures of our present history but by the requirements of general human happiness. Our religious task is to unify history. The mystic, as Hocking describes him, is armed with his moment of insight. He moves now to the prophetic task, which is the work of the kingdom, and this brings us to Christianity.

We have become accustomed to the universality of Hocking's concern. *The Meaning of God* is, after all, a book about what God means to all men, in all times, and in all places. Even the emphasis on mysticism is in keeping with this universality; the mixed company of Mohammed, Lao

Tze, Confucius, and John of the Cross confirms it. With the idea that mystery breeds prophecy, however, we find this universal truth necessarily embodying itself in a concrete situation. By touching on the significance of dogma and authority, Hocking brings us back to a problem which he seemed to have tried to avoid: the conflict among positive religions and positive claims to religious authority. If religion is to have a prophetic, world-unifying function, there must necessarily come a time when a particular religion will become the bearer of genuine, concrete universality.

Hocking first expressed his views on Christianity in an essay in the *Yale Divinity Quarterly* on the thorny theological issue, "How can Christianity Be the Final Religion?"[30] He finds the authoritative affirmation of finality nothing less than the "one mark of sincerity in a religion." This is not to endorse the claim that Christianity teaches "truth" in the form of a finally fixed metaphysics and ethics, nor is it even to affirm the final moral perfection of Jesus. It is rather to say that a particular person, Jesus Christ, becomes the necessary object of religious devotion. Christianity will be final because Jesus, as the Christ, "assumes an *office* which has been created by universal necessity and consent."[31] He performed a function which only one person could perform, one which is logically universal. But the final fact—that this particular person fulfills the universally necessary function— cannot be proved (since no universal function necessarily implies any particular functionary); it can only be believed.

Hocking first asks if there is such a necessary religious function, and, if so, what it is. Next he asks whether the individual person involved has consciously attempted to solve the religious problem by assuming the particular office. Then he seeks to show that this person is to be accepted by all men as the once-and-for-all performer of this particular religious office. This acceptance, and resulting affirmation, would be the one authoritative dogma of religion.[32] Hocking works out his doctrine in terms of what he calls a "dialectic of evil," which one could also call a dialectic of self-consciousness, or of self-valuation, which is also a dialectic of resentment. Man begins with a divided reaction to the factuality of his world. There is a tension between fact and destiny; what the world is, and what it is to be; between what the world is and why it should be as it is. Religion, Hocking contends, declares the question about the world to be a legitimate one, and it seeks to provide an answer.

The affirmation of the Greek—that gloriously once-born man, whose faith in his own value can be shaken neither by angry gods, nor tragedy, nor death itself—speaks for us all. Our very being in the face of fact is a noble achievement. But there follows on this boldness something which the pure classicist would call a failure of nerve. For Hocking it is a deeper sense of self which knows that even one's partial achievements cannot insure self-justification in the face of one's infinite ambitions; that success is always mixed with failure; that justice and injustice are a tangled web. This first stage begins with self-affirmation and ends in pessimism. Historically we move, with Hocking, from the Greek to the Roman world where, as Hegel said, the human soul could, for the first time, be thoroughly lost.

There is, Hocking feels, a natural relief from this pessimism, but it is found in the deeper pessimism of a sense of sin. Man is by nature as evil as he is good, and yet he takes the good as his standard; the act of perfection is the normal act—"if we do right, what thank have we,—that is to be expected of us, nothing less."[33] We feel that if an act of our own fails of perfection—as it continually does—it is our own fault, and under the spur of this realization, this "postulate of the Orient," our subjectivity deepens and our speculative activity necessarily continues. The increase of goodness in the individual, Hocking says, serves only to clarify this logic of defect.

> No man can attain subjective freedom, nor reach maturity of self-consciousness, without having thus taken upon himself in his solitary person the sins of humanity—because they are in very truth his own . . . And he has seen most truly to whom his sin has taken on an aspect more sinister, perhaps, than that of voluntary guilt—an aspect almost of physical evil, inherent in the condition of a limited spirit, propagated from member to member of the species; until something like the old question of justice rises within him, and he is capable of resentment because he is not God.[34]

The dialectic of evil ends in free self-alienation from God. Here the Nietzsche in Hocking comes out. Hocking can feel Nietzsche's resentment at the injustice of being tied up in the world's evil. He can appreciate the relief of being out from under the religious burden and the intoxicating enthusiasm for the world of the *Übermensch* where justice is made possible by a new morality. God must die because he has made an evil world and enslaved us with a morality of guilt. Nietzsche's *Übermensch* has freed himself from the ethos of conventional morality and established an original morality derived completely and spontaneously from his personal freedom. It is Nietzsche's free, spontaneous creativity— and his sensitivity to the workings of the creative process— which appeal to Hocking. The appeal is partly to Hocking's own poetic and artistic impulses, but especially to his religious instinct. Hocking sees that Nietzsche's *Übermensch* represents a secularized ideal of personal salvation, because he has "overcome the world" and been redeemed from the world's sin. Nietzsche is a child of God in a world where God is dead; his philosophy is *theologie ohne Gott.* Hocking was impressed with Nietzsche's atheism because it was completely serious. Having insisted on the validity of a negative pragmatism, he recognized the validity for morality and ethics of Nietzsche's attempt to eliminate the problem of evil by eliminating God. Hocking does not agree that the attempt is successful, but he insists on the pragmatic declaration that God is dead as the only ground upon which Christianity can begin to build a permanent structure. The reason for Hocking's surprising emphasis on the significance of atheism is his loyalty to pragmatism. In his view, a generalized "universal religion" actually does fulfill every human religious need except the redemption of evil.

The argument that Christianity can only build on an atheist structure—granted, the right kind of atheism—strikes us as more typical of the present day than of 1909. The "death of God" theology has popularized it, but earlier the same thought had been expressed by Samuel H. Miller, then Dean of Harvard Divinity School, in an address at Princeton Theological Seminary: "If so-called religious atheism marks the honest recognition of insufficient representations in the light of new dimensions of reality, then such an atheism is not by itself an irreligious stance. It is the movement of the spirit by which religion itself may be saved from itself."[35] Pessimism and doubt, Hocking argues, breed a sense of sin, and the sense of sin, in its turn, breeds resentment—that desire to be God which is the depth and limit of sin, but which is a required movement in the dialectic of salvation. Man at his Nietzschean extreme, man who would curse God because there is no true justice, is man who has moved beyond the point where a strictly universal religion can help him. Universal religion can make man aware of the inner conditions of both righteousness and happiness. In this sense, Hocking believes that all universal religion is but a variation on the theme of stoicism which has taught men how to be happy by teaching them how to forgive their own sins. They have been supported in this self-salvation by the assurance that they are, in fact, part of the divine being. Stoic man is totally self-reliant.

If man can be his own God, then any need for objective confirmation of his self-valuation *is* a failure of nerve. On the other hand, this proud confrontation of man with his destiny, this decision to make a creed out of *hubris* means that life is a battle against an essentially antagonistic world which can be kept at bay only by one's own self-affirmation. The world ultimately wins, as it did against Nietzsche—it is so much bigger than we are—but at least man in this extreme can be convinced of God's reality only by a power that is clearly other. And from Hocking's view, a genuine freedom requires precisely this grounding in objectivity. And what will this objectivity set us free for? For the prophetic task. God forgives man his sin, and in so doing endows him with divine power which is a power over nature and history. Power, Hocking reminds us, is not given for anything which one might arbitrarily choose, "but only for what the god in him shall choose. This endowment is to be an act of God, an act of forgiveness; a forgiveness which does not take place alone in God's thought, but is to make this material difference in the position of the individual in nature and history."[36]

But how, we ask, can one know that the event of God's forgiveness has actually taken place, or that there is even the possibility of such forgiveness? Hocking believes that this is not a matter for reflection, but for experience; one must be able to see in history itself an actual manifestation of prophetic power. It must be more than a chance occurrence whereby one asserts something which accidentally turns out to be the fact. It must come from one who assumes the office of God in history consciously, and who performs his actions with the sole intent of bringing prophecy itself to human self-consciousness. It would be the prophetic work of this particular human action to become a visible manifestation of divine forgiveness.

Christianity, Hocking points out, is not the first religion to conceive of a god who comes to human history in order to die for us, and thus place death under the power of spirit. Osiris, Adonis, Orpheus, Dionysius, Demeter, and Mithra bear vivid witness to the fact that this function of a religious official has become, in man's religious speculation, "the chief of all religious functions."[37] "But," Hocking states flatly, "these figures were all mythical."[38] What is required is the touch of literality. As symbols these myths are readily a part of universal religion, but they are ideals, not actualities. And as such they are less than serious, religiously speaking. It was the part of Jesus to transform this myth of the Messiah by taking the office seriously. Christ is the final religious figure because he set into history what Hocking calls the "dialectic religious act" as contrasted with the dialectic religious idea. He is final not as Jesus, but as the Christ. As Hocking explains it,

> By his own assumption of a positive relation to God, he made the supreme sanction for human life and suffering active, not contemplative or passive; and experiential, not merely ideal. He is final because in all these things he legitimately intended to be final; because he self-consciously assumed the office of God in human history, and thereby established the fact that through such assumption that entire certitude of action can come to men which alone can make

their situation ultimately endurable. He is thus the first of the prophets; the typical prophet, whose prophecy was none other than this, that through his deed the prophetic power may be the conscious possession of every human being however situated.[39]

But how does the cosmic demand for the spread of righteousness affect Christianity? And what is Christianity to make of man's antisocial impulses? Both of these are problems for "the Christian ambition."

Chapter XIV

THE CHRISTIAN AMBITION

FOR PHILOSOPHERS, AND INDEED FOR WRITERS, generally, the difference between great repute and obscurity is largely a matter of accident. Horace Kallen expressed this view in a discussion of Santayana's place in the history of philosophy:

> Somebody gets picked up; he has vocal and persuasive disciples; a school gets set up; reports are written—they may be forgotten altogether, or they may be carried on by organizations of power, the way Shakespeare is carried on, the way the Bible used to be carried on. Who reads the Bible now since the Church has lost control of education? And who would be reading Shakespeare now if there were not entrance examinations for college requiring the reading of two or three of Shakespeare's plays? The vehicles of communication and the relevancy of selected material are what makes the difference. What was Peirce's place in the history of philosophy? What was it in 1910? And then along came these kids who were sure that they knew more about Peirce than Dewey or James did, and provided the correct view of Peirce, having edited his works; and Peirce now has a vogue. Well, why does he have a vogue? Why Plato or Aristotle or anybody? Someone chooses to push the damn thing. The Madison Avenues of the world keep working.[1]

Kallen's comment is not quite as perverse as it reads, if one stops to muse on his phrase, "the relevancy of selected material." Melville won modest fame in his day for books which are now unread, only to have *Moby Dick* rediscovered years later as a great American novel. Why? A limited interest in whales and sea captains gave way to a widespread interest in symbolism about man's fate. Selected material from Melville's work is now relevant to contemporary problems and interests.[2] An accident, to be sure, but an accident of history—which brings us to Hocking.

Hocking's views on the Christian mission and the relationship between Christianity and other world religions began in a blaze of publicity with *Re-Thinking Missions.* Many people "pushed the damn thing" because they liked his views, and many others inadvertently promoted the book by condemning the author's beliefs as wicked. The "missionary spirit" appeals to American piety (there is something of the world-saver in most of us), and a book which knocked the missionaries was bound to arouse resentment and interest. But almost immediately after the storm over *Re-Thinking Missions* his influence fell off. Two years before Hocking delivered his Gifford Lectures in 1938, the English translation of Barth's *Church Dogmatics* (Vol. I, 1) appeared. Perhaps even more significant was the publication of Hendrik Kraemer's *The Christian Message in a Non-Christian World* which applied Barth's theological perspective to the problem of the Christian world mission. Hocking spoke for Liberalism, and Kraemer for a Biblical theology of *Krisis,* the new Protestant orthodoxy. Hocking followed the philosophical monism of Royce and Hegel and reflected the hopeful piety of his midwestern American upbringing. Kraemer, on the other hand, championed a radical philosophical dualism which was inherited from Kant and deepened by the sense of divine judgment and cultural despair which was sweeping continental Christianity. With the Nazis on the march in Europe, the theology of *Krisis* was clearly and obviously relevant, especially compared with Hocking's subtle and impressionistic talk about slowly emergent forms of world culture and common religious sensibility. Philosophers were turning from idealism to positivism or to existentialism and phenomenology. Theologians were discovering "the strange new world of the Bible" convinced, with Barth, that philosophy's Athens had nothing to do with theology's Jerusalem.

Had Hitler become a permanent fixture, continental neo-orthodoxy of the Barthian type would probably have lasted with him. Here was an either/or, man versus God situation if there ever was one. But the war—so horribly absorbing while we were engaged in it—now seems like something less than the definitive event in the twentieth Century. The larger significance of the last great war was its World proportions. It revealed a fatal flaw in the structure of Western modernity: the split between *res extensa* and *res cogitans*. Science and technology, freed from the control of metaphysics and religion, had equipped man's instinctive pugnacity with technological tools of terrible efficiency. This freedom had made industrialization possible, and with it a new and better dimension of human life. Under no circumstances could this freedom be relinquished. And yet this same freedom was now in danger of running amok. Without some new synthesis of technological values in the realm of *res extensa* and moral and spiritual values in the realm of *res cogitans* man's future stood in jeopardy. And within a few short years this problem, which had originally been internal to Western culture, became a world problem complicated by the population explosion, the collapse of colonialism and the rise of Asian nationalism, the racial conflict between white and black, and the economic conflict between a few rich nations and the masses of the world's poor. But these political, social and economic ventures depend for their success on some binding ingredient of the emerging world civilization. The required commitment to mankind cannot be fashioned in the workshop of the human will, on the purely pragmatic ground that we must all hang together or we will all hang separately.

A balance of terror in ethics is as tenuous as its counterpart in politics. As communication between two individuals cannot begin without a prior ground of communication to build on, so the communication between East and West, black and white, poor and rich requires ultimate recognition of a common ground which does, in actual fact, unite us all. It is this ultimate commitment on which Hocking has riveted his attention, and it is the emerging awareness of this world problem which has won for Hocking, Toynbee, Radhakrishnan and other philosophers of a world culture a new respect. As Hocking makes clear in *The Coming World Civilization* the ground of man's being is the only ground on which a world community can be securely built.

To be sure, the gods men worship are many, and no one of them is exclusively the god of the philosophers or the ineffable alone of the mystic vision. The Asian peasant cannot join with the New York industrialist on the basis of the ontological argument. Man's positive religions will not gracefully wither away, voted out by some world congress of religions. The ground must be found among the positive religions. It must represent both the genius of each and the meaning of all. It cannot be found in a jolly outreach of religious rotarianism. For a Christian, it is a new inwardness which goes more deeply into one's knowledge of Christ, finding that he is not restricted to the human bonds of *any* religion (even the one which bears his name) or *any* culture

(even that of the West in which he has been most cele-
brated). At the same time, however, it is a new openness to
those whose religion and culture are alien to our own. Aware
that religion is a cultural product, convinced that God has
not left himself without witnesses throughout his creation,
and taking seriously the promise that the Holy Spirit will
lead the faithful followers of Christ into new truth, Hocking
insists that our communication with men of other faiths expands our knowledge of God, as well as gives us an understanding of the other's experience of God. At work here is
his philosophical conviction that God is known to all men
in the common experience of knowing the world. But his
view is also based theologically on the incarnation of God
in Jesus Christ. He shares the Christo-centrism of Barth and
Kraemer, but he insists that God in Christ is incarnate in
the world, the *whole* world, not just in the Western Christian world and certainly not in any religion. Because we
have bound Christ to *our* culture and *our* religion Hocking
speaks of an "unbound Christ"[3] who is to be known outside
the bounds of Western Christianity. The Christian task is
to make Christ known in new contexts, as, for example,
Father Raymond Panikkar has done in his *The Unknown
Christ of Hinduism*.[4] This means a basic change in the
Christian understanding of mission. In the past the Christian
mission has been individualistic and exclusivistic. It has
sought to convert individuals by taking them out of the context of their old faith and culture and placing them in the
new context of a Christianity which almost inevitably reflected Western cultural thought forms and patterns of living. The new task as Hocking explains it, is not to bring
individuals to a westernized Christian religion, but rather
to enliven the presence of Christ who is already within Hinduism, Buddhism, Islam and other religions. This will in-

volve a "re-conception" of each religion, in which it discovers its own deepest genius, "the unbound Christ" within, who seeks to make himself known.

Hitler's "national Christianity" forced European theology into a radical rejection of all such syncretisms and adaptations of historic Christianity. Hitler sought to swallow up Christianity into the demonic secularism of National Socialism, and Christianity fought for its life by making a radical distinction between the gospel and the world. In this context Hocking's views seemed outdated and dangerously soft. But the religious crisis within the Christian West has now spread to a religious crisis among men of differing faiths which threatens to destroy post-colonial nation-building in Asia. The Hindu-Muslim conflicts in the Indian subcontinent and the Buddhist-Catholic conflicts in Vietnam are only the most vivid recent examples. Twenty years ago Hocking was regarded as the last of the old liberals. Today in Asia, where the spirit of ecumenicity is fostering new experiments in interreligious understanding,[5] Hocking has become one of the new pioneers. His influence grows not just because *The Coming World Civilization* is being read and some are eager to "push the damn thing." It grows because of the relevance of the book's material to current history.

The basic statement of his views on the Christian ambition comes in the concluding chapters of *Human Nature and Its Remaking*, which summarize his discussion of the problem of instinct.[6] If Christianity is to make a creative difference in an individual's life (and the book is, among other things, a philosophy of conversion) it must sublimate the destructive impulses associated with our sexuality, pugnacity, and ambition, without repressing them, in order that the basic will-to-power may find creative expression. Christianity finds a legitimate pugnacity opposing an enemy's ill will in the name of his more ideal self. It finds sex-love fulfilling itself by fostering the creative potentiality in the beloved. It finds the worldly ambitions of the Gentiles overcome in the spiritual ambition of being first in the kingdom—an ambition that requires becoming the servant of all. What initially appears as a *power-over,* ultimately finds its true satisfaction in a *power-for.* Christianity, Hocking says, converts the will to power in the world, which is ambition, into a "will to confer spiritual life." The Christian ambition lays hold on the world of spirit with such power that it weaves its very quality and principle into the fabric of our present human history. This not only transforms the passion of ambition in the public order; for Hocking it is the transformation of *all* the basic instincts.

> It is the same form of will as that which gave the final meaning to human love, the will to confer immortal life. It is likewise the last transformation of pugnacity, the will to displace evil with good. It is, in truth, *the point in which the meanings of all the instincts converge.* It is the positive meaning to the human will as a whole.[6]

The fulfillment of human instinct is provided in that venture which places Christianity in direct confrontation with the major living religions of the world, the world mission of the church. Mission sums up the whole human meaning of Christianity. If Christianity is relevant to human nature as a whole, it is relevant precisely as a fulfillment for the basic human instinct, the will to power. The total will to power must have a concrete historical form.[7] It is the function of Christianity to fulfill that world-unifying work which *The Meaning of God* discovered as the prophetic task of religion in history. But is Christianity doing its work well? The question was being asked with some urgency in the early thirties by a group of American laymen who had become concerned with the problem of missions. The problem, in a word, was money. Contributions to missions had fallen off sharply in the period just preceding the depression. This decline was enough in advance of the general decline in the American and world economy so that it could not be explained as resulting from it. What, then, were the reasons? No one was sure. Had missions outlived their usefulness? Were the churches simply doing a bad job of dramatizing missionary work, and informing people about it? Were the missions, as they were being run, doing the job that the people in the churches thought they ought to be doing, and was the decline in giving perhaps a protest against bad organization and poor personnel?

These were some of the questions in the minds of a small group of Baptist laymen—many of them prominent businessmen—who gathered in New York, at the invitation of Mr. John D. Rockefeller, Jr., on the evening of January 17, 1930, to hear an address by Dr. John R. Mott, the father of the Ecumenical Movement. Mott convinced the group that the missionary enterprise was being challenged on the field by numerous problems calling for important decisions. The sense of the meeting was that the American church was asking many of the questions which the group of laymen also had in mind. It was decided to seek an objective answer to the questions. What, in actual fact, was going on in the missionary movement? Should it be continued, and if so, what changes should be made? The venture was to be businesslike. American laymen had, in the past, invested a considerable amount of money in missions. Had it been well spent? Was it still a good investment? The Commission would present a report to the stockholders. Beginning as a Baptist group, the planners decided to expand in order to include members of other denominations.[8] While independent of the mission boards of the various denominations, the denominational boards were consulted and maintained a loose cooperation throughout the enquiry. Great emphasis was laid on scientific objectivity and impartiality, and the Institute of Religious Research was hired to make a preliminary study of the facts in the three areas selected for observation: Japan, China, and India-Burma. This fact-finding group was to be followed, a year later, by a Commission of Appraisal which would evaluate the facts and make a final report.

One of the first problems which the group faced after securing the funds for the project and being assured of the cooperation of the several mission boards, was the selection of the Commission members, especially the chairman. It was at this point that two recent articles of Hocking's on the religious situation in the Near East[9] were mentioned and the directors of the group wrote to Hocking offering the chairmanship. At the time, Hocking was on a sabbatical leave from Harvard, working in his library in Madison on the final version of *The Spirit of World Politics*. He made the trip to New York to talk to Mr. Rockefeller and told him frankly that he had many questions about the modern missionary movement and felt that, for this reason, he was not qualified for the job. Rockefeller replied that this was exactly the attitude the group was looking for, and that he trusted Hocking's objectivity as a scholar to help them produce a fair and honest report.

This attitude appealed to Hocking, as did the opportunity for travel and study in the Far East. On the other hand, the middle of one sabbatical is not an ideal vantage point from which to apply for another. Nonetheless, Hocking wrote his friend James Woods, Chairman of the Philosophy Department at Harvard, outlining the venture and seeking the Department's approval. In his letter, of November 14, 1930, he explained that he had been urged to take the position as chairman, "the more so because I told them that I have grave doubts about the value of Christian missions." He continues:

> They are willing that I should act in some independence of the committee, carrying my own introductions and meeting persons with whom I would care to converse; and that I should enlarge my conception of the theme of enquiry to include the general problem of the interaction of civilizations and races in the Far East; and that I shall go as a philosopher rather than a Christian. This would seem to allow me all desirable liberty of character and action, and to promise as fruitful an experience as I could devise. It grows directly out of my present work, and is an integral part of the work I have been doing at Harvard in the philosophy of religion, and of the work I desire to continue to do. I might regard it as a year of research in applied metaphysics, with the special theme of Christian missions to give it actuality.
>
> My own feeling is that there are few enterprises into which so much good energy has been thrown, with so much just enthusiasm in their general conception, and with so much misguided and bedeviled effort in their detailed execution, as Christian missions. If I can do anything to aid in giving that energy a more profitable turn in the next generation, it will be a deed worth doing.

The kind of "misguided and bedeviled effort" Hocking had in mind was spelled out by James Thayer Addison, in an article in the *International Review of Missions* for January 1938. Addison quotes a statement of an early missionary, Henry Martyn, which he takes as typical of the attitude of Christian missionaries toward non-Christian religions in the period preceding the middle of the last century. Martyn went to visit a temple in Serampore, India, and there discovered devout Indians worshipping a small black idol. Martyn wrote: "I shivered at being in the neighborhood of hell: my heart was ready to burst at the dreadful state to which the devil had brought my poor fellow creatures."[10]

Addison uses the quote to illustrate his point that the problem of the Christian relation to non-Christian religions during this period was decided in terms of the simple question: Who is responsible for the religious beliefs and practices of these people—God or Satan? If you were orthodox and in the majority, your answer—during this period—was Satan. Because Indian religion is so much of a piece with Indian culture, this inevitably meant that the white man's instinctive sense of superiority became strongly fortified by his theology. Even as late as 1896, James Dennis, who was a pioneer in social work, could still hold essentially this same view of other religions and cultures. He is responsible for this devastating analysis:

> The contribution of Buddhism to society is a paralysed personality; that of Confucianism an impoverished personality; that of Hinduism a degraded personality.[11]

During this early period the military metaphor prevailed in the missionary imagination. In 1837 Alexander Duff spoke of missionaries as

> a noble army [who] make known their presence by the terror of their power, in shattering to atoms the towering walls of China, and hoisting in triumph the banners of the Cross over the captured mosques of Araby and the prostrate pagodas of India.[12]

Even in the half-century preceding the report of the Laymen's Commission this military metaphor was not entirely absent; but a new appreciation of other religions was developing, stimulated by developments in scholarship dealing with the history of religions and also by a general liberalizing of Protestant theology. Gone was much of the theological enthusiasm for hell, and with it the conviction that the heathen were bound to roast there forever. Gone too was that narrow conception of revelation which credited the devil with inspiring all non-Christian religions. On the positive side was a growing conviction that God could not have left himself without witnesses, even in non-Christian lands. Addison comments:

If God has been revealing Himself in the hearts of men everywhere and always, it is natural to assume that much beauty and truth will have been appropriated and signs of it will be sought for. Once these signs are expected and gladly welcomed they seem to multiply in number, and so the testimony accumulates that God's Holy Spirit is at work even in the darkest places.[13]

Hocking decided that missions should continue. However, he did not feel they were worthy of support in their already established and questionable form. It was because he recognized the virtues, however well hidden, of the missionary concept, that Hocking asserted his belief that the concept be supported. This was not an easy judgment to make, nor an easy one for us to understand. The "missionary enterprise" under discussion was an entity somewhere between the actual mission movement (which Hocking thought was not worthy of support) and the potential that lies within it (and constitutes the element of hope for the entire enterprise) but which has not yet been realized. The major issue lay in the fact that the misisonary personnel did not impress the Commission, nor Hocking. He acknowledged that some missionaries were first-rate—large in spirit, capable, and devoted. But these seemed to make up the minority.

> The greater number seem to us of limited outlook and capacity; and there are not a few whose vision of the inner meaning of the mission has become obscured by the intricacies, divisions, fractions and details of a task too great for their powers and their hearts.[14]

An improved personnel was needed to cope with the new theological outlook, the emergence of a new and basic world culture, and the rise of nationalism, especially in the East— all new developments since missions had begun. Hocking emphasized those changes which we have already examined —the liberalization of the doctrine of hell, the growing concern with this world rather than the next—as representative of a shift from the negative to the affirmative side of the Christian message and as having the greatest bearing on missionary motivation. For him the new emphasis represented a maturity which was especially evident in the conviction that sincere and devout non-Christians are not necessarily cut off from eternal life and the supreme good.[15]

The second and most important single change on the mission field is the meeting of Eastern and Western cultures and the subsequent overcoming of the rift between them. Hocking is not convinced that the rift was ever as deep in actual fact as it was in the opinion of romantic writers and statesmen. But it is clear that certain elements of science, technology, art, trade, and literature are now common properties to both East and West in a way which has not been true of the past. Hocking also finds a growing consensus in regard to the values of democracy, general education, and problems of society such as the family, health, and population. He gives particular emphasis to one element in this whole complex of converging cultural influences which is ultimately basic:

> There is also generally speaking an openness of mind to the view that whatever is valid in morals needs something of the nature of religion to give it full effect in the human will. In many quarters one finds the idea expressed that this religious ingredient will not be identical with any of the positive religions now offering themselves; that there is a simpler, more universal, less contentious and less expressive religion coming into human consciousness which might be called the religion of modern man, the religious aspect of the coming world-culture.[16]

Here are echoes of that passage in *The Meaning of God* where he insisted, "There is, I say, a quiet and canny maturity of conscience abroad. . . ." the desire for "a simple thing, a common word, a slight increment of ultimate sincerity somewhere that can re-unify our roots with mother earth."[17] Hocking goes on to note that the modern missionary "must be prepared to deal with the critical thinking whose outcome is secularism, and what is perhaps even more severe a test, with the thinking which tends to the simple non-partisan religion of the modern man."[18] This "simple non-partisan religion" is neither all black nor all white. It is, first of all, one of the facts of contemporary religious life. As such, it holds a potential for world religious cooperation. If cooperation is a good thing then this religion of modern man is a good thing in so far as it represents a common element. But it is not, as it stands, good enough, and this fact will constantly try the ingenuity and faithfulness of the missionary. No operative religion can realistically be non-partisan, in Hocking's view, since it is only by taking part in particular historical action that religion can fulfill its proper function. Hocking finds both the fundamentalists and the modernists missing the point in regard to this religious phenomenon.

The third change with which the missionary movement must come to terms is the rise of nationalism. Within the wider movement of a growing world culture, Hocking also discerns an emphasis on national distinction which, far from being hostile to the world culture, is one of its outstanding characteristics.

> The newer nationalism is inclusive, not exclusive; it has learned to take what is universal, not as western, but as its own, and upon this basis to cultivate and strengthen its own distinctive tradition and art, hence the oriental states are, or are becoming, self-conscious and self-directing members of the world community.[19]

In their new independence, Oriental nations are critical of those Western countries which once seemed so superior to their own. A chief aim of this criticism, since World War I, has been to point out the failure of Christianity to dominate the social and economic policies of supposedly Christian nations. The significance of this failure for missionary strategy is an important point in Hocking's argument. Christianity must separate itself from its past identification with Western history and become truly universal, and therefore ready for indigenization into various cultures. The initial missionary contact with Asia was lacking in that wisdom, and early missionaries were repelled by what they saw of "heathenism," insisting on a clean break with the traditions of the past. Cruelty and strategical difficulties were occasioned by the necessity of giving the new converts a place to begin a new life; this inevitably meant relocating them in dependence on the mission (if not within the mission compound itself) in a situation which could not help but be rootless. But the central lesson which the early missionaries failed to learn was that, as their own faith announces, "God has not anywhere left himself without a witness."[20]

Here again Hocking insists on his major point, quoting C. B. Olds of Okayama: "we *are* brothers in a common quest, and the first step is to recognize it, and disarm ourselves of our prejudices."[21] What Christian Missions have tended to ignore, Hocking finds, is their common ground with other religions. The stronger a religion is, the more open it should be to explore this ground.

> If there were not at the core of all the creeds a nucleus of religious truth, neither Christianity nor any other faith would have anything to build on. Within the piety of the common people of every land, . . . there is this germ, the inalienable religious intuition of the human soul. The God of this intuition is the true God: to this extent universal religion has not to be established, it exists.[22]

But as it stands, this intuition is not enough. We are always to be at work rethinking our faith, searching for more light on its own deepest essence. "Reconception" develops out of the tension in Hocking's philosophy between the actual and the potential, the particular and the absolute, the initial vague perception of a whole idea which is the loom of all our idea-weaving, and the infinite task of the weaving itself, attempting to fill out all the endless spaces of the loom. The final truth, the absolute, which is true for all men and is therefore in reality "the New Testament of every existing faith" is thus the mind of God. This is not something which we can find or build or write in history. All men, Hocking feels,

have a common point of departure in their common knowledge of God, and the ultimate standard of reality and truth
is likewise this same God who is one God, and as such transcends every human conception of God. But we do not move
in the absolute. Our existence is in the "middle world" of
particulars. How shall we know God *here?* This is an issue
which must ultimately be decided, and which can be decided,
as Hocking sees it, only in terms of a single positive religion.
For him there has to be this decisive, positive, finality in religion. No theology, no system of ideas can ever be "the final
truth"; but Jesus Christ, "the human face of God," is the
living truth which every religion seeks. Hocking's theology
on this point is summed up in a story concerning the Commission's work.

> Let me tell you a little incident. . . . We went into a
> Buddhist temple seven miles out of Colombo. A number of
> us were there together. A few of us went into a room in the
> temple where there was a statue of Buddha, a long statue of
> sleeping Buddha. And at his feet there was another statue
> and we were told that that was a statue of Bodhisattva. And
> we said to the attendant priest, a simple person with a rather
> finely chiseled face, "Do you worship, do you pray to
> Buddha?" And he said, "No, we don't pray to Buddha.
> Buddha has entered Nirvana. He does not hear prayer. But
> we pray to the Bodhisattva." And we said, "Who is this
> Bodhisattva?" And he said, "The Bodhisattva is the Buddha
> of the future. He is now somewhere in the universe. Per-
> haps he will be taking human form and when he comes then
> all things will be at peace on earth and men will love one
> another." My companion said: "And does this coming of
> the Bodhisattva fill you with joy and peace?" He said: "I
> look for that coming, I hope for that coming." My friend
> said: "I join in that hope." And there was a little touch of
> sympathy that went between that simple priest of the
> Bodhisattva and this Christian, and I wondered at the time

if Christ had been there would he say: "My dear friend, you are worshipping the wrong person. You are on the wrong track." Or would he say: "Friend, I am He for whom you are waiting."[23]

I have already pointed out that Hocking's point of view implies a new idea of the Christian mission. The old colonialist goal was to convert individuals from one religion to another. Hocking's new goal is to honor these religio-cultural communities (Hinduism, Islam, Buddhism, etc.) and encourage each religion to reconceive its own essence, to discover its own cultural form of the common knowledge of God which all men share and the common presence of Christ which each religion must discover in its own terms. The significance of his view is that it avoids the impasse in modern thinking about the relationship between Christianity and other religions. What was once a war has now become a friendly athletic contest, but the conflict is unresolved, and Christianity remains theologically unequipped for life in the twentieth century with its religiously pluralistic mankind. Hendrik Kraemer's energetic scholarship won the day for the radical claims of the Christian gospel in the years just prior to World War II, but this "either/or" solution was never very satisfactory, even to Kraemer himself. As a polemical theologian he proclaimed the Christian faith triumphant over all religions; but as a Christian man he maintained his sympathy for men of other faiths and for the values of their traditions; and he never finally resolved this conflict.

In recent years two major alternatives for Christian strategy have emerged. Those who would withdraw from any contest with other religions see the Christian task in the world as one of witness or presence. Informed by the new spirit of peace-making among religions and honoring the humanity of all men, this view says in effect: "We must proclaim the good news in Christ and live the life to which he has called us, letting this witness work in the world as God wills." This view gives up any idea of "winning the world for Christ." It has the courage of its own doubts about the militant efforts of the past, but it offers no clear goal for the Christian's work in the world as far as relations with other religions are concerned. It is not really sure what the specific purpose of the Christian witness in the world is. It is content with the view that "God only knows," and the faith that he is somehow at work. This view is honest and humble, but it leaves the crucial question about point and purpose unanswered.

A second view is held by those who carry on the old campaign for a Christian world. Their drums are more muffled than in the militant years of the last century, and some distinguish between world conformity to the Christian religion, and world loyalty to Jesus Christ. Some want deeper bonds of brotherhood which will break down the walls between men of differing religions; but what they want most of all is a Christian church which will predominate in the affairs of men "from Greenland's icy mountains to India's coral strand." The first view makes dialogue possible, but does not make clear what we ought to talk about. This second view has a clear word, and the satisfaction of having hurled the word like a stone down into the midst of the congregation, as Karl Barth's famous metaphor has it. But the Bishop of Woolwich is right when he says, "If we say in effect, 'Take it or leave it,' they leave it. And if we content ourselves with saying that at any rate we have 'preached the gospel,' 'whether they hear or whether they forbear,' we shall find it increasingly difficult to carry conviction even with ourselves."[24] Is it possible, Hocking asks, for Christianity to rid itself of its exclusivism, and still preserve the integrity of the Christian message?

Hocking belongs in the company of Christian writers[25] who argue for a new kind of syncretism. Beginning with Kraemer's negative analysis of "religion," and yet doubting that religion and culture can be radically separated in Asia, their argument follows this conviction: that religion is neither as closely identified with faith as has been assumed in the past, nor is it as antithetical to faith as some of its critics assume in the present day. As the cultural matrix in which man's relation to God takes cultic shape, religion is more or less neutral, but one can approach any culture with the conviction that Christ is already present and at work in this context. Christian faith, says Hocking, has already exhibited a certain cultural adaptability, having migrated from its original Near Eastern Judaic context to a Western context which was partly Judaic and partly Greek and has now become almost thoroughly modern. We are tempted to ask: Is it possible for Christian faith to exist in an Indian Hindu context or a Ceylonese Buddhist context, or an Islamic context? If St. Thomas could use Aristotle's philosophy as a vehicle for the interpretation of the Christian Gospel (when Aristotle himself exhibited little interest in "religion") is there good reason to doubt Raymond Panikkar's thesis that a theology can be constructed in terms of the *Brahma Sutra*, or Kaj Baagø's thesis that the gospel of Christ can become indigenous in India in the form of a Hindu Christianity? If there can be a Christian Platonism, is there any definitive reason why there cannot be a Christian *Advaita* along the lines of Mark Sunder Rao's *Ananyatva?*

But these questions are all too hasty. Hocking indicates that any genuine religious cross-fertilization will depend

more on specific characteristics than on theoretical considerations. Here he is limited. He was not an expert in
comparative religion, although he read carefully and had a
shrewd eye for representative detail. His own, philosophi-
cally-oriented, Christian natural theology gave him a sympathetic point of contact with Asian religions. Compared
with writers like Hendrik Kraemer, however, he is less
knowledgeable, less authoritative and less systematic. He is
convinced that the detailed writings of most experts in the
field fail to give a sense of the actual Oriental scene. He
admits that the interpreter must penetrate surface variety to
find the central meaning of a religious tradition. But how
does one catch the motivating spirit of an alien religious
tradition? Hocking suggests that we should move away from
the too-ready general characterizations to the diverse details
of living religion in Asia.

> The *prima facie* diversity and confusion . . . remains an
> important part of the picture, especially when we attempt to
> judge those impending or possible relationships between
> religions with which our own study is concerned.
> For it is just on their growing edges, often by way of the
> gropings of deviating groups, that living religions are likely
> to encounter one another in new relationships. What these
> religions in their main features are reputed to be, I can as-
> sume and shall assume as known. I shall attempt rather to
> bring before you some relevant aspects of the actual religions
> which current expositions do not make prominent.[26]

In outlining and explaining these "relevant aspects,"
Hocking begins with "plural belonging."[27] In the West,
religious affiliation is exclusive. To claim more than one religious loyalty is to deny any. In the East, Hocking notes, a
good Confucianist regularly calls upon Taoist or Buddhist
priests to conduct a family funeral. So also in India; a Hindu

can speak of the Hindu-Buddhist civilization of India, and some Muslims claim that they, too, are Hindus. One can belong to more than one religion on the ground that each supplements the others; they do not compete. Hocking also points out the relative formlessness of Asian religions and the lack of administrative structure—as contrasted with the typical Western religious *organization*. In addition, he observes, a variety of human types are involved in the functioning of religious life in Asia; all of these are semi-autonomous, yet all have appropriate religious authority operating without a clear organizational charting of their respective places and responsibilities. There are priests and monks, not always in agreement as to the nature of the truly religious life. There are, especially in India, "lay mystics" (as Hocking calls them), a motley and sometimes extravagant group, who are nevertheless significant for the creatively experimental nature of their living and thinking. A fourth factor, Hocking notes, is that there are scholars, many of whom represent the growing edge of their particular religious tradition. And finally, he submits, there are the people themselves. In the West, these laymen of the churches may not be as theologically articulate as the professional clergy, but they are of comparable social, economic, and educational background. In Asia, this group represents the masses—a peasantry whose religion runs more to superstition and magic than to logical thought, and whose convictions, practices, and experience may be removed from those of the scholars and priests. Hocking puts special emphasis on the importance of this group, for he finds in them that inarticulate religious sense of the presence of God in man's immediate world which is the central focus of his own religious philosophy.

He describes this inherent religion of the common people as remarkably similar the world over, despite the differences among the *formal* religions to which the people belong. He goes on:

> This is due in part to the neglect of their education of which we have spoken—the mental gulf between the instructed priests or monks, and the uninstructed commoners, peasants, artisans, whose religion takes the form of the lore of family and neighborhood. The people know little of the theologies professed by the specialists. They may not so much as know the name of their own religion; for to them, it is not "Hinduism" nor "Shinto," it is simply religion, or perhaps simply tradition, for they know no other.[28]

Finally, Hocking points out the ambivalence of the intellectual element in Asian religious thought. Asian religions are both more reflective, rational, and philosophical, and at the same time less dogmatic about this doctrinal characteristic than are the Semitic religions of the West.

> [The Semitic religions] never resort to argument, nor establish doctrine on human experience. They are built of history, poetry, aphorism, prophecy, exhortation, dogma, command. They appeal to faith, that is, to recognition, intuitive insight, the voluntary leap of trust in the prophetic speaker, surrender to the divine will (conveyed in the word "Islam") as represented by the human medium. In this sense, all Semitic scriptures are Islamic, including Judaism and a portion of Christianity.[29]

This is one of his major arguments with Hendrik Kraemer, who "stigmatizes the religions of the farther East as based on naturalism and human effort rather than on supernaturalism and divine grace. For my part I confess that it is just the honouring of thought and of human effort as a factor—never the whole—of religion which in the religions of India and China bring me a sense of freedom and self-respect, as if the use of reason were not a religious misdemeanour."[30] For Hocking, this indictment of Kraemer's is not only bad theology, it is symptomatic of the Western intellectualization of reason which began with the rationalism of Descartes—for whom philosophy was a science stripped of all ethical, emotive, or religious connections. The Orient seems to Hocking to be wiser in honouring the uses of reason, while at the same time restoring its relation to feeling, and subordinating it to faith. As a result, Eastern religions are both more philosophical and less dogmatic than those of the West. What are we to make, Hocking muses, of the fact that Indian philosophy proposes six different systems of interpretation for the Hindu tradition, and regards all of them as orthodox? His answer is not a major evaluation of the traditions of Eastern religious thought. He simply observes that these traditions are immune to logical or systematic disproof, because each one cannot be identified with a single metaphysical position. He goes further and submits that no religion, whether Western or Eastern, can be identified with a doctrinal formulation. Whether or not a particular individual may be regarded as a faithful representative of his own religious tradition is never essentially a matter of the way he formulates his religion intellectually.

Hocking emphasizes this point for several reasons. He takes pains to show that the elaborate theological refutations which Western Christians have made of Oriental religions have been ineffective because they have been beside the point. (He also implies that secular ideologies, such as communism, are likely to be equally ineffective insofar as they mount a rational attack on religion.) Positively, however, he is eager to show that Oriental religions display considerable plasticity to change. Unlike Hegel, who argued that the deficiencies of one tradition are overcome by the validity of a truer and more effective one, Hocking argues that the dialectic of change operates within each tradition. He recognizes that Christian missions in the Orient have had considerable effect on Oriental religious life. This effect is best seen in the reforms which have been stimulated within the Oriental traditions and not in the number of converts which have been won for Christianity.

Hocking's point about the subordinate role of doctrine in religious life has always been something of a truism in regard to Oriental religions. On the other hand, the Christian tradition of the West has had periods which were notable for heresy trials and pronouncements of anathema on orthodox views. But today it is increasingly difficult to regard a doctrinal position as a definitive test for the validity of an individual's religion. Even Hendrik Kraemer, who had once described Hocking's views as devoid of genuine Christian insight, later confessed that Hocking was "as a man, a shining example of truly Christian urbanity."[31] The words "as a man" form the crux of the matter. There is no meeting of religions, much less a meeting of theological interpretations of "religion." There is only a meeting of people who have different religious customs, intuitions and ideas. For this meeting, psychological sensitivity is probably as important as theological erudition. Perhaps more than anything else, an evaluation of an alien religious tradition requires an openness to the validity and truth of a man's religious life, even when one rejects his doctrine and perhaps even his feeling about God and the world. Without the touch of humanity which this kind of spirit bestows, even the most perceptive scholarship is in danger of missing the point. Arend van Leeuwen's book, *Christianity in World History*, for all its brilliance and wisdom, illustrates this danger.

Van Leeuwen has a good deal in common with Hocking:

the conviction that Christianity has "parented" much that is important to contemporary technocratic society; a positive view of secularization; and emphasis on Christianity's creative role in a "planetary world" or "world civilization." At the same time, however, van Leeuwen makes a more radical and systematic distinction between the culture and history of the West, which was determined by Israel and Christianity, and that of the East, which was not. For him the world view of the West is "theocratic"; the world view of the East is "ontocratic."[32] Following Barth and Kraemer, van Leewen believes that it is the transcendence of God over man and the world which is the culturally distinctive characteristic of the Judeo-Christian tradition. The transcendence of God over man protects man's freedom because it distinguishes God from the world and gives man an area in which to work out his salvation faithfully. Thus the West avoids the "cosmic despotism" of the oriental state, made possible because oriental religiosity equates divinity with being, finds divinity everywhere immanent in the world, and consequently invests the state with despotic divine powers.

Van Leeuwen believes that religion, as one finds it in the Orient, is essentially nihilistic, but also essentially outdated. It is representative, he feels, of the Neolithic era of human culture, which was essentially "agricultural-cum-pastoral," whereas the present era is technocratic. Because the ontocratic world is impregnated with God, man can deal with this world only religiously and ritualistically. Man is swamped by God and hence not free to deal with the world in terms of those uses developing out of his free, independent creativity. In a "theocratic" world, however, a transcendent God gives the world over to man. Man has elbowroom in which to work. His world is now secular rather than religious: that is, it is no longer impregnated with God. It is this secular freedom which is the distinguishing mark of a civilization influenced by Christianity, and it is this same freedom which has made Western technology possible. Here Hocking and van Leeuwen have much in common. But, like Kraemer's *Christian Message in a Non-Christian World,* van Leeuwen's book takes as its overall purpose the task of dealing firmly with the suggestion that Christianity should form a "common front" with other religions in order to face the growing secularism and materialism of the modern world.

Fortunately, van Leeuwen's book accomplishes much more than this stated purpose and is especially important as a way of approaching Hocking's views. Hocking, of course, doubts that religion is a primitive expression of culture due to dissolve under the acids of modernity or of neo-orthodox theology. For all that they share in common, he is at odds with van Leeuwen over many of the same issues which forced his debate with Kraemer: the dialectical relationships between history and nature, theology and philosophy, Western Christianity and Eastern religions. Is a synthesis of some sort valid? Hocking believes that it can be; van Leeuwen does not. Two significant and major distinctions between Hocking and van Leeuwen are noteworthy.

One is in Christology. For Hocking, Jesus Christ is both the personal saviour of the Methodist experience meeting, and the *logos* of the Western philosophical tradition. Christ is known directly to him as personal saviour in the experience of worship, and indirectly as *logos* in his experience of God in the natural world. For van Leeuwen, neither personal piety nor natural theology is ground for a valid Christology. Christ is supremely the "historical event" in which God's working in history is made plain. For Hocking it is the personal experience of the "unbound" person of Christ which will redeem the world. For van Leeuwen, it is rather

Christian history, in which Christ is the definitive event, which is redemptive.

Second, van Leeuwen is concerned about a confrontation between two systems of thought and belief—theocracy and ontocracy. Hocking is concerned about relations among people. Van Leeuwen announces an expansion or invasion by the West, with its Christian heritage, of the East—a move which ultimately destroys religion, the guardian of the ontocratic world view. Because the ontocratic and theocratic views are mutually exclusive, he is not interested in dialogue with other religions, although he recognizes a need to understand them. Because dialogue is a process in which the participants learn from each other, even though they represent different points of view, van Leeuwen is concerned for "dialogue" with secularized Western technocracy, for here Christianity has something to learn as well as a responsibility to fulfill.

Hocking believes that if one is going to give a systematic account of the heart of a particular religious tradition, one must be careful that the system is built up from within. He distinguished two types of system by their respective methods. The system from without operates deductively from a preconceived notion of how things are (as does van Leeuwen's "strictly theological thesis") and, because of its commitment to this notion, tends to find itself on a theory-proving venture, rather than on a fact-finding one. The system from within operates inductively on the basis of experience and, because of its commitment to experience, tends to use the categories which it discovers there always with the reservation that they should be open to rethinking, remaking and reconceiving. One might describe the system from within as empathic. It takes the alien tradition seriously, recognizing that it fulfills genuine needs and reveals viable realities to the people who have identified themselves with it. It does not mean that the systematizer must be without religious convictions of his own which are counter to those which he is investigating. It does mean that he must be willing to suspend his own belief for a season in order to identify with the life and faith of these alien people. The critical difference between Hocking and van Leeuwen is summed up in this methodological contrast. Van Leeuwen hobbles his superior scholarship with a system of interpretation which is largely from without. Hocking, given his limitations, works at a system of interpretation which is as far as possible from within.

No man is entirely free of his preconceptions, however, and Hocking has romanticized the simple, natural religion of the Asian peasant. The rapidity of social change in Asia makes any prediction about the future of Oriental religion speculative and dogmatic. Certainly modernization has made the life of the Asian peasant less primitive than it was even thirty years ago when Hocking wrote *Living Religions and a World Faith*. Rural electrification brings radio to the village, and with it a growing commercial and political consciousness. Mass education encourages elements of rationality and tempers intellectual traditionalism and superstition. The "revolution of rising expectations" is underway in at least some areas of Asian life, challenging tendencies toward fatalism. Modern communications help make possible a "global village" which is, in fact, not the traditional village at all, but a secular city. Does this mean the end of religion, or only a new challenge to the dialectical process of religious reconception in Asia?

For his part, Hocking feels that much of the uniqueness of a specific culture derives from the merger of traditional philosophy and social ideas with religious ideas and practices.

While the prophetic consciousness creates a tension between religion and culture, he believes that religion is always the deepest dimension of culture. He liked, admired, and defended cultural diversity, and fought against the idea that a world civilization would mean that all cultures would be molded into a westernized megalopolitan homogeneity. Cultural diversity is one of the things that makes life interesting. For Hocking, it was also an impressive testament to human creativity that there should be so many different ways to make music and bake bread. He saw immediately that if cultural diversity is to be preserved then religious diversity must also be preserved. But he recognized that, for all the diversity of religious life, there was also the thread of a common human experience of God, out of which might be woven the fabric of a common religious life, if only the right weaver could take up the task. He believed that the coming world civilization requires such a fabric; that a world civilization is not only the great adventure of our day, but also our only hope for survival.

Christianity may well be able to do the weaving, Hocking hopes and believes, not only because Christ is the redeemer of all men, but because Christianity is the one historic religion which has come to terms with modernity. Through the secularization of Western culture, Christianity has been set free for genuine universality. The diverse religions begin with an element of unity in the thread of common experience of God which the mystics celebrate. The mission of Christianity is to encourage each religious tradition to find, within its own life and developing out of the common thread, a common ultimate meaning which is the unbound Christ. This common religious commitment need not destroy religious diversity. Hocking sat loose to "religion," believing that men could celebrate their commitment to

God with those diverse outward and visible signs which were indigenous to their culture, and still have a common inward and spiritual grace which was truly of God.

The Christian ambition is not to achieve power over men of other religious traditions through the world wide rule of an imperial Christianity. The Christian ambition fulfills the will to power in a way that is not competitive. The way to save one's life is to lose it; the way to gain power is to give it away; the way to exalt Christianity is to strip it of its imperialism, make it serve the Hindu, the Muslim, the Buddhist, and thereby confer on them the power of the unbound Christ who will, in his own time, make himself known as the one for whom men of all religions and no religion have waited.

Chapter XV

THE COMING WORLD CIVILIZATION

"A GREAT PROCESSION OF HUMANITY . . . Men like souls walking." This is Ernest Hocking's description of the vision which came in the midst of his conversion experience at the age of twelve. It marks the beginning of his personal discovery of mankind. Seventy-five years after that experience, the outlines of Hocking's vision have been filled in. A new figure of universal man begins to emerge: He is a post-modern man who is both scientist and inward visionary, in the manner of Teilhard de Chardin; politically he is a nationalist committed to internationalism, a democrat who cherishes the variety of culture patterns among the *demoi* of the world, as did Nehru; intellectually he is a metaphysician whose synthesis honors the objective reality of nature, the subjective reality of the self and the world context which gives them integrated meaning. Having traveled the length of modernity's subjectivism Hocking's universal man has come to an intersubjectivity based on the availability of a common, objective physical world to each experiencer. Physicist, poet, and philosopher join in a common awareness that the world of nature which the physicist analyses, the poet celebrates, and the philosopher seeks to understand is, in its wholeness, a world given by a world-making, world-sustaining power.

Post-modern, in Hocking's thought, should not be confused with post-Christian—a term representing the view that Christianity no longer informs the basic convictions of contemporary Western man, and that it has been replaced by secularism. When *The Coming World Civilization* appeared in the middle fifties, Christian writers were still largely critical of Western secularization. Hocking was prepared to regard secularization as an advance, however, not only because it gave a rightful autonomy to the culture which Christianity had parented, but especially because it had destroyed the identification of Christianity with Western culture and thus given Christianity an opportunity to express its inherent universalism. Secularization, according to Hocking, has not killed Christianity; it has freed Christianity. He is more cautious than those who see the hand of God everywhere at work in secularism. Most thoroughgoing secularists are much more aware of the pitfalls of post-modern culture than the "Christian secularists" have thus far been, and Hocking stands with the thoroughgoing secularists in a recognition of these dangers. Hocking also has the advantage of being a serious philosopher of history. Hocking's *The Coming World Civilization* represents the "conspectus of a life's work."

Talk of a post-modern period, or what Hocking calls a "passage beyond modernity," requires a characterization of the modern period, which is perhaps best studied in terms of its product, the free individual.[1] Individualism, Hocking notes, is an element of the crisis of modernity. The state, having encouraged the development of creative individuality, and having recognized its dependence upon this creative capacity for its own life, finds itself unable to command that capacity. The state can penalize, but the individual alone can change himself. The state can lead an individual to the point where he can see the best that his culture has to offer, but it cannot stuff goodness into him. The state's touch on family life, Hocking points out, is equally impotent. It can establish legal forms through law and recognize that the morale of the family is crucial to the morale of the larger community, but it cannot legislate love or guarantee happy childhoods. And in recreation, the free play of freedom, the state can provide endless amenities, but cannot guarantee anyone a good time. The state, as state, has no enforceable standard. From its own resources the state cannot even assure the viability of its own system of law; it must, finally, rely on the good will of its citizenry.[2]

Hocking is convinced that secular modernity, in freeing the individual from the domination of supernatural, supra-individual authority, has left him wondering what it is that he really wants, without giving him the means to decide. Modernity has produced a deepened, subjective sensitivity, which is the potential source of creativity. Against corporate domination of all kinds the individual stands free. But "what is he standing for? and what is he standing on?"[3] Hocking says he stands on his right to be an individual and free. And yet he is not concerned with his own interest, but with a right which belongs to all others in similar situations. Seeming to stand alone, he yet insists that an inner certitude of personal right is felt by others, and known to be common to all. Thus Hocking can say that there is *"a vein of non-solitude* [in] *the solitary ego."*[4] Here, again, is the paradox of Descartes' solitude, whereby an intensely inner experience connects him with an infinite outside. If analyzed and understood, this world-connection might re-establish the individual's bearings and re-animate his motivation. In a world of atomic individuals, however, relativism reigns supreme because objective values are psychologized into matters of personal desire. Hocking remarks:

And with this abandonment of man's native rapport with the whole, the nerve of worth in his own living and acting silently ceases to function. Here, I venture to think, is the root of our malady.[5]

The solution to this crisis is not some new cultural or religious heteronomy. We cannot retrace the way we have come, by a "return to the religious element in the premodern civilization."[6] And so Hocking says: "If we believe, as I certainly do, that the advances of modernity are genuine, and must enter into the body of whatever faith mankind can hold, we cannot disregard modernity's philosophical quandaries."[7]

Having split off value and meaning from fact, and having suffered a failure of motivation bred by the resulting moral relativism and metaphysical isolation, modern man—the secular individual—seeks to solve these quandaries by moving toward the recovery of his broken metaphysical connections with the world. It is this move which constitutes the "passage beyond modernity." Hocking finds it, for example, in current philosophies of law and the state. Convinced that the will to obey is rooted neither in the individual's sense of contractual obligation nor in any simple fear of reprisal, contemporary political theory now recognizes that man's world view is the ultimate and permanent source of this will. Professor Robert MacIver argues that the "web of government" derives its authority in part from an element of myth.[8] For Hocking, of course, this is not enough, but it is a move in the right direction, from "psychological debility" to the "outer air of speculative metaphysics."[9] It recognizes that solipsism simply cannot explain the fact of government and the complex, interrelated loyalties and responsibilities which sustain it.

Hocking notes that the social sciences have also confronted

the problem. An attempt was made prior to the turn of the century to explain individual selfhood not as something unique but as a manifestation of social forces such as language, custom, and traditional belief. Margaret Mead and James Mark Baldwin discovered much useful truth by following this path, but the journey required a gradual capitulation of "the proud and pregnant loneliness of free individual creativity and right"—a loss which modernity can ill afford.[10] On the other hand, Hocking contends that where individual experience has been honored in Western thought, it has long been necessary to go outside the bounds of individual experience and posit some *a priori* rooted in the world beyond the individual in order to find a basis for relationships between man and man, and between man and his world. Plato, dedicated to the recovery of *arete* (virtue) in the political life of Athens, rejects Socrates' optimistic assumption that the common ground of morality can be uncovered in the thought and experience of the individual, if only disciplined dialectic can be allowed to probe through the deceits of *doxa* (opinion). Rather, the source of the common good is to be found in the realms of being, in the pristine, transcendent *eidos* (idea), which common experience knows only as a flickering, distorted shadow. Descartes' pronouncement that mind and nature are of radically different kinds frees an empirical science from the medieval view that nature is sacrosanct, a living expression of purpose on the part of a personal God. The relationship between man and his world is broken, and Descartes' only repair is in reason's attempt to establish a God who assures us that our world is real. Kant's social philosophy, Hocking feels, comes closest to finding relationship in experience. Kant finds a sense of duty in man's immediate experience, but to find the sustaining source behind this sense of duty he must posit God, who serves as the cause of this experienced effect.

In the passage beyond modernity, Hocking points out, man's commitment to individual experience has been recognized, and the logic of solipsism has been taken more seriously. This is evident in the work of the early Bertrand Russell and the later Husserl. But a study of the logic of solipsism, as we have noted earlier, reveals an inner inconsistency. The argument that one is incurably alone assumes that one knows what aloneness is, and this knowledge, in turn, depends upon its opposite, i.e. not being alone. Thus, Hocking explains, philosophy at the turn of the century inclined toward simple repudiation of solipsism, substituting alternative theories of knowledge, such as Bergson's intuitionism. Here the intuitions of the mind coincide with their objects in nature and society as well as with the semipurposive *élan vital* which integrates them. Intuition thus captures its objects by the force of its transcendence over them, and solves the intellectual problem by disqualifying the "intellect" in metaphysics. The new realism of this period (represented by R. B. Perry, W. P. Montague, E. B. Holt, and others) also repudiated solipsism, affirming the power of self-transcendence as a natural capacity of human knowledge. Meanwhile, Hocking goes on, Royce, Simmel, and others attempted the underlying issue of how we can know another mind in the first place, and tended to follow Kant in shifting the problem from pure reason to the practical realm of morals. The resulting argument was that we *ought* to acknowledge other minds, even though we cannot hope to experience them directly. Husserl, emphasizing the "intentional" element in thinking, first suggested an "egological" solution, and then later proposed an ambiguous "monadological intersubjectivity." It was left to Whitehead to offer the most radical solution. He promoted a rejection of the causal theory of perception in favor of "prehensions," which make possible a direct awareness of one's objects.[11]

Hocking, however, finds modernity's best insight not in a simple repudiation of solipsism, but in the path of inwardness followed by Camus and Marcel. Hocking declares: "Solipsism is overcome, and only overcome when I can point out the actual experience which gives me the basis of my conception of companionship."[12] Here he restates his basic argument, emphasizing the fact that consciousness does not take its sense experience aesthetically, but rather feels obligated to *think* a world. "My impulse to live by thinking, rather than by sensing alone, is a *response* to a felt purposiveness of the real with which in experience I have to do."[13] This sounds like Kant, but it is more. To Kant's sense of duty Hocking adds a sense of destiny, of "faith-in-opportunity" which is "a hopeful launching out on the effort to achieve the costly happiness of becoming what I am destined to become." With this assurance, and its verification in experience "we have passed beyond modernity into the postmodern era."[14]

There are, of course, secular optimists who rejoice in release from the chains of metaphysics and religion, and see no problem in modernity; and hence they have no need for anything beyond. Theirs is a post-existentialist, secular stoicism, devoid of *angst*. They find the furniture of immediacy comfortable enough. Raging against the dying of the day is patently futile, and therefore silly. Experience is a surface and its tangibilities suffice for a good life. For his part, Hocking is, of course, convinced that the metaphysical question about the meaning of life is serious. He would agree with Crane Brinton that "metaphysical anxiety is . . . a very real thing in our Western culture."[15] But Hocking never insists that everyone shares this anxiety. He does not say, as Sartre does, "Of course, there are many people who are not anxious; but we claim that they are hiding their anxiety, that they are fleeing from it."[16] He agrees with Dietrich Bonhoeffer that in our world "come of age" one has no business insisting that people really feel sinful or anxious when they themselves deny it. The fact that the philosopher or theologian has an answer to questions of anxiety and sin does not justify the assumption that everyone is asking the questions.

Hocking's appeal is not to his dogma but to our experience. It is an open appeal. He says, in effect: "This is my experience; is it yours also? Has it *man* in it? This is what I believe it means; doesn't this explanation also make sense of your experience?" The question is always accompanied by the certainty derived from past experience, but the tool of reconception is always in hand. The only thing that could prevent the possibility of answers within such a conversation is the refusal to think things through. And no philosopher has a solution for this refusal. Hocking believes that life itself is asking the questions. The reflective spirit faces the question of man's inwardness; one must answer in order to keep faith with one's own experience. The social activist faces the question of his own motivation; what does it mean to be a member of a society? What does action aim at? What is the value of work? The scientist, hopefully adventuring in the wilderness of natural fact, must decide the relationship between a purposeful science and a purposeless world. And because science is the most prestigious venture of modernity, it is Hocking's allusion to the questions involving natural science which is most likely to clarify the metaphysical purview of contemporary secularism.

The empirical conscience of modern science, Hocking indicates, has taught man to take his experience of the world realistically. The world has neither quality nor value in itself. These elements are derived from the perceiving subject. In itself, the cosmos is a realm of fact and event—one which is mathematical in process, empty of choice, devoid of purpose. Directed with such success toward the workings of physical nature, the empirical conscience has lately turned to man himself as an object within nature, claiming in its psychology, sociology, and anthropology a science of man. Viewed as an object in nature man exhibits the characteristics of the whole; his value-setting is, itself, "a product of valueless necessity."[17] On the other hand, modern solipsism claims the entire realm of value for the I-think. Modernity is thus left with two radically contrasting views of the self: self is either devoid of any real value, or it is the only source of all values. And neither view provides a substantial basis for the concept of rights common to all men which is so much a part of the modern world view. In this way Hocking points to the essential dilemma of modernity: it cannot abandon its empirical conscience, but its empirical conscience cannot sustain its own hard-won doctrine of individual human rights. It is this idea of rights as common to all men which is becoming part of a worldwide political pattern and which is crucial to the development of the coming world civilization.

Hocking's problem is to sketch in the details of a view which does not deny the validity of the scientific world picture. He is convinced that the scientific world picture has its own integrity and is itself a major achievement of modernity. Granted, it makes it impossible for modern man to claim his world as a home. The cosmos of *res extensa* is indifferent to human fate, as much modern writing on the lostness of the human soul has recognized. The dilemma which it presents is unique to Western Civilization, for the West developed the astrophysics of an inanimate nature implied in Cartesianism. But the scientific world picture is an abstraction, Hocking points out. It omits quality and volition from a universe in which quality and volition exist. It is not valid when applied to that natural data in which volition is alive—most obviously in man. Yet it is a necessary abstraction for "it is only an inanimate world segment that can be exploited for human [scientific] ends without consideration or compunction." To re-animate nature, as G. T. Fechner and Whitehead seek to do, is to give over "a genuine and world-changing advance."[18] Man himself, however, is both a natural being and a nature-transcending being. Insofar as he is end-seeking, loving, purposive, he is beyond the purview of a truthful science. The enthusiasm of science, bred from its astounding successes in dealing legitimately with the natural world, has, however, fostered an untruthful implication that man is only a creature of nature. This Western malady now threatens to infect the cultures of the East as they absorb the science and technology born in the West. The spread of this infection can be halted only by the adoption of a view of man and his destiny which reminds science of its own limitations and, at the same time, offers a viable interpretation of man's world-connection which supplements, but is consonant with, the necessary abstraction of the scientific world picture. This conviction can come, Hocking feels, only from a positive religion. The problem facing Christianity is whether or not it can reconceive its own message so that it can come to terms with that malaise which is the negative side of secularism, and, at the same time, show itself to be genuinely universal—and not simply Western. In order to do this it must offer itself to all men as something which *belongs to them* as men in their own cultural and historical situation, not as something either borrowed or imposed from the outside. Hocking finds that the responsibility for healing modernity's metaphysical malaise belongs peculiarly to Christianity because it has been involved, as no other religion has, in the development of modernity and of its scientific method.

Why, one might ask, should modern science and technology have arisen in the West rather than elsewhere? A more limited question has been raised by several philosophers—notably Whitehead in *Science and the Modern World*—and that is whether Christian thought played any part in this technological development. The suggestion that it did is historically reasonable, if only because the seeds of scientific investigation were sown so soon after the medieval period in which Christianity was the definitive element in Western culture. Hocking notes the obvious dependence of Descartes' *Cogito* on Augustine's *Si fallor sum*. He finds more pervasive, however, the influence of Christian morals on the scientist's conception of his own task. In the Christian exhortation that it is only in losing one's life that one can find it, Hocking sees the model for Bacon's dictum that in order to master nature we must first learn, empirically, to obey her. Hocking sees a further influence of Christianity in Kepler's concept of the *verae causae* of physical processes as homogenous with their effects, and in his conviction that only a mathematical idea of nature as a closed group was consonant with the perfect law which is the thought of God. It is against this background that Hocking speaks of Christianity's "parenthood" of modernity and of Christianity's present responsibility in the light of this relationship. He is not claiming, as do some enthusiasts in contemporary Christian theology, that Christianity is the "cause" of modern science, and that technology's triumph over nature is but a belated recognition of God's command to Adam to have dominion over all the earth.

The desire to bend nature to human purposes is not something that man derives from his religion, but rather from the challenge of his natural condition. The fact that the West has been more successful in this task than, say, India, owes partly to the fact that the geography of western Asia, Europe and North America has been more responsive to man's desire to affect and transform. Hocking simply observes that Christianity has made an important contribution to the development of the modern ethos. The Christian tradition does indeed have its otherworldly elements. It is notable among the world's religions, however, for the seriousness with which it takes man's involvement in nature, even to the point of finding God in the world, not as an *avatar* or a Gnostic "appearance" but as an incarnate Lord. For this reason, Hocking states, Christian thought is not free to retreat into dualism, rejecting modernity's "lean and mind-swept system of nature" as mere *māyā*. It has played a part in fostering the scientific world view. It can no longer claim, as the medievals did, that the detailed rhythms of nature are theologically purposive; nor can it, with Spinoza, regard God as simply another name for nature. Nature's autonomy must be honored, but the divided consciousness of man must find a perspective which can include both himself and his world in a context of ultimate meaning. Before sketching Christianity's role in the coming world civilization, Hocking glances briefly at its relationship to modern thought as it developed the two foci of Descartes' philosophy and evolved its characteristic social institutions.

In philosophy, while Hobbes developed the purely objective half of Descartes' dualism, and Malebranche and Berkeley developed the purely subjective side, the early modern period was unwilling to forego the attempt to relate them. Locke, Spinoza and Leibniz were pioneers in this effort which was later continued in the work of Kant and Hegel, Royce, Bergson and Whitehead. Similarly Christianity, having fought the early efforts of science to gain autonomy, gradually gave up the idea that here was a "warfare between science and religion." While the problem of relationships between science and religion remains, Christianity has accepted the responsibility of incorporating scientific findings into its world view, including even those ideas—the theory of evolution is a prime example—which threatened to destroy Christianity's understanding of itself. Hocking believes that this rapprochement was demanded by the fact that Christianity's own empirical conscience had helped to foster a value in the scientific enterprise. Christianity now rests its case on its relevance to man's experience. Empiricism, broadly conceived as an empiricism of meaning, constitutes a bond between Christianity and scientific thought and is broken only when "empiricism is mounted, as positivism has attempted, on the vanishing knife edge of 'the given,' the ideal 'sense datum' from which all thought, all interpretation, all meaning is banished—that is to say, on the meaningless."[19]

On the subjective side of the Cartesian dualism, the I-Think represented a triumph of spirit over matter, and hence a refuge from the purely mechanical in thought and society and a clear emphasis on the importance of the individual and a basis for the individual's demands for his just right. Christianity was naturally drawn to it. The emphasis on subjectivity was not only crucial to German Idealism and later idealists, such as Royce, Bradley, and Bosanquet but also to the pragmatisms of Dewey and James, the operationalism of Bridgman's post-relativity physics, and at key points in the mathematically oriented philosophies of Russell and Whitehead. But insofar as idealism was infected with solipsism, it was necessary for Christianity to "cleanse its skirts of idealism." This necessary reaction of Christianity against idealism, still going on among many contemporary Christian theologians, has clouded the relationship between religion and philosophy with the influential assertion that there is no such relationship. Hocking counters:

> I am far from proposing that it is primarily through philosophy that Christianity meets the issues presented by modernity. Philosophy is but a rude and remote indicator of the secret struggles of countless human souls carrying on the query-laden enterprise of living under existing conditions. Religion meets these struggles directly. But the philosophy that lives, lives only because those who struggle find it helpfully interpreting that struggle. It is not something apart from religion—it is an organ of the human thought without which religion is but a blind survival impulse, sometimes usurping the name of "faith"—which is never blind. Christianity, holding itself duly independent of philosophy (and on occasion unduly despising it), has no choice but to come to terms with the concepts which the time spirit finds expressive of its own groping for light.[20]

Beginning with the reality of the I-Think, modern philosophy sought to fulfill a long-standing philosophical ambition for a synthesis of idealism and realism, a dream which motivated the objective idealisms and absolute idealisms following Kant and was partly realized by the later Schelling. Hocking notes that what nineteenth-century philosophy required, however, was a new relationship with contemporary science, such as philosophy had known in the two centuries preceding it. He points to the labors of Fechner, Poincare, Lotze, and Royce, and perhaps especially those of Charles Peirce and Whitehead, as being in this direction. Professional philosophers were joined in this effort by a generation of physicists, notably Nils Bohr, Max Planck, Werner Heisenberg and C. F. Weizsaecker, all of whom recognized the necessity for a common venture between philosophy and the physical sciences. But, Hocking points out, perhaps the most decisive step in the development of a philosophy adequate to the full range of man's experience was to come not from the absorption of scientific technique, but from a deeper analysis of the empirical principle itself. This analysis came into modern thought through Kierkegaard and the existentialists, among whom Hocking finds Marcel and Gilson the most creative representatives today. Hocking believes that "this movement substantially promotes a reconception of Christianity pointing beyond the limits of the modern era, preserving it from an ultimately devastating antisubjectivism."[21]

As with science and philosophy, so with almost every other area of Western life: "It is perhaps fair to say that there is no phase of western culture that has not been nursed by this religion into a renewal of life after the Dark-Age period of confusion." The birth of scientific method, Hocking explains, is only the most recent and most dramatic example: "We might have taken law, education, the family, forms of property, architecture, engineering, music . . . Here, as elsewhere in the world, all of these arts have borne marks of their religious parentage, and religious expression has been modified by occupation with these arts."[22] That these different phases of culture now stand free of Christian dominance is only proper. That Hocking is convinced of their need for rootage in religion we have already seen in earlier chapters. Does this mean a return to Christianity? Does Hocking want a Christian society rather than a secular society? The question is basic, despite its lack of subtlety. He certainly does not want a return to medievalism. By the same token, he is not so enamored of contemporary secularism that he fails to see the need of its autonomy for rootage in the universal. Hocking looks to a post-modern culture in which—to borrow Tillich's terminology—the heteronomy of medieval Christendom's domination over culture and the autonomy of contemporary culture's rootlessness will be superseded by a "theonomy" in which cultural freedom will be grounded in a freely accepted world faith. It will not be a reductionist religion-in-general but that apprehension of the "unbound Christ" which is known to everyman in the "common mysticism" of his knowledge that God is in the midst of his perceived world.[23]

Hocking clearly proposes what used to be called a natural theology, and which today sometimes goes under the title of general revelation. How does this relate to the heart of the Christian faith which is not natural but historical—not given to everyman but given rather to a few in the form of a special revelation? On the philosophic side this question seeks the relation between nature and supernature. He recognizes the validity of what Santayana called "animal faith" and insists that man's faith exhibits the characteristic of all human mentality, namely a sense of the whole present in every part of man's experience. Here is its tie to philosophy, and Hocking asserts that there is a basic "continuity between 'natural piety' as piety toward nature and whatever is honestly 'mystical' in man's spontaneous reverence toward the world."[24] The boundary between the natural and the supernatural (like that between fact and self), is actually a double boundary. Man, in the course of his natural use of reason, defines what he means by nature and in the process leaves himself out of the scope and purpose of that nature which he defines. This nature is the realm of natural necessity, of causes—a closed group of events ruled tightly by natural law.

However, Hocking continues, man himself is not caused by this realm of nature to do the defining in the first place. In the process of setting up the cause-tight closed group which is nature, man himself remains free, and in that act is, in the strict sense, "super" natural. Hocking is careful in his view of natural religion. Because "the faith of the Christian is continuous with the nature faith by which all men live," Christianity *"is the making-fully-explicit of this universal faith. It is therefore present in some degree wherever religion is present."*[25] Thus Hocking brings us to the role of the Christian religion in a multireligious world, offering its own essence as the binding ingredient of the coming world civilization.

Christianity, Hocking believes, gives promise of being able to fulfill its inherent universality not by pretending that it has no historical background in the West (no positive religion can simply shed its historical markings), but by carrying out the work of reconception in such a way as to reach beyond its own cultural limitations. In adapting the concept of experience from existentialism, Christianity gives evidence of a passage beyond philosophical modernity. In ending its warfare with science and in seriously attempting to maintain relevant connections with the life of the modern world, Christianity moves beyond modernity's narrow concept of experience toward a widened empiricism which can include both the cause-tight, purposeless world of science and the open, purposeful world of man's destiny. Christianity, Hocking feels, is aware that the purposeful has need of the purposeless in order to fulfill its own purposes. And in its growing openness to its own conviction that God is not without witnesses in other religions and cultures, Christianity begins to live in terms of its inherent universality. But Hocking recognizes that in the meeting place of world religions there is inevitable conflict among various claims to universality. He seeks to temper this conflict with three postulates governing the relations among religions. The first of these is that "the true mystic will recognize the true mystic."[26] Spiritual men of one tradition have regularly been recognized and moved by spiritual men of other traditions. The relationship between Gandhi and C. F. Andrews is but one illustration. This kind of personal kinship is as much an earmark of the present day meeting among men of different faiths as were the conflicts which characterized such meetings in the past. The attainment of what is often simply called peace leaves a mark which other attainers from other traditions intuitively recognize. These are people for whom renunciation has bred insight, and, as Hocking notes, they make contact with other religious traditions in their experience of creative suffering.

The second of his postulates is: "Every Man's religion must be 'a' religion having its own simplicity of essence and its own integrity."[27] Here he restates the opposition to Christian exclusivism which he shares with Toynbee and Radhakrishnan and which he spelled out in detail in *Living Religions and a World Faith*. The method of achieving a world faith by the way-of-radical-displacement, Hocking asserts, denies the knowledge of God available to every man both from his experience of the world and by the fact that the unbound Christ is present in a hidden manner in his own religious tradition. On the other hand, Hocking opposed the old liberal ideal of a religious synthesis on the basis of the lowest common religious denominator—religion-in-general. Although it is possible to infer from *Re-Thinking Missions* that Hocking is advocating a synthesis of this sort, he took pains to correct this misinterpretation in *Living Religions and a World Faith*.

What is needed in the religious world is dialogue, and neither the way-of-radical-displacement nor the way-of-synthesis are dialectical enough to provide for it. Displacement wants no dialogue; it wants only to preach the word, and have those who heed it join the exclusive community of true faith. Synthesis needs no dialogue; it announces that all are one, and having made this announcement, finds nothing more to talk about.[28] Dialogue, for Hocking, is an adventure in broadening one's own experience as a prelude to a deepening of the "essence" of one's own religious understanding.[29] The way of reconception is really a dialectic of religious inwardness, a conversation between one's broadening experience of other religions and one's deepening awareness of their relation to the germ of faith in the heart of one's own. Hocking has even charted the growth of understanding and the manner in which the base of one's own religious understanding may be expected to broaden (see diagram on page 306).[30]

He admits that any reaching out to another religious tradition involves a preliminary or tentative syncretism. The reaching is justified only insofar as it integrates these new findings into its own religious essence. Borrowing then becomes the beginning of a thinking process. Either the new thing discovered belongs "uniquely to the religious organism from which it came—in which case you must adopt *that* unity—or it belongs to *yours*—in which case you must reconceive the essence of your own faith, to include that new element."[31] In the midst of this reconceiving work one must recognize, Hocking says, that no religion can claim to be the only way to God, partly because religions express various cultural values. He does not believe, however, that all ways are equally good; he is not even convinced that all ways are good. Hocking believes that the "equality of all religions"

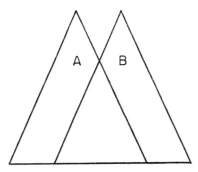

The Way of Radical Displacement

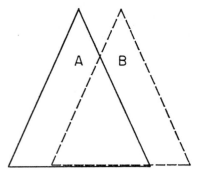

1. Two religions, A and B, are represented as being partly coincident or overlapping in their present teaching and character. The subsequent diagrams will represent the three ways to a world faith which we have now discussed, as practised by A—religion B being assumed for simplicity's sake to remain passive.

2. A hardens its own outline, excluding all of B except what is now included in A.

The Way of Synthesis

The Way of Reconception

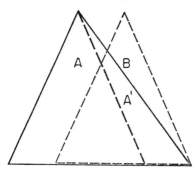

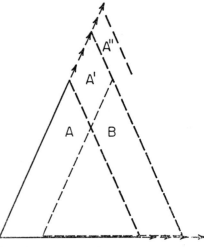

3. A reaches over to include what it finds valid in B, but with some distortion in its own shape.

4. The apex of the cone A, its conceived essence, moves upward, until without distortion the cone A includes what is valid of B, and indefinitely more, as self-understanding deepens.

doctrine leads to "Indifferentism that evades deep-going issues."[32] His point here is that no religious tradition is totally unredeemable, any more than any individual sinner is totally unredeemable. Are there, then, no distinctions to be made among religions? Jainism, I might point out, teaches a profound antihumanism, an ascetic titanism of the *Tirthankara* who transcends even the gods, and a concept of an eternal bliss which is almost indistinguishable from a naturalistic conception of death.[33] These views are profoundly antithetical to Hocking's own religious perceptions. But if one could ask him outright whether a religion like Christianity is not actually superior to Jainism, he would answer that the wrong question had been raised. The wrong question allows for a dismissal of Jainism and the Jains as a lesser breed, whereas both the coming world civilization and the evangelical task of Christianity are served by finding that point within the Jain understanding of his religious situation which can lead him to reconceive that situation and which can lead the Christian to discover a deeper dimension of his own faith. Unless one is prepared to return to the older view that non-Christian religions are of the devil, God must somewhere be present in the world of the Jain; it is the task of faith in the Christian to find that witness and to give glory to God as he is present there.

Hocking has led us to the third of his postulates: "To every man belongs the full truth of religion." What he has in mind is that every man knows something in his own tradition which calls and claims him, which for him is the way, the truth, and the life. Hocking agrees that his claim for universality on behalf of any particular way is valid, insofar as "it is the Way *already present in all,* either explicitly or *in ovo.*"[34] Because the germ of world faith exists in every religion, there is something in each religion which participates in the Being of God.

We cannot gather from Hocking's statements that the developing world community is likely to eliminate religious diversity, for diversity reflects the characteristic expressions of various cultures, and religion will always be related to its cultural environment in order to remain relevant to its life. Hocking looks for a willingness of each to learn from the other, and even to worship with each other. The ecumenical spirit infects the world's living religions as well as diverse Christian bodies, and radical experiments are being made in communion between men of different faiths.[35] What Christianity brings to an encounter with the spiritual iron of Eastern religious asceticism is its maturity, its ability to unite the opposites of life's dialectic—the natural with the supernatural. As far as Hocking can see, Christianity is the only religion which has been compelled to come to terms with a

> rationally convincing and technically triumphant naturalism, with the mind-body realism from which modernity springs, with a psychology of great prowess, value, and depth which can implicitly present a human nature devoid of freedom in plausible defiance of what everyone knows, with a social science whose strong and valid sense of relativity is prepared to sweep away every absolute as mischievous arrogance, including those absolutes on which its own judgments of relativity must be based. I will not say that Christianity is unitedly equipped with the answers. I will say that the answers are at hand within its immediate context and are being recognized. And it becomes, therefore, the opportunity—not the boast—of Christianity to lend its maturity to all religions.[36]

In other words, it is Christianity which has had to face the secularism of modernity. Because it has accepted the challenge of that secularism and recognized its possibilities, it is equipped to pioneer in the passage beyond modernity. Indeed, Hocking makes it clear that "in so far as the world faith for the arriving civilization must be a mature faith, finding its way to a natural union of the natural and the supernatural, it is possible to say that this religion under whatever name will necessarily be in substance Christian."[37] Whether it will be called "Christian" or not is something which worries many[38] but Hocking counsels the Christian not to be anxious:

The time is ripe for that radical reconception of which we have spoken, whereby the concept of the Christ is extended to include that unbound Spirit who stands and has stood at the door of every man, and who, in various guises still appears to him who opens, both as an impersonal word and as a personal presence. As such a presence, he relieves at a stroke that sense of the measureless vastness of the world in which the individual soul finds itself a negligible atom, hopelessly lost. It is this, intrinsically incredible, personal address of the immensities of the cosmos and of history— the necessary and sufficient answer to the quantitative revelations of astrophysics—which, I surmise, will tend to identify the resulting world faith.[39]

In conclusion, Hocking draws together the chief concerns of his entire philosophical work, arguing that it is religion which, in clarifying the "unlosable essences" which are shared by all, will be able to provide new vitality for the motivations of mankind which have been so disturbed in the modern period. Christianity will

summon man to give himself to his science without reserve and without despair, knowing that the purpose of science cannot involve the banishing of purpose from the cosmos, and that the empiricism of sense data is but a limiting edge of the widening empiricism of the ontological passions, including those of the lover, the artist, and the prophet, which open the door to reality.

It will sustain that integrity of volition which the state must assume and cannot by itself command. Each individual person, being summoned to find in the apparent disorder of human history a *telos* with which he can co-operate, and in so doing to find the worth of his own existence, will discover in his will-to-participate in a world task a nonpolitical basis for those legal rights which, taken as costless gifts of nature, work for the corruption of the political community. It will uphold the dignity of the individual human being by upholding his responsibility. For it will leave in his hand the freedom to respond or not to respond to the call to co-operate with the divine purpose. This unique trust of freedom, vested in no other creature, marks both his nobility and his peril, his fitness to maintain and his capacity to destroy the oncoming civilization. It will assure the individual that his use of this freedom, his disposition of his own solitude, is the instant concern of the center of all Being.

It will also assure him that the way of his duty is at the same time the way of such happiness as can come from loving and being loved, from the full employment of one's powers, and from an inner peace. But it will deal with him on the basis of a profound honor: it will promise him no escape from pain and ill fortune; it will offer him the Cross—his own. Its way to happiness is the path of a will to create in love, which is inseparable from a will to create through suffering. But that will, like love itself, is touched with the light of immortality.[40]

Conclusion

TOWARD A WORLD PERSPECTIVE
IN PHILOSOPHY

HOCKING LEFT NO SCHOOL but instead a host of strikingly diverse individuals who have been helped to a solution of their own philosophical problems by his leading. The Hocking *Festschrift* bears eloquent testimony to this influence: from C. T. K. Chari, a South Indian Brahmin whose reading of Hocking led him to a reevaluation of the *Viśistādvaita* tradition of *Vedānta*;[1] from Gabriel Marcel, the French existentialist, for whom *The Meaning of God* meant deliverance from "a prison in which I was afraid I would suffocate";[2] from Frederick Werner, a young American physicist who sees in Hocking's conception of the self new implications for quantum theory;[3] from philosophers in fields as varied as religion, law, science and Oriental studies. In each case, Hocking's conceptualizations helped an individual with his own set of problems. It is possible to be helped by Hocking without becoming a Hockingian in the process. This fact points up what is both the strength and the weakness of Hocking's philosophical system.

The charge of eclecticism against Hocking, while invalid, resulted from the looseness of Hocking's system. The outlines are sketched with a broad brush, casting key ideas in a seemingly occasional context. In addition, the ideas that others took from Hocking were not usually detailed solutions to specific problems. His followers, each in a singular way, found themselves pointed in new directions, exploring new areas along promising lines which had previously escaped them. Marcel is a case in point. He had been trying to make sense of experience by the use of a transcendent *a priori* principle of immanence. Hocking convinced him that the meaning of experience is to be found in the contextual stuff of experience itself, and not by going above it to call down an idealistic *deus ex machina* to solve the problem.

Hocking has been more of a pioneer than a settler. He recognized, in the "Envoi" to *The Coming World Civilization,* that this summary book lacked "the connective tissue" which is the mark of definitive studies.[4] He was aware that, although *The Meaning of God* was indeed definitive for his religious philosophy, he had never completed the detailed work on his basic metaphysics which would have served to tighten up the system. It was this unfinished business, I think, that Charles Hartshorne had in mind when he commented that Hocking's philosophy was never technical enough. Hocking never wrote the systematic treatment of his metaphysics which he owed to the Gifford people (not to mention himself), because there were other immediate pressing human problems which represented a more clamant need. And, more to the point, he readily became involved in affairs which were caught in the net of his broad interests but which were distractions from the job of systematizing those interests and tightening the lines of the net.

Events involving the Laymen's Commission investigating foreign missions provide us with an example of Hocking's problem. James Woods, I suspect, never grasped the proportions of the project which Hocking had dimly in mind and into which all his interests fed. What resulted, of course, was one of the first American philosophies of history and culture. Woods' own views on what Hocking should be doing were rather conventional and academic, but he did see that Hocking was essentially a metaphysician. When he expressed regret that Hocking was getting involved in too many peripheral things, he was reminding Hocking that a system-builder has architectural responsibilities. Metaphysics is indeed an out-of-doors business, and many contemporary philosophers have spent too much time sharpening their tools and too little time working with them. Hocking's problem has been the reverse. It was only toward the end of his life that he began carving out his basic categories of fact, field, and destiny in detail. His system of categories was never as tight as it should have been. But this looseness leads to the strength which counteracts the weakness. While Hocking was quietly trying to find a way to integrate the full range of human experience and diverse characteristic human enterprises, most of his contemporaries remained caught up in modernity's fruitful but fragmented bifurcation of nature.

The I-Thou philosophers, from Sartre to Buber to Emil Brunner, convinced many that the human situation was essentially personalistic and that to be alive was to hurt. Then it turned out that the relationship between I and Thou was a "confrontation" which one might find "nauseating," as Sartre did, or intensely moving, as Buber did; in neither case was it very promising as far as the human community was concerned. It was too narrow and too abstract. This is not the stuff that simple friendship—the most common social bond—is made of. We don't "confront" our friends. And we *are* deeply concerned with science, an attitude which the I-Thou philosophies ignored. On the other hand, "scientific" philosophies of all sorts continued to ignore the way modern men were *feeling* about themselves. These philosophies concentrated rather on the analytical function of pure reason and the prospect of further achievement in the relationship of the I with the It—man's dealing with nature. But when atomic physicists began publicly searching for answers to the political and ethical problems posed by atomic power, it became apparent that science was involved in a matrix of social issues to which no purely scientific philosophy was entirely adequate. The existentialists made it sound as though real philosophy was dying, and the modern world going completely to smash. The scientific philosophies made it sound as though real philosophy had been invented only in 1920 and that the contemporary scientific enlightenment was endlessly promising. Each side tended to write off the other.

Hocking shows us how Western modernity has recognized the need to resolve the internal conflicts which are evidenced in these conflicting philosophies. There has been outside pressure toward this same end. The collapse of colonialism and the subsequent Asian renaissance has begun to shake Western thought from its internecine parochialism. It is now increasingly evident that if philosophy is going to be of any use to anybody, it must provide a coherent way of dealing with a wide range of human problems. This realization derives also from the West's new post-war economic and political involvement in Asia. The spectre haunting Asia is social, political, and intellectual anarchy. Hence the great philosophical need is for an integrating perspective, one which does justice to man's relationship to the natural world and to the resulting science and technology which figure so prominently in both the East and the West. This integrating perspective must also come to terms with the social problems of diverse races, religions, linguistic groups, and economic classes, as well as to the hopes and fears of the independent individual who everywhere increasingly refuses to be totally identified with any of the social groups in which he participates.

The great strength of Hocking's metaphysics—providing, as it does, a framework which integrates his insatiable creative and critical interest in everything from the mystical vision to freedom of the press—is that it proves him to be among the few contemporary philosophers equipped to deal with the problems just outlined. In the introduction to *The Meaning of God,* Hocking had given notice that he was attempting what Andrew Reck has called "the irenic perspective of the Olympian"[5] when he insisted that idealism and realism must go together, that the finished pragmatist best knows the need of the absolute and the finished idealist best knows the need of the realistic elements of experience. He continues:

> I know not what name to give to this point of convergence, nor does name much matter: it is realism, it is mysticism, it is idealism also, its identity, I believe, not broken. For in so far as idealism announces the liberty of thought, the spirituality of the world, idealism is but another name for philosophy—all philosophy is idealism. It is only the radical idealist who is able to give full credit to the realistic, the naturalistic, even the materialistic aspects of the world he lives in.[6]

Two things are at stake here: one is the scope of Hocking's thought, what he has called a widened empiricism; the other —intimately related—is his implied definition of philosophy as an enterprise which, as such, has something to say. Hocking argues that philosophy breeds on diversity of thought and rejects orthodoxies, that philosophy has its chief value in raising the level of reflection rather than in producing definitive results, and that there is no universal philosophy or perennial philosophy which can claim special authority. His central argument is simply that philosophy, which is "the examination of beliefs," requires at least three presuppositions, without which there can be no motivation for the examining process. These are: that things have a meaning, that we are competent to grasp at least some of that meaning, and that the effort to do so is worthwhile and should be made.⁷ These assumptions reject the view that "philosophy is a sort of personal artistry in the making of world-pictures, or a forefated expression of temperament."⁸

As I understand Hocking's confession of dissatisfaction with the phrase "widened empiricism," it was in recognition that his prior conviction that things have a meaning is not, strictly speaking, empirical. It is an instinctive human assumption. Philosophically this conviction functions as a hypothesis, a belief to be examined; it opens itself to the test of logic and experience. It follows that, short of a discovery which would negate philosophy as such—that is, the discovery that things have no meaning—any philosophical position which is "meaningless" must be excluded. Hocking's dialectic is simply the argument that solipsistic idealism and naturalistic realism are both meaningless because both are logically contradictory and neither does justice to what we experience. Solipsism is meaningless because it cannot explain how we know other selves, even though—by virtue of its attempt to communicate with them—it inadvertently confesses that it believes in them. Extreme naturalism is meaningless because it treats human meanings as cosmic accidents and thereby vitiates the meaning of its own contentions.

Philosophy, Hocking contends, is an examination of what we really believe. This is not to say that solipsists and extreme naturalists do not believe what they say, but rather that logic and experience prove that their contentions are not believable in their own terms. To be sure, philosophy cannot give us a belief in God, as far as that goes; but it can prove that God is believable. What widened empiricism does is to insist on the full range of experience as the testing ground of our beliefs. The reason that solipsism and an extreme naturalism have been perpetuated is that we have acquiesced in their selection of a particular area of experience within which to work. As a result, both are abstractions from what Hocking calls, simply, human experience —the inclusive category which covers fact, field, and destiny. Hocking's approach to experience is inductive and goes beyond naturalism and realism by finding natural objects inextricably linked with an other mind which is their source.

The interdependence of I, Thou, and It in Hocking's metaphysics integrates not only the three major objects of human attention; it integrates also what would appear to be the distinctive concerns of the major world cultures of China, India, and the West. Problems in East-West philosophy have come into the forefront of philosophical work everywhere. The explorations are recent, and it is too early to look for a consensus or even a definitive statement of the problems involved. But we are working toward a time when invidious attempts to prove the superiority of one tradition over another will be past, and the beginnings of a world perspective in philosophy will be possible. Toynbee, Northrop, Gerald Heard, Radhakrishnan, E. A. Burtt, Wing-Tsit Chan, P. T. Raju, Charles Moore, and others have already made notable contributions to this venture.[9] One of the most suggestive recent contributions is Huston Smith's "Accents of the World's Philosophies."[10] Admittedly "working in broad strokes and risking oversimplification to keep the outlines clear"[11] Smith offers an analysis of central philosophical motifs in the three major existing world cultures. Perhaps he shows us most pointedly where Hocking's system leads and how we can approach a world perspective in philosophy.

Rejecting the possible thesis that racial characteristics are responsible for differing cultural capacities and interests, Smith turns instead to environmental factors as a key to various cultures. He finds it significant that Western culture was born in the "fertile Crescent," where nature invited and rewarded the advances of man. Smith takes it for granted that the development of Western science is well known and turns instead to the implications of an early and basic interest in nature for Western religion and philosophy.[12] Because Western philosophy regards physical nature positively, it tends to be:

(1) Realistic in ontology. On the whole, it rejects the Platonic identification of being with intelligible and stable ideas or forms and joins Aristotle in giving purchase to matter.

(2) Hylomorphic in anthropology. Man is composite in nature, constituted of soul and body. Both are real and ultimate aspects of his nature.

(3) Sense-involved in epistemology. Knowledge originates in sensible things and is, in the main, about sensible things.[13]

What is true in philosophy, Smith points out, is equally true of Western religion. Christianity, as William Temple's well-known maxim has it, "is the most avowedly materialistic of all the great religions."[14] Notable is the Christian doctrine of the resurrection of the body. Life after death is in some sense physical, in keeping with the doctrine of the incarnation of God in the physical world. Thus, Smith affirms, the entire arc of Western thought is oriented toward nature.

"Western man has been, *par excellence,* the natural philosopher."[15]

The main concern of China, on the other hand, has been in social philosophy. Chinese culture, like that of the West, is riverine in its origins, but these rivers brought both blessings and scourges. Chinese naturalism tends to be that of the artist and the romanticist, not of the scientist. Nature can be communed with, reverenced, or intuited. When it comes to man's attempt to make nature obey him, however, Smith finds the Chinese attitude somewhat fatalistic: "Those who would take over the earth/ And shape it to their will/ Never, I notice, succeed."[16]

There has been, then, no notable Chinese science. China excels, rather, in the philosophy of man in society. Smith finds China's definitive historical event in the infamous "time of troubles" between 700 and 200 B.C. This was the era of "the Warring Kingdoms" which posed a question for subsequent generations of Chinese philosophers: "How can we live together without destroying one another?" Smith follows this with a quote from Arthur Waley: "All Chinese philosophy is essentially the study of how men can best be helped to live together in harmony and good order."[17] In other words, the order which Chinese philosophy sought was not in nature but in society. Carefully systematized are the "five great relationships": father and son, elder brother and younger brother, husband and wife, friend and friend, ruler and subject.[18] The principle of right order in these relationships is summed up in the ideal of *li,* or propriety.[19] On this basis China constructed the most extensive of human civilizations, boasting the incredible achievement of a dynastic political rule—the Chinese Empire—which lasted from 221 B.C. to 1912 A.D. Although constantly open to invasion along its vast open frontier, China absorbed barbarian hordes with perhaps the most thorough indigenization in cultural history.

Smith turns last to India and finds nature particularly forbidding to the Indian. Here he proposes a theme which has recently been expanded at length and with considerable virtuosity by India's finest English essayist, Nirad Chaudhuri, in his *The Continent of Circe*.[20] Any interest which the originally world-affirming Arayans may have had in nature was defeated by the brutal Indo-Gangetic plain. The Indian view of nature is therefore characterized by the conviction that the world is "ungovernable and, in some strange way, unreal."[21] The laws of nature are *māyā* or illusion. Society presented comparable problems to the Indian, chiefly in the color-culture barrier between Aryan and Dravidian which persists to the present. The major thrust of Indian thought has been inward toward the psychological problem of self-knowledge in man. Inner certainty, it is believed, will help maintain man against the assaults of nature's brutality and society's inherent conflicts. India seeks *mokṣa* (release) for the individual *ātman* (soul) from the bonds of life in this world of suffering. To perfect one's inner being is to discover one's identity with the holy world power (*Brahmā*). Through this power one breaks the chains of *māyā* and is freed for the mystical peace which passes all understanding.

In conclusion, Smith observes that neglect of natural problems has left India and China wanting in scientific development, struggling with an impossibly low standard of living. And yet the West's failure to deal with social problems —as the fragmented and continually changing map of Europe bears eloquent testimony—has been equally dramatic.[22] The fratricidal warfare of the years since 1914 is only the most recent example of endemic Western social divisiveness. Smith takes it as typical that the West should produce, in Marxism, a social theory which reduces sociology to economics, implying that the material problem is basic to all social life. He sums up by saying that "each of the world's three great traditions has achieved notable results with one of man's basic problems, but has been brought to the brink of ruin by not attending sufficiently to the other two. The obvious conclusion is that an adequate culture must strike all three notes as a chord."[23]

Implied in Smith's thesis is the need for a philosophy which takes as its chief business the fundamental integration of selfhood, nature, and society. Hocking's philosophy fills that need. Virtually no other contemporary thinker has matched the balance and scope of his thought. This newest challenge to philosophy thus restates the oldest of all philosophical challenges—the need to do justice to the full range of human experience. This has never been merely a technical problem for philosophy; and today it is a problem of critical human importance. The era of a single civilization is already upon us. Meetings of East and West are underway: the changing attitude of the West's hitherto militant Christian mission to the East; the development of social, political, and economic relationships; brave but bedeviled beginnings in a world political organization; increasing awareness of, interest in, and tolerance toward various cultures; and, perhaps most significantly, the gradual discovery of mankind as a human commitment which lays its claim upon us all. Within the last thirty years, however, the meetings have brought more darkness than light. Where there has been good will it has too often been frustrated by a lack of understanding. The much-needed understanding of cultural differences and a perspective which integrates their several concerns, will not, in itself, solve the problem of conflict between East and West. It is still true that philosophy bakes no man's bread. But man does not live by bread alone. In both East and West he lives also by an understanding of himself and his relation to his world, to his neighbors, and to God. It is these three basic relationships that formed the central concern of Ernest Hocking's long life of philosophizing.

Chronology

Selected Bibliography of Hocking's Works

Notes

Index

Chronology

THE LIFE OF

WILLIAM ERNEST HOCKING

1873	Born in Cleveland, Ohio, son of William Francis Hocking and Julia Carpenter Pratt.
1889	Graduates from Joliet High School, Joliet Illinois.
1889–1893	Works as surveyor, map-maker, "printer's devil," illustrator, to earn money for college.
1894	Enters Iowa State College of Agriculture and the Mechanic Arts as student of engineering.
1895–1898	Teaches at Duncan's Business College in Davenport, Iowa. Becomes Principal of School No. 1 in Davenport.
1899	Enters Harvard College.
1902–1903	After graduating from Harvard, spends a year studying in Germany at Göttingen, Berlin, and Heidelberg.
1904	Receives his Ph.D. from Harvard and becomes instructor at Andover Theological Seminary.
1905	June 28: marries Agnes Boyle O'Reilly.
1906	Joins philosophy department at the University of California.
1908	Becomes Assistant Professor of Philosophy at Yale.

1912   *The Meaning of God in Human Experience* published.

1914   Joins philosophy department at Harvard.

1918   Appointed inspector of "War Issues" courses by U.S. Army, which resulted in the publication of *Morale and Its Enemies*. *Human Nature and Its Remaking* published.

1920   Becomes Alford Professor of Natural Religion, Moral Philosophy, and Civil Polity.

1928   *The Self, Its Body and Freedom* published.

1929   *Types of Philosophy* published.

1930–1932   Appointed chairman of Laymen's Foreign Mission Inquiry; travels in Asia and becomes principal author of *Re-Thinking Missions*.

1936   Hibbert Lecturer at Oxford and Cambridge, England. Lectures published in 1940 as *Living Religions and a World Faith*.

1937   *Thoughts on Death and Life* published, *Lasting Elements of Individualism* published.

1938–1939   Gifford Lecturer on "Fact and Destiny" at University of Glasgow, Scotland.

1942   *What Man Can Make of Man* published.

1943   Retires from Harvard.

1944   *Science and the Idea of God* published.

1947–1948   Guest Professor at University of Leiden.

1947   *Freedom of the Press: A Framework of Principle* published.

1949   Lectures at Goethe Bicentennial in Aspen, Colorado, on "Binding Ingredients of Civilization."

1954   *Experiment in Education* published.

1956	*The Coming World Civilization* published.
1957	*The Meaning of Immortality in Human Experience* published.
1959	*Strength of Men and Nations* published.
1966	June 14: Hocking's death at his home in Madison, New Hampshire.

SELECTED BIBLIOGRAPHY OF
HOCKING'S WORKS

For a complete bibliography of Hocking's works, see Richard Gilman's "Bibliography of William Ernest Hocking from 1898 to 1964" in *Philosophy, Religion and the Coming World Civilization: Essays in Honor of William Ernest Hocking*, ed. Leroy S. Rouner (The Hague: Martinus Nijhoff, 1966), pp. 465-504.

"Action and Certainty," *Journal of Philosophy*, XXVII (April 24, 1930), 225-238.

"The Binding Ingredients of Civilization," in *Goethe and the Modern Age*, ed. Arnold Bergstraesser (Chicago: Henry Regnery, 1950), pp. 252-283.

"Chu Hsi's Theory of Knowledge," *Harvard Journal of Asiatic Studies*, I (April 1936), 109-127.

The Coming World Civilization. New York: Harper and Bros., 1956.

"Dewey's Concepts of Experience and Nature," *Philosophical Review*, XLIX (March 1940), 228-244.

Experiment in Education. Chicago: Henry Regnery, 1954.

"Fact and Destiny," *Review of Metaphysics*, IV (September 1950), 1-12.

"Fact and Destiny (II)," *Review of Metaphysics*, IV (March 1951), 319-342.

"Fact, Field and Destiny: Inductive Elements of Metaphysics," *Review of Metaphysics*, XI (June 1958), 525-549.

Freedom of the Press: A Framework of Principle. Chicago: University of Chicago Press, 1947.

"From the Early Days of the 'Logische Untersuchungen'," in *Edmund Husserl 1859-1959: Recueil commémoratif publié à l'occasion du centenaire de la naissance du philosophe* (The Hague, Martinus Nijhoff, 1959), pp. 1-11.

"How Can Christianity Be the Final Religion?" *Yale Divinity Quarterly,* V (March 1909), 266-288.

"How Ideas Reach Reality," *Philosophical Review,* XIX (May 1910), 302-318.

Human Nature and Its Remaking. New Haven: Yale University Press, 1918.

Lasting Elements of Individualism. New Haven: Yale University Press, 1937.

Living Religions and a World Faith. New York: Macmillan, 1940.

Man and the State. New Haven: Yale University Press, 1926.

"Marcel and the Ground Issues of Metaphysics," *Philosophy and Phenomenological Research,* XIV (June 1954), 439-469.

The Meaning of God in Human Experience: A Philosophic Study of Religion. New Haven: Yale University Press, 1912.

The Meaning of Immortality in Human Experience. New York: Harper and Bros., 1957.

"Metaphysics: Its Function, Consequences, and Criteria," *Journal of Philosophy,* XLIII (July 4, 1946), 365-378.

Morale and Its Enemies. New Haven: Yale University Press, 1918.

"On Royce's Empiricism," *Journal of Philosophy,* LIII (February 2, 1956), 57-63.

"The Ontological Argument in Royce and Others," in *Contemporary Idealism in America,* ed. Clifford Barrett (New York: Macmillan, 1932), pp. 45-46.

Preface to Philosophy: Textbook (with others). New York: Macmillan, 1946.

The Present Status of the Philosophy of Law and of Rights. New Haven: Yale University Press, 1926.

"Response to Professor Krikorian's Discussion," *Journal of Philosophy,* LV (March 27, 1958), 274-280.

Re-Thinking Missions: A Layman's Inquiry after One Hundred Years (with others). New York: Harper and Bros., 1932. (Hocking is author of Chaps. 1-4.)

Science and the Idea of God. Chapel Hill, N.C.: University of North Carolina Press, 1944.

The Self: Its Body and Freedom. New Haven: Yale University Press, 1928.

"Some Second Principles," in *Contemporary American Philosophy: Personal Statements,* ed. George Plimpton Adams and William Pepperell Montague (New York: Macmillan, 1930), I, 383-400.

The Spirit of World Politics: With Special Studies of the Near East. New York: Macmillan, 1932.

Strength of Men and Nations. New York: Harper and Bros., 1959.

"Theses Establishing an Idealistic Metaphysics by a New Route," *Journal of Philosophy,* XXXVIII (December 4, 1941), 688-690.

Thoughts on Death and Life. New York: Harper and Bros., 1937.

Types of Philosophy, 3rd ed., with the collaboration of Richard Boyle O'Reilly Hocking. New York: Charles Scribner's Sons, 1959.

"What Does Philosophy Say?" *Philosophical Review,* XXXVII (March 1928), 133-153.

"What is a Lost Soul?" *Chicago Theological Seminary Register,* XXIII (March 1933), 9-10.

What Man Can Make of Man. New York: Harper and Bros., 1942.

NOTES

Abbreviations Used in the Notes

CWC	*The Coming World Civilization*
HNR	*Human Nature and Its Remaking*
LEI	*The Lasting Elements of Individualism*
LRWF	*Living Religions and a World Faith*
MATS	*Man and the State*
MGHE	*The Meaning of God in Human Experience*
MIHE	*The Meaning of Immortality in Human Experience*
PRCWC	*Philosophy, Religion and the Coming World Civilization: Essays in Honor of William Ernest Hocking*
RTM	*Re-Thinking Missions*
SBF	*The Self, Its Body and Freedom*
SMN	*Strength of Men and Nations*
TP	*Types of Philosophy*

Introduction: The Formative Years

1. Anecdotes for which no reference is given are from the author's notes on personal conversations with Hocking. In each case Hocking verified them and gave permission for their publication. Much of the material in this Introduction appeared originally as "The Making of a Philosopher: Ernest Hocking's Early Years," *PRCWC*, pp. 5-22, and is used with permission.

2. "Some Second Principles," *Contemporary American Philosophy: Personal Statements*, ed. George Plimpton Adams and William Pepperell Montague (New York: Macmillan, 1930), I, 385-386.

3. *MGHE*, pp. xiv-xv.

4. Quoted by Whit Burnett in "Philosopher of a Single Civilization" in *This Is My Philosophy* (New York: Harper and Bros., 1957), p. 287.

5. "Some Second Principles," *Contemporary American Philosophy*, I, 387.

6. *MIHE*, pp. 213-214.

7. It was while principal of P. S. No. 1, Davenport, Iowa, that he published his first philosophical essay, a criticism of the Dewey-McClelland method of teaching number, entitled "What is Number?" *Intelligence: A Journal of Education*, XVIII (May 15, 1898), 360-362.

8. "From the early days of the 'Logische Untersuchungen'" in *Edmund Husserl 1859-1959* (The Hague: Martinus Nijhoff, 1959), p. 6.

9. *Ibid.*, p. 4.

10. *MGHE*, pp. ix-x.

I. The Influence of Royce and James

1. "Some Second Principles," *Contemporary American Philosophy*, I, 391.

2. During his stay in Davenport, Iowa (1898) he outlined and began a book on analytical geometry. The text and drawings are in his own hand, and are bound and deposited in the Hocking library in Madison, New Hampshire.

3. "The Elementary Experience of Other Conscious Being in Its Relations to the Elementary Experiences of Physical and Reflexive Objects," unpub. diss., Harvard University, 1904.

4. See "The Group Concept in the Service of Philosophy," *Journal of Philosophy, Psychology, and Scientific Methods,* III (August 2, 1906), 421-431.

5. For the material on the development of Royce's philosophy I am particularly indebted to John E. Smith, *Royce's Social Infinite* (New York: Liberal Arts Press, 1950).

6. Herbert Schneider, *History of American Philosophy* (New York: Columbia University Press, 1946), p. 488.

7. Quoted in Smith, *Royce's Social Infinite,* p. 93, *Cambridge Philosophical Transactions,* X, 339.

8. Royce's reference to an idea as a plan of action is a reminder that he always considered himself a pragmatist "up to a point."

9. New York: Macmillan, 1914, II, 231.

10. "On Royce's Empiricism," *Journal of Philosophy,* LIII (February 2, 1956), 61.

11. "The Elementary Experience of Other Conscious Being," p. iv.

12. *The Varieties of Religious Experience* (New York: Longmans, Green, 1902), p. 6.

13. From a letter to Miss Frances R. Morse, April 12, 1900. Quoted in Ralph Barton Perry, *The Thought and Character of William James* (Boston: Atlantic-Little, Brown, 1935), II, 326-327.

14. See Herbert Schneider, *Religion in 20th Century America* (Cambridge, Mass., Harvard University Press, 1952), pp. 173ff.

15. See "A Union for Ethical Action," with Howard Woolston (privately printed, 1904), 17 pp. Woolston was the principal founder, but Hocking is the author of "The Principles of Union," pp. 1-5, and co-author of the "Plan of Organization," pp. 12-17. The Union was designed for young men who would "choose their life work with a sense of its significance for the general welfare and advance," and therefore, eventually

"create a nation morally significant in history." The pamphlet is deposited in the Andover-Harvard Library of the Harvard Divinity School.

16. *MGHE,* pp. xxiii-xxiv.

17. The first series of Gifford Lectures was summarized in two articles in *Review of Metaphysics:* "Fact and Destiny," IV, (September 1950) 1-12; and "Fact and Destiny (II)," IV, (March 1951), 319-342. The second series is summarized in *PRCWC,* pp. 423-463. The relevant statement (p. 463) reads: "Thus, the Absolute permeates the texture of history. Without it there can be no stable conviction; without conviction, no courage; without courage, no craving for adventure; and without ever renewed adventure, no history worth recording."

18. *MGHE,* p. xxxii.

19. Perry, *The Thought and Character of William James,* II, 670.

20. A student in Royce's metaphysics class at Harvard, 1914-1915, recalls: "James had died; but he was still alive in Royce's mind: Royce could not state his own position on almost any topic without first stating James'." Walter Marshall Horton, "Tambaram Twenty-Five Years After," *PRCWC,* p. 225. James was instrumental in bringing Royce to Harvard from California, and their influence on one another's thought took place in the context of firm friendship. In the introduction to his *Philosophy of Loyalty,* p. x, Royce wrote: "Had I not very early in my work as a student known Professor James, I doubt whether any poor book of mine would ever have been written." James' reply, prompted by his genius for friendship, is noteworthy; typically, he could not resist needling Royce about the Absolute: "I am quite overwhelmed by the oriental hyperbole of your page *x* to me-wards. That the world owes your books to *me* is too awfully gracious a saying! But I thank you for the beauty of spirit shown and for the honor. I am sorry you say we don't see truth in the same light, for the only thing we see differently is the Absolute, and surely such a trifle as that is not a thing for two gentlemen to be parted by. I believe that at the bottom of *your* heart *we* see things more alike than any pair of philosophers extant! I thank you anyhow from the bottom of mine." Quoted in Perry, *The Thought and Character of William James,* I, 821-822.

21. See Perry, *The Thought and Character of William James,* I, 778-824.

II. Dialectic

1. Hocking's approach differs from most current discussions of the other mind's problem, which tend to center on purely logical and verbal problems. The traditional alternatives to the logical-verbal approach have been either the ethical one, such as Royce's, arguing that we *ought* to deal with other human beings *as if* they were persons like ourselves; or the aesthetic approach by way of a metaphorical or analogical relationship. Hocking's conviction that ordinary experience is metaphysical leads to an approach whch is a metaphysics of common sense and which combines elements of ethics and aesthetics with logic. Since this problem is the central issue of his metaphysics, his approach to it provides the key example of what he means by a "widened empiricism" and by his assertion that pragmatic realism, idealism, and mysticism are integrally related. For Hocking, philosophy is "the examination of beliefs," and it is possible to come to a knowledge of those other minds which most of us sincerely believe in because feeling, which plays a large role in that belief, reaches its natural terminus in idea. "All feeling means to instate some experience which is essentially cognitive; it is idea-apart-from-its-object tending to become idea-in-presence-of-its-object, which is 'cognizance,' or experiential knowing" (*MGHE*, p. 68). Epistemological problems are therefore neither purely logical nor simply psychological. They are problems of an experience which includes both.

For a discussion which is sympathetic to Hocking's see Donald Williams, "Preface to Privacy," *PRCWC*, pp. 81-94. Williams admits to "having long availed myself of [Hocking's] clues without following all his dialectic," and describes his essay as "a sort of convergence of considered results of traditional and educated common sense with the technical philosophical alternatives open to a realistic empiricism" (pp. 81-82). For a readable examination of the current discussion in its historical context, see Margaret Chatterjee, *Our Knowledge of Other Selves* (Bombay: Asia Publishing House, 1963). For a sampling of the current discussion, see also "Symposium: The Other Minds Problems," *Journal of Philosophy*, LXII (October 21, 1965); included are: Paul Ziff, "The Simplicity of Other Minds," pp. 575-584; Alvin Pantinga, "Comment," pp. 585-587; and Sidney Shoemaker, "Ziff's Other Minds," pp. 587-589. For a fuller statement of Pantinga's views, see his "Induction and Other Minds," *Review of Metaphysics,* XIX

(March 1966), 441-461. Richard Rorty discusses the identity theory and related problems in the philosophy of mind in his "Mind-Body Identity, Privacy, and Categories," *Review of Metaphysics*, XIX (September 1965), 24-54.

2. "Marcel and the Ground Issues of Metaphysics," *Philosophy and Phenomenological Research*, XIV (June 1954), 439-469.

3. *Ibid.*, p. 441.

4. *Ibid.*, p. 461.

5. *Types of Philosophy*, 3rd ed., with the collaboration of Richard Boyle O'Reilly Hocking (New York: Charles Scribner's Sons, 1959), pp. 186-187.

6. *MGHE*, pp. 265-266.

7. From a letter to a friend whose name has escaped Hocking's memory. The copy of the letter has no salutation, but is dated "1920."

8. *MGHE*, p. 266.

9. *Ibid.*, p. 261.

10. *Ibid.*, p. 84.

11. *Ibid.*, p. 92.

12. *Ibid.*, p. 95.

13. *Ibid.*, p. 97.

III. Thesis and Antithesis: Natural Fact and Personal Will

1. New York: Alfred A. Knopf, 1962.

2. *MGHE*, p. 230.

3. *Ibid.*, p. 3.

4. See pp. 9, 103, 137, 149, 150, 229, 242-243, 298, 301ff, 422, and 515.

5. See "Logic or Beauty?" letter to the editor, *Scientific Monthly*, LXXIX (October 1954), 269, in which he argues that beauty, when understood as power, is an influential factor in the acceptance of some scientific theories.

6. *MGHE*, p. 118.

7. *What Man Can Make of Man* (New York: Harper and Bros., 1942), p. 51.

8. Noting that Karl Barth was the architect of a twentieth century theological revolution, and that Paul Tillich was Barth's most influential opponent, Dillenberger points out that "while theologians and scientists previously crossed into each other's territory, Barth and Tillich have so separated these spheres that they have disregarded the knowledge of the world contributed by natural science." *Protestant Thought and Natural Science* (Garden City, New York: Doubleday, 1960), p. 262.

9. "Fact and Destiny (II)," *Review of Metaphysics*, IV (March 1951), 324.

10. *Ibid.*, p. 320.

11. Willem Zuurdeeg, review of Jules Lawrence Moreau, *Language and Religious Language*, and Frederick Ferré, *Language, Logic and God*, in *Religion in Life*, XXX (Autumn 1961), 623-624.

12. *MGHE*, p. 140.

13. *Ibid.*, pp. 145-146.

14. Whether Bultmann's philosophical theology is "subjectivist" or not depends on whether one is prepared to credit the idea that what seems subjective is really objective "in the theological sense." For a highly influential criticism of Bultmann's position from the Protestant side, see Ian Henderson's pioneering monograph for English speaking readers, *Myth in the New Testament* (Chicago: Henry Regnery, 1952). For a defense of the divine objectivity of "event" as the key category in Bultmann's thought, see the Roman Catholic scholar, Father L. Malevez, S.J., *The Christian Message and Myth* (London: S.C.M. Press, 1958). In many ways the best book on Bultmann available in English is Stephen Neill's translation of Giovanni Miegge, *Gospel and Myth in the Thought of Rudolph Bultmann* (London: Lutterworth Press, 1960).

15. *MGHE*, p. 150.

16. *Strength of Men and Nations* (New York: Harper and Bros., 1959), p. 1.

17. *MIHE*, p. 243.

IV. *Monism, Pluralism, and the Absolute*

1. *MGHE*, p. ix.

2. *TP*, p. 3.

3. See Gabriel Marcel, "Solipsism Surmounted," *PRCWC*, pp. 23-31.

4. *CWC*, Study II, "Passage Beyond Modernity."

5. James A. Martin, Jr., *Empirical Philosophies of Religion* (New York: King's Crown Press of the Columbia University Press, 1947), p. 14.

6. *MGHE*, pp. 167-168.

7. See William C. Greene, *Moira: Fate, Good and Evil in Greek Thought* (Cambridge, Mass.: Harvard University Press, 1944), p. 4. "That this is on the whole a good world, and that man is on the whole happy, we are generally agreed; at least man struggles to prolong life as if it were worth living."

8. *MGHE*, p. 178.

9. *Ibid.*, p. 181.

10. *Ibid.*, p. 182.

11. Quoted in *MGHE*, p. 184, from *A Pluralistic Universe* (New York: Longmans, Green, 1909), p. 111.

12. Hegel, *Werke*, vol. VII: *Vorrede zur Rechtsphilosophie* (Berlin: Bruno Cassirer, 1916), p. 17.

13. The renewed interest in Hegel has produced a major re-evaluation of his thought in Walter Kauphmann, *Hegel* (Garden City, New York: Doubleday, 1965). Kauphmann notes: (p. 381): "It is . . . essential to translate *Wirklichkeit* and *wirklich* as actuality and actual, not as reality and real. . . . Hegel's notorious equation of the actual and the rational is not a sanctification of the *status quo*; in his terminology, most states are not fully actual and rational."

14. *MGHE*, p. 131.

15. *Ibid.*, p. 135.

16. *Science and the Idea of God* (Chapel Hill: University of North Carolina Press, 1944), pp. 77-78.

17. *MGHE,* p. 205.

18. This statement, later published under the title "What is a Lost Soul?" *Chicago Theological Seminary Register,* XXIII (March 1933), 9-10, followed one of Hocking's Alden-Tuthill Lectures at the Chicago Theological Seminary, January 24–26, 1933. The text of Hocking's address had contained a reference to "lost souls," and in the question period an impassioned listener challenged him to define the phrase. The drama of the occasion was heightened as Hocking stood silent for a long moment thinking out his reply. Ward Madison, Hocking's secretary for the work of the Laymen's Commission, made a verbatim transcript. Although Hocking later made a few editorial changes, the statement is essentially as he gave it on that occasion.

V. *Selfhood, Nature, and Other Mind*

1. *MGHE,* p. 270.

2. *Ibid.*

3. *Ibid.,* p. 273.

4. "Marcel and the Ground Issues of Metaphysics," *Philosophy and Phenomenological Research,* XIV (June 1954), 450.

5. "Fact and Destiny," *Review of Metaphysics,* IV (September 1950) 5. Hocking quotes this same comment of Whitehead's in a slightly different form in his essay, "Marcel and the Ground Issues of Metaphysics," cited above.

6. Andrew Reck emphasizes the originality of these categories of fact, field, and destiny in his analysis of "Hocking's Place in American Metaphysics," *PRCWC,* pp. 32-47.

7. "Fact and Destiny (II)," *Review of Metaphysics,* IV (March 1951), 325.

8. The observation of fact "is a part of the steady enjoyment of being alive." "Fact and Destiny," p. 3.

9. *Ibid.* p. 5.

10. "Marcel and the Ground Issues of Metaphysics," p. 326.

11. "Fact and Destiny (II)," p. 326.

12. *Ibid.*, p. 327.

13. "Marcel and the Ground Issues of Metaphysics," p. 453.

14. *MGHE*, p. 284.

15. *CWC*, p. 33.

16. "Marcel and the Ground Issues of Metaphysics," pp. 454-455.

17. *Ibid.*, p. 455.

18. *Ibid.*

19. *Ibid.*, p. 456. This argument, which he makes tentative with the question "could we be still ourselves if the world were thus changed?" has a bearing on his treatment of evil. The problem of evil assumes that God *could* have made the world more congenial if he had wanted to, say by the elimination of disease. This would be an exercise of his omnipotence. But the terms of the problem also assume that this change would not have necessitated *our* being basically changed. Hocking does not deny that existential evil is a problem which each of us must come to terms with, both in the lives of men and of nations. However, the implication here is that, as a logical problem, the problem of evil suffers from faulty formulation. For the view that the problem of evil is essentially a logical problem, see Walter Stace, "The Problem of Evil," *PRCWC*, pp. 123-134.

20. "Marcel and the Ground Issues of Metaphysics," p. 457.

21. *Ibid.*, p. 458.

22. *MGHE*, pp. 286-287.

23. "Marcel and the Ground Issues of Metaphysics," p. 459.

24. *Ibid.* p. 460.

25. *MGHE*, p. 287.

26. On this point see Charles Hartshorne, "Idealism and Our Experience of Nature," *PRCWC*, p. 72: "Hocking also defended, with James, causally transcendent freedom for man as well as for God. Thus he avoided the 'block-universe,' the theory of exclusively internal

relations, which in England particularly has so often—but illogically— been taken as a corollary of the view that mind is the ultimate explanatory principle. The connection between (a) the rejection of mere matter and (b) the universal denial of external relations and contingency seems to have been the merest historical accident. It certainly does not follow from any conceptual necessity."

VI. Our Knowledge of God

1. This has validity, even though we are sometimes more sure of the reality of another individual than we are of ourselves. Hocking says, "I may call upon my friend to assure me of my own sanity, by acknowledging as real for him also an object of mine which I fear may be an hallucination." But, at the same time, "I am more likely to judge *his* sanity by his assent to the reality of objects which apart from him I regard as unquestionably real" (*MGHE*, p. 292).

2. *MGHE*, pp. 294-295.

3. *Ibid.*, p. 295.

4. *Ibid.*, p. 296.

5. "The statement that God is being-itself is an unsymbolic statement." *Systematic Theology*, Vol. I (Chicago: University of Chicago Press, 1951), p. 238.

6. "I do not say that the Absolute is equivalent to God. I say that God, whatever else he may be, must needs also be the Absolute" (*MGHE*, p. 206).

7. *Ibid.*, pp. 296-297.

8. *Systematic Theology*, I, 205. Elsewhere Tillich argues that, by the same token, God is not to be regarded as eternal essence.

9. Ultimately, however, "Brahman has nothing similar to it, nothing different from it, and no internal differentiation, for all these are empirical distinctions. Brahman is the non-empirical, the non-objective, the wholly other, but it is not non-being. It is the highest being." Radhakrishnan and Moore, *Source Book in Indian Philosophy* (Princeton: Princeton University Press, 1957), p. 507.

10. "Idealism and Our Experience of Nature," *PRCWC*, pp. 72-73. Commenting on Tillich's doctrine of God, Hartshorne notes: "Tillich never reaches a clear notion of the root of contingency in creativity; he speaks sometimes quite like an Augustinian determinist. He never clearly envisages the issue between classical and neoclassical views, whether of God or the creatures. And the idea of a God who responds lovingly to the world is lost in the indifferent absoluteness of 'unconditioned' being." *The Logic of Perfection* (La Salle: The Open Court Publishing Co., 1962), p. 144.

11. *MGHE*, pp. 298-299. Hocking later qualified this space-time monism.

12. *Union Seminary Quarterly Review*, XVIII (November 1962), 1-21.

13. "The Ontological Argument in Royce and Others," in *Contemporary Idealism in America*, ed. Clifford Barrett (New York: Macmillan, 1932), pp. 45-66.

14. *Ibid.*, p. 62.

15. The reference is to Professor Royce's lecture of February 29, 1916, in "Philosophy 9" at Harvard. A transcription of student notes is deposited in Widener Library. In the lecture Royce discussed the realist-idealist conflict by contrasting his own views with those of Santayana, as expressed in Santayana's paper, "Some Meanings of the Word 'Is'," *Journal of Philosophy* (February 4, 1915). For a discussion of the differences between Royce and Santayana, see John H. Randall, Jr., "Josiah Royce and American Idealism," *Journal of Philosophy*, LXIII (February 3, 1966), 57-83.

16. "The Ontological Argument in Royce and Others," p. 64.

17. *Ibid.*

18. *Ibid.*, p. 65.

19. *MGHE*, p. 306.

20. *Ibid.*, pp. 306-307.

21. *Ibid.*, p. 310.

22. Hartshorne regretfully (but firmly) classes Hocking with that

large and distinguished company of philosophers who have never really understood the historic ontological argument.

23. *MGHE*, p. 310.

24. *Ibid.*, p. 202.

25. *Ibid.*, p. 312.

26. *Ibid.*, p. 315.

27. *Ibid.*, pp. 314-315.

28. *CWC*, p. 36.

29. *MGHE*, p. 323.

30. *Ibid.*, p. 326.

31. *Ibid.*, p. 329.

32. *Ibid.*, p. 335.

33. *Ibid.*, p. 336. In working out his philosophy of worship, he defines religion as "anticipation of an ultimate attainment" (a theologizing of the metaphysical inter-relationships among Fact, Field, and Destiny), and offers a "theory of alternation" between work and worship.

34. *Indian Philosophy* (London: George Allen and Unwin, 1962), I, 197.

35. "Solipsism Surmounted," *PRCWC*, pp. 68-69.

36. John H. Randall, Jr., *The Making of the Modern Mind* (Cambridge, Mass.: Houghton Mifflin, 1940), Bk I, p. 36.

37. "Idealism and Our Experience of Nature," *PRCWC*, pp. 70ff.

38. *Ibid.*, pp. 77-78.

39. *Ibid.*, p. 79.

40. "Chu Hsi's Theory of Knowledge," *Harvard Journal of Asiatic Studies*, I (April 1936), 121.

41. "Response to Professor Krikorian's Discussion," *Journal of Philosophy*, LV (March 27, 1958), 278.

42. *Ibid.*

VII. The Human Individual

1. See *MGHE*, pp. 485-514.

2. *MGHE*, p. 189.

3. *HNR*, p. xi.

4. See especially "Theses Establishing an Idealistic Metaphysics by a New Route," *Journal of Philosophy*, XXXVIII (December 4, 1941), 688-690; and "Fact, Field and Destiny," *Review of Metaphysics*, XI (June 1958), 525-549.

5. For recent philosophical discussion of this problem, see *Journal of Philosophy*, LIX (July 19, 1962) 393-409, for Anthony Quinton, "The Soul"; LXI (September 3, 1964), 461-475, for Bernard Berofsky, "Determinism and the Concept of a Person"; and LXII (March 4, 1965), 111-128, for Virgil C. Aldrich, "Reflections on Ayer's *Concept of a Person.*" See also *Review of Metaphysics,* XVII (September 1963), 49-66, for Paul Feyerabend, "Materialism and the Mind-Body Problem"; and pp. 33-48 for P. T. Raju, "The Nature of the Individual"; XVII (December 1963), 171-186, for Grace A. De Laguna, "The Person"; XVII (March 1964), 340-360, for Robert R. Ehman, "A Defense of the Private Self."

6. *SBF*, p. 53.

7. *Ibid.,* pp. 53-54n.

8. *Ibid.,* p. 59.

9. *Ibid.,* pp. 62-65.

10. *Ibid.,* p. 67.

11. *Ibid.,* pp. 67-68.

12. *Ibid.,* p. 81.

13. *Ibid.,* p. 83.

14. *Ibid.,* p. 85.

15. *Ibid.,* pp. 90-91.

16. *Ibid.*, p. 101.

17. *Ibid.*, p. 105.

18. *Ibid.*, p. 110.

19. *Ibid.*, p. 112.

20. *Ibid.*, pp. 112-113.

21. *Ibid.*, p. 120.

22. *Ibid.*, p. 123.

23. *Ibid.*, pp. 134-135.

24. *Philosophical Review*, **XXXVII** (March 1928), 145.

25. *Ibid.*, p. 146.

26. *SBF*, p. 159.

27. *Ibid.*, pp. 161-162.

28. *Ibid.*, p. 164.

29. *Ibid.*, p. 166. This is not, however, the first time he had speculated along these lines. In *MGHE* he remarked almost casually (p. 143): "I have often wondered whether in these supermundane matters the universe may not be so nicely adjusted (and withal so justly) that each man finds true the things he believes in and wills for; why should not everyman find his religion true, in so far as he has indeed set his heart upon it and made sacrifices for it?" In *MIHE*, published almost fifty years after *MGHE*, he picked up the thread of this speculation and applied it to the idea of immortality. He insists (p. 244): "Without broaching theological issues, [our philosophical analysis] notes the possibility of a self-executing justice in the world-process, whereby what we refer to as the Will of God appears to each soul as the necessary outcome of its own willing: no soul shall perish but by its own consent."

30. *MIHE*, pp. xiv-xv.

31. **XXXVIII** (December 4, 1941), 689-690.

32. *Ibid.*, p. 688. He was as good as his word, although it was seventeen years before he published "Fact, Field and Destiny: Inductive

Elements of Metaphysics," *Review of Metaphysics*, XI (June 1958), 525-549. The most complete statement of his position is Chapter V, "The Philosophical Analysis," in the section entitled "The Relativity of Death" in *MIHE*, pp. 220-244.

33. "Theses Establishing an Idealistic Metaphysics," p. 688.

34. *Ibid.*, p. 689.

35. *Ibid.*, p. 690.

36. "Fact, Field and Destiny," p. 532.

37. *Ibid.*

38. *Ibid.*, p. 533. This argument harks back to the discussion of communication in *MGHE*, where he had argued that existence is always social or it is never social, since social relationship has to have some ground of communication to build on. This ground must be already given; it cannot be built, for in order to build it it would be necessary to have some common ground to begin building on. He says, "Yet I confess that I cannot find a genuine social experience at all, except as a continuous experience" (*MGHE*, p. 269).

39. "Realization" is a key term in Hocking's vocabulary. In his philosophy of mysticism it refers to the mystic's experience of "realizing" the divine presence in his own experience. Here, however, it has the more literal meaning, "to make real in existence."

40. *MIHE*, pp. 229-230.

41. *Ibid.*, p. 231.

42. *Ibid.*

43. Commenting on the originality of Hocking's basic metaphysical categories of "Fact, Field and Destiny," Andrew Reck notes:
The category of Field . . . invites comparison with analogous categories in other American systems. It has much in common with Peirce's thirdness—the enveloping universality, but since Hocking's conception of the category of Field culminates in the Self, Peirce in his more realistic moments might have dissented. The mentalistic features of the Field suggest similarities between this category and Santayana's Realm of Spirit, but with one great difference. Whereas

Santayana's Spirit is quiescent and passive, so that it can contemplate but it cannot do; Hocking's Field construed as the Self is the essence of creativity as well as of structure. Northrop's conception of the ultimate microscopic atom in *Science and First Principles* (1931) and Ushenko's conception of patterned vectors of power in *Power and Events* (1946) divide between them aspects unified in Hocking's conception of Field. In *Modes of Being* (1958) Paul Weiss's category of Existence approximates Hocking's category of Field, since Existence in Weiss's system, like Field in Hocking's system, denotes embracing structure plus creativity. But there the similarity ends. Weiss's "four-fold universe" contains three other categories besides Existence, and features Hocking assigns to Field are distributed among these other categories, particularly to those modes of being Weiss calls Actuality and God. As in the case of the category of Fact, so in the case of the category of Field, Hocking's metaphysics categorizes the world induced from experience in a singular fashion. The category of Field is akin to the Whole of Absolute Idealism, but it is a whole construed in terms of modern physics, in terms of space-time systems and electro-magnetic fields of energy. The category of Field has most in common with the Omega System De Witt Parker expounded in *Experience and Substance* (1941). Unlike the Whole of Absolute Idealism and its reinterpretation as the Omega System of Parker, Hocking's Field is bounded by two other categories. It is a Field which contains Fact; and it is a Field which points to Destiny. ("Hocking's Place in American Metaphysics," *PRCWC,* pp. 44-45.)

44. *MIHE*, p. 232. For his anatomy of imagination, see Chapter XIII.

45. *Ibid.*, p. 233.

46. Werner's paper was preceded by numerous lengthy conversations with Hocking—the two were summer neighbors in Madison, New Hampshire—and was extensively revised after Werner made a special trip to Madison to read it to Hocking. See *PRCWC,* pp. 95-120.

47. Frederick Werner, "Integrity," *PRCWC,* p. 102.

48. *Ibid.*, p. 105.

49. *MIHE*, p. 232.

50. "Integrity," p. 100. Werner's reservation about Hocking's meta-

physics is that Hocking's field is an exclusively classical space. Hocking's metaphysics remains "unfinished" in his view because he has not shown how concrete freedom actually joins idea with fact in the "will-act." An extremely bold and imaginative thinker himself, Werner suggests that "If aspects of [Hocking's] further thinking could be regarded as formally identical with some features of the objectively verified physical theory of Quantum Mechanics, they would have firmer roots in what Hocking calls the "obduracy of Fact," and thereby gain deeper significance" ("Integrity," p. 114). He goes on to suggest that the problem of the "closure" of a mathematical set, which he has closely identified with the self's deciding on or "realizing" one of the possible worlds which it contemplates, is at the heart of both the observer-observed problem in physics and the body-mind problem in a philosophical psychology. He notes, hopefully, that "If the observer-observed problem and the mind-body problem can be shown to be formally identical, a solution of one would provide for a solution of the other" ("Integrity," p. 116). I agree with Werner that Hocking has not shown how concrete freedom produces the will-act. His hope that philosophical problems can be solved through solution of the analogous problem in physical theory, however, seems to me to be too sanguine.

51. "Fact, Field and Destiny," p. 544.

VIII. The Human Individual

1. *HNR*, p. 18.

2. *Ibid.*, p. 38.

3. *Ibid.*, p. 41.

4. *Ibid.*, p. 64.

5. *Ibid.*, pp. 64-65.

6. *Ibid.*, p. 70.

7. *Ibid.*, pp. 71-72.

8. Quoted in my "The Making of a Philosopher," *PRCWC*, pp. 16-17.

9. *HNR*, pp. 72-73.

10. In a note on Jung's definition of the libido as "that energy

which manifests itself by vital processes, which is subjectively perceived as aspiration, longing and striving," Hocking welcomes the perception of unity in psychology which the doctrine represents. He takes obvious satisfaction in the fact that a unified psychological theory is not the prerogative of a monistic metaphysics, citing Buddhism as an example. But the Freudian doctrine of the libido still strikes him as misleading. He comments (*HNR*, p. 77): "Sex-love itself which to the Freudian mind seems the deepest thing in human nature is far better placed as an expression of this will; for what more profound assertion of power is our nature capable of than in that impulse which, assuming responsibility for the life and welfare of another, may also summon a new life into existence? The greatness of the sex-motive lies in the junction which it is able to effect between the human and the superhuman ranges of power. But to invert the relation and make all will a form of 'libido' is simply ex-centric; and can yield at best a ptolemaic system of psychology."

11. *HNR*, p. 147.

12. *CWC*, p. 7.

13. So Aristotle begins Book Alpha of his *Metaphysics* by reviewing the ideas of his predecessors.

14. *HNR*, p. 177.

15. *Ibid.*, p. 178.

16. *Ibid.*, p. 179.

17. *Ibid.*, p. 180.

18. For example, at a time when it was still popular for Christian writers to bemoan the rise of secularism, Hocking wrote (*CWC*, p. xii) that "the partial de-Christianization of the West brought about by the various secular movements is destined to work not only to the net advantage of the West, but also to that of a reconceived Christianity."

19. In *The Lasting Elements of Individualism* Hocking also notes a growing Oriental individualism which is central to the Asian revolution of this century; but, unlike those who argue that the East has borrowed its individualism from the West, he is convinced that Oriental individualism is an indigenous response to the post-colonial requirements of Asian nation building.

20. *LEI*, p. 17.

21. *Ibid.*, p. 27.

22. *Ibid.*, p. 18.

23. *Ibid.*, p. 22.

24. When *LEI* was published (1937), Hocking was still of the view that "The necessity for reliance on his reason as he leaves the shelter of fixed group-belonging and its authority lies upon all men so separated, and implies a native fund of reason qualitatively the same in all" (p. 35). It is clear from *Strength of Men and Nations* and *The Coming World Civilization*, written from the other side of the irrationalistic outburst of the Second World War, that he no longer believes that the "native fund of reason" is qualitatively the same in all men.

25. *LEI*, p. 30.

26. *HNR*, p. 185.

27. *Ibid.*

28. *Ibid.*, pp. 191-192.

29. *Ibid.*, p. 193.

30. *Ibid.*, p. 195.

31. *Ibid.*, p. 200.

32. *Ibid.*, p. 201.

33. *Ibid.*, pp. 207-208.

IX. Education

1. "What is Number?" *Intelligence: A Journal of Education,* XVIII (May 15, 1898), 360-362.

2. See note 13, Chapter I, above.

3. New Haven: Yale University Press, 1918. The "Bibliography of William Ernest Hocking from 1898 to 1964," compiled by Richard C. Gilman, lists *Morale and Its Enemies* as entry no. 51 with the follow-

ing note (*PRCWC*, p. 474): "Much of the background for this volume was gained during Hocking's experience at the British and French fronts in France during the summer of 1917. An introductory "Note of Acknowledgment" announces that "Some of the substance of this book has already been presented in the form of lectures to the Training Corps at Williams College in the winter of 1917, and as the Bronley Lectures at Yale in the spring of 1918. I also presented for preliminary criticism by the service a set of psychological theses in *The Infantry Journal* for April, 1918."

4. "The Religious Function of State Universities," *University of California Chronicle*, X (October 1908), 454-466.

5. "What is College for? The Place of Preparation," *Education*, XXXV (January 1915), 287-300; "The Culture Worth Getting in College," *School and Society*, III (January 15, 1916), 80-84. Other papers on education include: "What are Human Motives Today?" *Religious Education*, XVIII (February 1923), 24; "The Creative Use of the Curriculum," *Progressive Education*, III (July-August-September 1926), 201-206; "The Arteries of Education," *Simmons College Review*, IX (August 1927), 1-11; "The Place and Scope of Missionary Education," *Educational Yearbook, 1933: International Institute of Teacher's College, Columbia University*, ed. I. L. Kandel, (New York: Bureau of Publications, Teacher's College, Columbia University, 1933), pp. 5-31; "Can Values be Taught?" *The Obligation of Universities to the Social Order*, ed. Henry Pratt Fairchild, (New York: New York University Press, 1933), pp. 332-350; "What Has Philosophy to Say About Education?" *Harvard Alumni Bulletin*, XXXVII (November 2, 1934), 161-164; "The Beginning of Wisdom," *Bulletin of the Association of American Colleges*, XXI (May 1935), 296-300; "Philosophy and Religion in Undergraduate Education," *Bulletin of The Association of American Colleges*, XXIII (March 1937), 45-54; "How Can Our Schools Enrich the Spiritual Experience of Their Students?" *Beacon* (October 1943), 195-206; "Teaching in Dutch Universities," *Main Currents in Modern Thought*, VII (Autumn 1949), 95-96. This last entry is a shortened version of an article which appeared under the title "Dutch Higher Education—Comparative Impressions of a Visiting Harvard Professor" in the *Harvard Educational Review*, XX (Winter 1950), 28-35. It was also represented in part in *Higher Education*, XI (January 15, 1950), 113-114; "The New Way of Thinking," *Colby Alumnus*, XXXIX (July

15, 1950), 3-7, given as the commencement address at Colby College, June 12, 1950.

6. *Experiment in Education: What we can Learn from Teaching Germany* (Chicago: Henry Regnery, 1954).

7. The manuscript is mimeographed, in two parts, and is on deposit in Widener Library of Harvard University. Part I, 46 pages, is dated 1952; Part II, 83 pages, is dated 1954. Three paragraphs from Part I (pages 11a and 11b) were reprinted, under the title "The Eighth Grade," in *Why Teach?* ed. D. Louise Sharp (New York: Henry Holt, 1957), pp. 98-100.

8. For example, "What is Number?" See note 1, above.

9. For example, Chapter XXX, "Education," in *HNR*, pp. 226-253.

10. There is not a genuinely nasty word in all of Hocking's published work—something of an achievement for a philosopher. His typical reply to criticism is first to give credit where it is due and then modestly to urge the query which seems to him most problematical for the critic's case. See, for example, his "Response to Professor Krikorian's Discussion," *Journal of Philosophy*, LV, (March 27, 1958), 274-280.

11. *HNR*, p. 227.

12. *Ibid.*, p. 231.

13. See Hocking's "Can Values be Taught?" in *The Obligation of Universities to the Social Order*, ed. D. Fairchild (New York: New York University Press, 1933), pp. 332-350.

14. *HNR*, p. 234.

15. See *The Necessary and Sufficient Conditions of Human Happiness* (Stanford: Stanford University Press, 1907) and also Chapters XI and XXXII, and Appendix II, of *MGHE*.

16. *The Necessary and Sufficient Conditions of Human Happiness,* p. 236.

17. *Ibid.*

18. *Ibid.*, p. 239.

19. *Ibid.,* p. 240.

20. *Ibid.,* pp. 241n-242n.

21. *Ibid.* p. 241.

22. *HNR,* p. 244.

23. *HNR,* p. 245.

24. *Ibid.,* p. 248.

25. *Ibid.,* p. 250.

26. Socrates rejects Protagoras' view that virtue can be inculcated through imitation, and thus taught. For Socrates, virtue can only be remembered; but the Socratic midwife *can* help bring ideas to birth in others, through the probing of "dialectic." In this limited sense, virtue can be approached through the right kind of teaching. Hocking takes the same position, and in so doing strengthens his case against a thoroughgoing secularism. The dangers of indoctrination through the urgent presentation of values and beliefs are fewer than the secularist supposes. As any parent learns, it is not even possible to mold one's children's ideas permanently.

27. *HNR,* p. 252.

28. *Experiment in Education,* p. 12.

29. Published in English by the U.S. State Department (1943), under the title *National Socialism.*

30. *Experiment in Education,* pp. 32-33.

31. *Ibid.,* p. 34.

32. *Ibid.,* p. 36.

33. *Ibid.,* p. 37.

34. *Ibid.,* p. 49.

35. *Ibid.*

36. *Ibid.,* p. 288.

37. *Ibid.*

38. *Ibid.,* p. 156.

39. *Ibid.,* p. 161.

40. *Ibid.,* p. 163.

41. *Ibid.,* p. 162.

42. *Ibid.,* p. 163.

X. *Law and Human Rights*

1. During the brief employment at Andover Seminary which followed the completion of his dissertation, he had also served as an instructor at Harvard, offering a seminar in nineteenth-century British philosophy.

2. See, for example, his "Answer to a Threat" (letter to the editor of the *New York Times,* October 25, 1920, p. 14); "The Diplomacy of Suspicion and the League of Nations," *University of California Chronicle,* XXI (April 1919) 83-95.

3. See his "Is the Group Spirit Equivalent to God for All Practical Purposes?" *Journal of Religion,* I (September 1921), 482-496; "Les Principes de la Méthode en Philosophie Religieuse," *Revue de Metaphysique et de Morale,* XX (October-December 1922), 431-453, trans. Gabriel Marcel; "Illicit Naturalizing of Religion," *Journal of Religion,* III (November 1923), 561-589; "The Religion of the Future," *Religion and Modern Life* (New York: Charles Scribner's Sons, 1927), pp. 343-370.

4. *The Present Status of the Philosophy of Law and of Rights* (New Haven: Yale University Press, 1926).

5. "Ways of Thinking About Rights: A New Theory of the Relations Between Law and Morals," in *Law: A Century of Progress, 1835-1935,* vol. II: *Public Law and Jurisprudence* (New York: New York University Press, 1937), pp. 242-265.

6. See *Library of the Tenth International Congress of Philosophy,* ed. P. W. Beth and H. J. Pos (Amsterdam: North Holland Publishing Co., 1949), I, 556-559.

7. "How Ideas Reach Reality," *Philosophical Review,* XIX (May 1910), 302-318.

8. *Ibid.*, p. 310.

9. *Ibid.*, p. 310, n. 1. One might add that contemporary Westerners, puzzling through the enigmas of "the Asian mind," might well gain as much understanding from examining the unique features of contemporary Asian nationalism as from the more popular investigations in the field of sociology. For a study which touches on this possibility, see Carl Friedrich, "Pan-Humanism, Culturism and the Federal Union of Europe," in *PRCWC*, pp. 330-339, especially p. 332.

10. "How Ideas Reach Reality," p. 312.

11. *The Present Status of the Philosophy of Law and of Rights*, p. 39.

12. *CWC*, pp. 49-50.

13. The conservative Swiss farmer is a notable example. Standing on his "rights," he has thus far prevented the completing of an *autobahn* through Switzerland.

14. *The Present Status of the Philosophy of Law and of Rights*, p. 58.

15. *Ibid.*, p. 62.

16. *Ibid.*, p. 64. Hocking's views are somewhat to the right of today's "automatic liberals" but well to the left of Aristotle's social snobbery.

17. *Ibid.*, p. 65.

18. *Ibid.*, p. 67.

19. *Ibid.*, p. 71.

20. *Ibid.*

21. *Ibid.*, p. 74.

22. *Ibid.*, p. 75.

23. *Ibid.*, p. 76.

24. *MATS*, p. 39.

XI. The State and Democracy

1. The invention of new terminology, or the re-casting of familiar terms in a new context (for example, Tillich's use of "autonomy," "heteronomy," and "theonomy"), sometimes provides a useful and intelligible

shorthand; but this valid use of jargon is relatively rare. More common is that clever sloppiness which presents as entirely unique and original an idea which simply lacks refinement to its basic elements. Although metaphysically poles apart from the no-nonsense tradition of British empiricism from Hume to the present, Hocking shares its respect for the English language.

2. *MATS*, pp. 15-16.

3. *The Problem of Christianity*, II, 27; quoted in *MATS*, pp. 351-352.

4. *A Pluralistic Universe*, pp. 289-292; quoted in *MATS*, p. 353. Hocking notes: "James is here thinking not of the political but of the religious super-self. But the conception of the state as a super-mind has been aided throughout its history by religious conceptions."

5. *MATS*, p. 360.

6. *Ibid.*, p. 364.

7. *Ibid.*, p. 371.

8. *MGHE*, p. 521n.

9. *MATS*, p. 373.

10. *Ibid.*, pp. 377-378.

11. *Ibid.*, pp. 175-195.

12. *Ibid.*, p. 185.

13. *Ibid.*, p. 193.

14. *SMN*, p. 98.

15. *Ibid.*

16. *Ibid.*, p. 100.

17. *Ibid.*, p. 102.

18. *Ibid.*, p. 108.

19. *Ibid.*, p. 111.

20. *Ibid.*, p. 113. Hocking specifies these as "including the functions of well-informed thinking, of earning a living, and of sharing in the control of his own government."

21. *Ibid.*, p. 113.

22. See Chapter X for Hocking's reference to *"die tragende Idee,"* which he translates loosely as "the loadlifting idea."

23. *SMN*, pp. 117-118.

24. *Ibid.*, p. 284n.

25. I owe this story to D. T. Niles of Ceylon.

26. *MATS*, p. 289.

27. *Ibid.*, p. 293.

28. *Ibid.*, p. 294.

XII. Art and Destiny

1. *TP*, p. 213.

2. *MIHE*, p. 243.

3. See Chapter XV for Hocking's discussion of "the Christian ambition."

4. See *MGHE*, p. xiv.

5. Notably p. 399. "And it seems to me that [Christianity] is also right in saying that [God] must suffer; and not alone with us (as any god must who knows what is going on) but also for us, and *at our hands.*"

6. By contrast, see the indices of *Experiment in Education,* and *The Coming World Civilization.*

7. See especially, *TP*, pp. 299-306.

8. "The International Role of Art in Revolutionary Times," *Modern Age: A Conservative Review*, IV (Spring 1960), 129.

9. *Ibid.*, p. 130.

10. *HNR*, p. 317.

11. *Ibid.*

12. The NBC Television series "Wisdom" included a program devoted to Hocking and his thought, filmed at Hocking's farm in Madison. Hocking told the story during the interview and illustrated it with an on-the-spot drawing.

13. *HNR*, p. 318.

14. *SMN*, p. 121.

15. He feels that relativism has been particularly damaging to America's aesthetic self-confidence. He was much impressed with the response to Van Cliburn's Tschaikowsky Prize performance in Moscow some years ago (*SMN*, p. 28): "For the American public, and for our present argument, the striking thing in the Russian response to the Van Cliburn performance is its uninhibited spontaneity, with the complete and normal certitude of popular judgment. We had given him earlier a kindly hearing and some praise, and had let him pass on: it was the Moscow public that estimated his true proportion."

16. See Chapter VI.

17. See Chapter V, note 19.

18. *CWC*, p. 41.

19. "The International Role of Art," p. 132.

20. *CWC*, p. 42.

21. "The International Role of Art," p. 133.

22. Here is another bond between Hocking and Tillich, and between both of them and the Biblical tradition. Tillich says that every man has an "ultimate concern" and that whatever he calls it, it constitutes his "religion." Hocking says that every man operates with some idea of the whole, and that this idea is the most important element in his belief about the world in which he lives. The Biblical tradition knows nothing of atheism in the technically literal sense. Man will have his gods (and goddesses); the question is whether the god we worship is God indeed. There is, therefore, only one sin in the Biblical view of life, and that is idolatry. Whether one's catalog includes seven deadly sins, or seventy times seven, each individual sin is but a bow in the direction of some false god. Convinced that man is a religious animal, both Hocking and Tillich approach "secularization" in a more gingerly

fashion than Van Buren, Cox, Munby, Jarrett-Kerr, and their kin. Hocking and Tillich are dialecticians, they cannot help but see something of value in modern "atheism"—Camus is a good example. (Tillich even applied his dialectical "yes" and "no" to the "death of God" theology.) As a category of historical interpretation, both Hocking and Tillich find secularization clearing away considerable cultural dead wood; but both remain philosophers of *religion*, and the idea of a religionless Christianity does not, in the last analysis, make any more sense to Hocking than it does to Tillich.

23. *MGHE*, pp. 13-14.

24. *Ibid.*, pp. 462-484.

25. *Ibid.*

26. Andy Warhol, however, defends his Coke bottles and Brillo boxes as items of contemporary beauty which we must love and learn to live with. Here secularized art reveals a trace of metaphysics.

27. "Fact, Field and Destiny," p. 544.

28. *Ibid.*

29. *Ibid.*

30. *Ibid.*, pp. 544-545.

31. *Ibid.*, p. 545.

32. *Ibid.*, pp. 546-547.

33. *MGHE*, p. 470.

34. *Ibid.*, p. 471.

35. *Ibid.*, p. 472.

36. *Ibid.*, p. 473.

37. *Ibid.*, p. 475.

38. *Ibid.*, p. 477.

39. *Thoughts on Death and Life* (New York: Harper and Bros., 1937). The volume includes the Ingersoll Lecture on the immortality of man, entitled "Meanings of Death," which was given at Harvard

in 1936, and the Hiram W. Thomas Lecture, entiled "Meanings of Life," which was given at the University of Chicago in the same year.

40. *MIHE* is a revised and enlarged edition of *Thoughts on Death and Life*, cited above. The new material includes the preface and three additional chapters, one of which, "The Relativity of Death," was delivered as the Forester Lecture on Immortality at the University of California, Berkeley, in 1942. A 35-page summary of the book appears in *Tomorrow*, Vol. 6, No. 1 (Winter 1959).

41. See, for example, Reinhold Niebuhr, *The Nature and Destiny of Man* (New York: Charles Scribner's Sons, 1951), II, 294-298, 311-312; Emil Brunner, *The Christian Doctrine of the Church, Faith and the Consummation* (London: Lutterworth Press, 1962), pp. 408-414; Paul Tillich, *Systematic Theology*, (Digswell Place, Eng.: James Nisbet and Co., 1963), III, 433-452. Karl Barth's references are more extensive, but then Barth *is* more extensive. Remembering the centrality of the concern for "the life of the world to come" in earlier periods of Christian history, I hazard the generalization that there has never been less serious and sustained interest in this doctrine among Christian writers than at present.

42. For a recent statement of Corliss Lamont's views, see "Mistaken Attitudes Toward Death," *Journal of Philosophy*, LXII (January 21, 1965), 29-36. A fuller statement of his view is to be found in his *The Illusion of Immortality*, (New York: Philosophical Library, 1959).

43. The spatial idea which he rejects is the "single space" of classical physics.

44. *Journal of Philosophy*, XXXVIII (December 4, 1941), 688-690.

45. *MIHE*, p. 233.

46. *MIHE*, p. 247.

47. Charles Hartshorne doesn't believe that anyone really could want to be anything but finite. He sees permanence for selfhood in the idea that God remembers us eternally, after we are gone. Hartshorne confesses that this seems to him a perfectly just disposition of his own destiny. The characteristic feature of Hocking's treatment, however, is that he never appeals to his own claim to immortality, but the claim of those he loves, as seen through his love for them. Hartshorne's

view is that *God* has our eternal life, not that we have it, since there is no "we" after death. For a criticism of Hartshorne's view that old people are always more or less bored with life, since zest is overcome by repetition, see Corliss Lamont's article, cited above, note 42.

48. *MIHE*, pp. 250-251.

XIII. Religion, Mysticism, and the Prophetic Consciousness

1. Presumably the "death of God" theology is a radical revolt against "religion." But if God is gone, and with him both an intellectually defensible faith and an eschatologically concrete hope, what is left that justifies calling one's views a theology? "Christianity" remains as an emphasis on the importance of love; the only saving attitude toward oneself, one's neighbors, and the world. Having lost everything else— God, world-view, ethical system, Biblical authority, faith, and hope— the one thing the death-of-God theologian has left is his "religion."

2. Kraemer, *Religion and the Christian Faith* (Philadelphia: Westminster Press, 1956).

3. Smith, *The Meaning and End of Religion* (New York: Macmillan, 1962).

4. *Religion and the Christian Faith,* especially pp. 191-196.

5. *The Meaning and End of Religion,* p. 194.

6. See Horace L. Friess's review of Smith's book in *Journal for the Scientific Study of Religion,* IV (Spring 1965), 261-262. Friess admits (p. 262):

> It may well be true that "Christianity, Buddhism, and the like" are vague and uncertain whether as substantial entities or historical existences. Yet within these vague, general aggregations, particular churches and quite specific systems of religion have from time to time arisen, and have achieved at least the status of a definite historical existence. Is it likely that the future has in store an "end of religion" and of "the religions" in this sense? What organizations it does bring will depend, I would think, on an untold variety of factors affecting the social and cultural life of mankind, rather more than on the methods and semantics proposed by scholars for studying the same.

Ironically, Friess feels that Smith's attack on the idea that religion has an essence is itself "more academic (in the weak sense) than its theses warrant, and largely because the relevant phenomena of society and culture are only minimally or implicitly considered."

7. *LRWF*, pp. 67-142. Hocking would agree with R. H. L. Slater that he and Smith are not as far apart as their different vocabularies would make them seem. See Slater's "Religious Diversity and Religious Reconception," a comparison of Hocking's views and Smith's book, in *PRCWC*, pp. 250-262.

8. See Ramesa-Chandra Majumdar and others, *An Advanced History of India*, 2nd ed. (London: Macmillan, 1950), pp. 3-8.

9. *MGHE*, p. 31.

10. *Ibid.*, p. 14.

11. *Ibid.*, p. 238.

12. *LRWF*, p. 26.

13. *Ibid.*

14. *MGHE*, p. 349.

15. *Ibid.*

16. See p. 23 above.

17. See John Dillenberger and C. Welch, *Protestant Christianity* (New York: Charles Scribner's Sons, 1954), pp. 217-224, and especially p. 218: "In effect, the liberal doctrine of immanence involved the breaching of the traditional distinction between natural and supernatural."

18. Marcus Cunliffe, *The Literature of the United States* (London: Penguin Books, 1954), chap. 6.

19. C. T. K. Chari, "Human Personality in East-West Perspective," *PRCWC*, p. 381.

20. This criticism has also been directed against Hocking himself. See James Alfred Martin, *Empirical Philosophies of Religion* (New York: King's Crown Press of the Columbia University Press), pp. 14ff.

21. *MGHE*, p. 358.

22. *Ibid.,* p. 357.

23. *Ibid.,* p. 366.

24. The "artificial self" is not necessarily a "bad" self. It is natural to human nature to remake itself (see Chapter VIII). It is only when it is devoid of its natural source of creative remaking that the artificial self founders (see *MGHE,* p. 430).

25. *MGHE,* p. 448.

26. *Ibid.*

27. *Ibid.,* p. 460.

28. *Ibid.,* p. 509.

29. *Ibid.,* p. 521.

30. *Yale Divinity Quarterly,* V (March 1909), 1-23.

31. "How can Christianity Be the Final Religion?" p. 9.

32. *Ibid.,* p. 12.

33. *Ibid.,* p. 14.

34. *Ibid.,* p. 16.

35. Samuel H. Miller, "Revolution and Religion," unpublished address given at Princeton Theological Seminary, June 6, 1961.

36. "How Can Christianity Be the Final Religion?" p. 19.

37. *Ibid.,* p. 20. See also Reinhold Niebuhr, *The Nature and Destiny of Man* (New York: Charles Scribner's Sons, 1951). p. 16: "One can find some degree of Messianism in every culture in which history is taken seriously."

38. "How Can Christianity Be the Final Religion?" p. 20.

39. *Ibid.,* pp. 22-23.

XIV. The Christian Ambition

1. Horace Kallen, *Dialogue on George Santayana,* ed. Corliss Lamont (New York: Horizon Press, 1959), pp. 89-90.

2. In 1951 Perry Miller announced to his class in American literature at Harvard that his generation had found Widener Library's single copy of *Moby Dick* catalogued under "Information on Whaling and Fisheries."

3. *CWC,* pp. 98-99, 100n, 138.

4. Father Raymond Panikkar, *The Unknown Christ of Hinduism* (London: Darton, Longman and Todd, 1964).

5. See, for example, Panikkar's *The Unknown Christ of Hinduism* (cited above); the "Religious Quest of India Series" of the YMCA Publishing House, Calcutta; Bishop A. J. Appasamy's works, notably *Christianity as Bhakti Marga,* and the "Indian Christian Thought Series" of the Christian Institute for the Study of Religion and Society (Bangalore, South India), especially no. 2.: Mark Sunder Rao's *Ananyatva* (1964), and no. 5 by "Two Pilgrims of the Way," *The Mountain of the Lord: Pilgrimage to Gangotri* (1966). There are also numerous Hindu writings on Christian themes by Swami Vivekananda, Mahatma Gandhi, and others. See, for example, Swami Prabhavananda's *The Sermon on the Mount according to Vedanta* (London: George Allen and Unwin, 1964).

6. *HNR,* p. 376.

7. *Ibid.,* p. 377.

8. There were finally seven in all: the Presbyterian Church in the U.S.A.; the Reformed Church in America (Dutch Reformed); the United Presbyterian Church; the Methodist Episcopal Church; the Congregational Churches; the Protestant Episcopal Church; and the Northern Baptist Denomination.

9. "The Working of the Mandates," *Yale Review,* December 1929; and "Palestine: An Impasse?" *Atlantic Monthly,* July 1930.

10. James Thayer Addison, "The Changing Attitude Toward Non-Christian Religions," *International Review of Missions* (January 1938), 111.

11. Quoted *ibid.,* p. 113.

12. *Ibid.*

13. *Ibid.,* p. 116.

14. *RTM,* p. 15.

15. *Ibid.,* p. 19.

16. *Ibid.,* pp. 20-21.

17. *MGHE,* p. ix.

18. *RTM,* p. 21.

19. *Ibid.,* p. 22.

20. *Ibid.,* p. 31.

21. "A Venture in Understanding," quoted in *RTM,* p. 31.

22. *RTM,* p. 37.

23. From Ward Madison's stenographic record of Hocking's comments at a meeting of the Laymen's Commission with representatives of the several mission boards at the Hotel Roosevelt in New York in December of 1932. The meeting was called to discuss the Commission's report *Re-Thinking Missions.*

24. John A. T. Robinson (Bishop of Woolwich), *The New Reformation* (London: S.C.M. Press, 1965), p. 33.

25. See note 5, above.

26. *LRWF,* p. 67.

27. *Ibid.,* pp. 69-93.

28. *Ibid.,* pp. 88-89.

29. *Ibid.,* pp. 95-96.

30. *Ibid.,* p. 96.

31. *PRCWC,* p. 235n.

32. Arend van Leeuwen, *Christianity in World History* (New York: Charles Scribner's Sons, 1964). For "theocracy" see especially pp. 46-104; for "ontocracy" see especially pp. 148-196.

XV. The Coming World Civilization

1. *CWC,* pp. 21-42.

2. *Ibid.,* pp. 8-13.

3. *Ibid.,* p. 21.

4. *Ibid.,* p. 22.

5. *Ibid.,* p. 23.

6. *Ibid.,*.pp. 25-26.

7. *Ibid.,* p. 26.

8. *Ibid.,* p. 29.

9. *Ibid.,* p. 30.

10. *Ibid.,* p. 31.

11. *Ibid.,* p. 34.

12. *Ibid.,* p. 35.

13. *Ibid.,* p. 40.

14. *Ibid.,* p. 41.

15. *PRCWC,* p. 319.

16. Sartre, *Existentialism* (New York: Philosophical Library, 1947), p. 22.

17. *CWC,* p. 56.

18. *Ibid.,* p. 61.

19. *Ibid.,* p. 70.

20. *Ibid.,* p. 79.

21. *Ibid.,* p. 77.

22. *Ibid.,* p. 82.

23. Here Hocking gives one of the clearest statements of what he really means by "the mystic" (*CWC,* pp. 100-101):
For the "mystic" here is simply that "any man" in any religion who opens the door of his self-built enclosure, and sees the world, perhaps for the first time, in his own experience, as not his alone but God's world, and therewith every man's world, as held in God's care, the ego's personal entity included.

Such seeing is not a rare and privileged event: it is not unnatural; it is a passing from the unnatural to the natural and true. It is present in some degree in every wakening of the mind to love, and every opening of the eyes to beauty: no one is so poor as not to have felt *their* light and their liberation—even though it be true that most forget . . . *To hold to the meaning of this disclosure* of the Real is the work of faith. And with that faith, and the reborn love of life it brings, the will to create through suffering raises its head. The world view of Christianity and its code, as we have said, are inseparable.

24. *CWC,* pp. 102-103.

25. *Ibid.,* p. 113.

26. *Ibid.,* p. 142.

27. *Ibid.,* p. 145.

28. This is one of the pitfalls of Radhakrishnan's neo-Hinduism. See S. J. Samartha, *Introduction to Radhakrishnan: The Man and His Thought* (New York: Association Press, 1964), pp. 104ff.

29. In *Living Religions and a World Faith* (p. 191) Hocking comments: "The word 'essence' refers to this generating principle [of religious life], the simple germ from which the many expressions are derived and can therefore be understood. As every living thing has its germ-cell-group, so has every project, undertaking, institution, historical movement its essence." This idea of "essence" is clearly a long way from the abstract conceptualism of Feuerbach which Wilfred Cantwell Smith opposes. In order to make clear that the term is concerned with the dynamics of *living* religion, rather than with a static philosophical abstraction, Hocking defines "essence" with a *biological* analogy.

30. LRWF, pp. 194-195.

31. *CWC,* p. 147.

32. *Ibid.,* p. 146.

33. See especially Heinrich Zimmer, *Philosophies of India* (New York: Pantheon Books, 1951), pp. 181-279.

34. *CWC,* p. 149.

35. One report gives detail to what, in Hocking's thought, remains a

broad outline. In *The Mountain of the Lord: Pilgrimage to Gangotri* (Bangalore, South India: The Christian Institute for the Study of Religion and Society, 1966), p. 32, two Roman Catholic *sanyassis*, one a priest and the other a monk, describe their pilgrimage, in the company of Hindu *sanyassis*, to the headwaters of the sacred Ganges.

36. *CWC*, p. 161.

37. *Ibid.*, p. 162.

38. Bishop Lesslie Newbigin feels that Hocking leaves the issue of Christ's lordship over the religion of the coming world civilization as "a haunting question." See James Edward Lesslie Newbigin, *A Faith For This One World?* (London: S.C.M. Press, 1961), pp. 46ff.

39. *CWC*, pp. 168-169.

40. *Ibid.*, pp. 185-186.

Conclusion: Toward a World Perspective in Philosophy

1. See C. T. K. Chari, "Human Personality in East-West Perspective," *PRCWC*, pp. 381-397.

2. See Gabriel Marcel, "Solipsism Surmounted," *PRCWC*, pp. 23-31.

3. See Frederick Werner, "Integrity," *PRCWC*, pp. 95-120.

4. *CWC*, p. xiii.

5. See Andrew Reck, "Hocking's Place in American Metaphysics," *PRCWC*, p. 34.

6. *MGHE*, pp. xix-xx.

7. "What Does Philosophy Say?" *Philosophical Review*, XXXVII (March 1928), 141.

8. *Ibid.*, p. 133.

9. Of particular interest in this growing literature are Warren Wagar, *The City of Man* (Boston: Houghton Mifflin, 1963); and William S. Haas, *Destiny of the Mind, East and West* (London: Faber and Faber, 1956).

10. Huston Smith, "Accents of the World's Philosophies," Publications in the Humanities, No. 50, Department of the Humanities, Massachusetts Institute of Technology, 1961. Reprinted from *Philosophy East and West* (April-July, 1957).

11. *Ibid.,* p. 7. Smith's pleasant diffidence hides impressive credentials. Chairman of the Department of Philosophy at Massachusetts Institute of Technology, he was born and brought up in China, has been a frequent visitor to India, and is an acknowledged specialist in comparative philosophies and religions. See his *The Religions of Man* (New York: Harper and Bros., 1958); and *Condemned to Meaning* (New York: Harper and Row, 1965).

12. He spells out these implications in more detail in "Valid Materialism: A Western Offering to Hocking's Civilization in the Singular," *PRCWC,* pp. 354-368.

13. "Accents of the World's Philosophies," p. 9.

14. *Ibid.,* p. 9. See William Temple, *Nature, Man and God* (London: Macmillan, 1953), p. 478.

15. "Accents of the World's Philosophies," p. 10.

16. *Ibid.,* p. 11. Quoted from "Tao Tê Ching," in *The Way of Life According to Laotzu,* trans. Witter Bynner (New York: John Day, 1944), p. 43.

17. "Accents of the World's Philosophies," p. 11.

18. *Ibid.,* p. 12.

19. All of which gives rise to the famous remark: "The Chinese have no philosophy, they have manners."

20. Nirad Chaudhuri, *The Continent of Circe* (London: Chatto & Windus, 1965). Chaudhuri is a totally individualistic Indian intellectual who is thoroughly Hindu. His book is well informed, perverse, and passionate: the most stimulating essay extant on contemporary India.

21. "Accents of the World's Philosophies," p. 13.

22. *Ibid.,* p. 18.

23. *Ibid.,* p. 19.

INDEX

Absolute, the, 68-85; Royce on, 16, 17, 18; James on, 28-30, 200; Tillich on, 105, 107; in Indian philosophy, 106-107, 116; in Plato, 189; in contemporary ethics, 191; and American educational program in Germany, 183-184; and reflection, 229-230

Absurd, the, 216, 220; redemption of, 221. *See also* Camus, Albert

Addison, James Thayer, 265-267

Advaita Vedānta, 52, 106-107. *See also* Hinduism

America, *see* United States

American Philosophical Association, 139

Andover Seminary, 12

Andrews, C. F., 304

Anxiety, metaphysical, 216, 293-294. *See also* Solitude

Aristotle, 16, 56, 118, 161, 195, 209, 228

Atheism, 252. *See also* God, death of

Augustine, 237, 297

Baagø, Kaj, 275

Bacon, Francis, 297

Baldwin, James Mark, 291

Barth, Karl, 236, 257 258, 260, 274

Bergson, Henri, 45-46, 299

Berkeley, George, 45, 79, 120, 298

"Block universe," 101

Bodhisattva, 272. *See also* Buddhism

Body-mind problem, 129-138

Bohr, Niels, 143

Bonhoeffer, Dietrich, 235, 294

Brahmanism, 106-107, 114-115, 320. *See also* Hinduism

Brinton, Crane, 293

Brunner, Emil, 313

Bruno, Giordano, 231

Buber, Martin, 313

Buddhism, 272-273. *See also* Oriental religions

Bultmann, Rudolph, 63-64

Burma, 264

Calvinism, 227, 236. *See also* Puritanism

Camus, Albert, 216-217, 219-222, 226

Chardin, Teilhard de, 287

Chari, C. T. K., 243, 311

Chaudhuri, Nirad, 320

China, 264, 319-320. *See also* Oriental religions

Christ, *see* Jesus Christ

Christianity: church, 2, 27, 245, "empirical conscience" of, 54-55, 63-64; Westernness, 260-261; and modernity, 285, 296-310; and philosophy, 300; and natural piety, 302-303 Christian missions, 27, 215, 240, 262-286; new view of, 260-261, 321; and will to power, 262. *See also* Laymen's Commission

Colombo, Ceylon, 272

"Commotive process," 199, 211

Communication, 41, 42, 86-88, 90, 101, 202; Royce on, 21

Community: Royce on, 17, 18-19, 20, 91; scientific, 19-20; Christian, 26-27, 165; Hocking's experience of,

40-45, 86; metaphysical basis for, 90-100, 108, 117-118, 127; and art, 218-222; and religion, 248, 256-286; world, 287-310
Constitutions, political, 190
Contract theory (of the state), 203-204
Conversion, religious, Hocking's experience of, 1-4, 287
Courage, 105, 221-222
Cox, James, 188
Creativity: and Royce's theory of interpretation, 20; and inspiration, 44, 149-152; and reality, 67, 72, 75, 83, 89, 134-135; and art, 215-226; and destiny, 226-234; and salvation, 250-252
Culture, 169-170, 172, 192; and art, 217-221; and Russian revolution, 219; East-West, 268-270, 296; and religion in Assian modernization, 284-285
Cunliffe, Marcus, 243

Dedekind, Julius, 16
Dennis, James, 266
Descartes René: *Cogito ergo sum,* 32, 79, 94, 100, 112-114, 289, 297, *see also* Solitude; on "clear and distinct ideas," 53-54; dualism of *res extensa* and *res cogitans,* 117, 118-119, 121
Despair, 76-77
Destiny, metaphysics of, 3, 5-6, 146; Hocking's personal, 67; and adventure, 29; Hegel on, 38; and resentment, 62; and despair, 76-77; and love, 81-82; and divine attention, 84-85; and individualism, 127-128; and education, 180; and art, 215, 227-228; and immortality, 231-234. *See also* Fact; Field theory; Will-to-power
Determinism, economic, 209-211. *See also* Marxism
Dewey, John, 215, 247
Dillenberger, John, 55
Dostoevsky, Fyodor, 194
Dream, 217-218

Dualism, 131, 133. *See also* Descartes, René
Duff, Alexander, 266

Eating, philosophy of, 158
Eclecticism, 31, 101, 311
Empiricism: and mysticism, 23-24; and knowledge of other minds, 40, 42-45; and "literality" in religion, 50-58, 83, 88-102; as openness, 103-105; and the ontological argument, 108-123; and selfhood, 138-139, 141-142; and concrete freedom, 148-149, 232-233; in legal theory, 189-190; and creativity, 224-225; and prophetic power, 246-255; and Christianity, 299; and existentialism, 301; "widened," 309, 315-317
Equality, social, 166
Extra-sensory perception, 54
Evil, 73-77
Existentialism, 97, 105, 216-217, 219-222, 314; and solipsism, 220; and the reconception of Christianity, 301

Fact, metaphysics of, 88-93, 117-123, 128; and the absurd, 220; in art, 223; and destiny, 234, 250. *See also* Destiny; Field theory
Fear, 159; of hell, 3; "realism" as fear, 223. *See also* Anxiety
Feudal system, 164-165
Feuerbach, Ludwig, 237
Field theory, metaphysics of, 128; and selfhood, 139-149; Maxwell's theory, 147; self as "vinculum" in, 148-152, 232; in art and creativity, 225. *See also* Destiny; Fact
Forgiveness, 253-255
Freedom: individual, 139, 148, 166-167; concrete, 150-151, 232; political, 196-198, 207-211; and sin, 251; and salvation, 253. *See also* Creativity
Freud, Sigmund, 132-133, 136-137, 217-218

Gandhi, M. K., 304
Geometries, non-Euclidean, 145
Germany: Hocking's graduate study in, 7-8, 10; scholarship of, 68; re-education of after World War II, 171-172, 180-186, 190, 216, 220
"Global village," 284-286
God: as objective Other, 1, 3-4, 50-51, 55, 103-123, 127; and mysticism, 23; in "natural religion," 26; and community, 41; in medieval thought, 56-57; as subjective postulate, 62-64; and evil, 74-75, 148; as will, 76-77; as divine attention, 83-85; Kingdom of, 165; and artistic creativity, 224; for mystic and prophet, 235-255; in non-Christian religions, 267, 271-286, 305-310; death of, 251-252, 363n1, *see also* Atheism. *See also* Christianity; Oriental religions; Religion
Grotius, Hugo, 237
Group mind, 199-201

Habit, 134-135
Hammarskjold, Dag, 244
Happiness: in teachers, 174-175; and personal destiny, 227, 246
Hartshorne, Charles, 107-108, 120-121, 122, 123, 130, 131; on creativity, 224; on Hocking's philosophy, 312
Harvard College: Hocking's student days at, 7, 11, 12, 15, 22, 26, 27; Hocking's teaching career at, 143, 187, 264, 265
Hegel, G. W. F.: deductive system of, 34, 61; and idealism, 65; on *wirklich*, 78; on immediacy, 110; on non-contradiction, 140; on economic theory, 209; on cultural development, 279-280
Heidegger, Martin, 199
Hell, 3, 216
Heraclitus, 227
Hinduism, 52, 106-107, 116, 227, 239, 260; *avatar*, 298. *See also* Oriental religions
Hilter, Adolph, 182, 183, 184, 190,

192, 258; and "national Christianity," 261
Hobbes, Thomas, 119, 203, 209
Hocking, Agnes Boyle O'Reilly, 12, 44, 157, 171
Holt, E. B., 292
Holy Spirit, 2, 267, 309
Howison, George Holmes, 188
Hume, David, 32, 74, 75, 89, 225
Husserl, Edmund, 8, 10, 11, 51, 292
Hylomorphism, 318

Idealism, 3, 64-65, 66-67, 101, 107-108; subjective, 22, 39, 48, 64-78 *passim*, 111, 138, *see also* Solipsism; absolute, 30, 68-85, 193, 202-203
Idee, die tragende (the load-lifting idea), 184-185
Immortality, 231-234, 310
India, 261, 264, 277, 320
Individualism, Western, 165-167; and modernity, 288-295
Induction, 230-231
Infinite, 16-17, 19-21, 47
Inspiration, 228-231
Instinct, 136-137, 153-158
International Congress of Philosophy (Amsterdam, 1949), 188
Interpretation, Royce's doctrine of, 18-19
Intuitionism, 46. *See also* Bergson, Henri

Jackson, Mr. Justice, 183
Jainism, 307. *See also* Oriental religions
James, William, 7, 15-31 *passim*, 68, 243; on the Absolute, 77-78, 82, 200; James-Lange theory, 132; method of, 216
Japan, 264
Jesus Christ, 55, 216, 249-250, 254-255, 259, 274; the "unbound Christ," 260, 282, 302, 304; Raymond Panikkar's "unknown Christ" of Hinduism, 260; "the human face of God," 272, 273; as *logos*, 282; as historical event, 283

John Birch Society, 208
Journal of Philosophy, 144

Kallen, Horace, 256-257
Kant, Immanuel, 79, 182, 203, 222, 257, 291
Kennedy, John, 67
Kepler, Johannes, 297
Kierkegaard, Sören, 61, 72-73, 184
Kraemer, Hendrik, 235-236, 237-238, 257, 260, 273-278 *passim*, 280-282 *passim*

Ladd-Franklin, Mrs., 93-94
Lamont, Corliss, 231
Langer, Suzanne, 215
Law, 160, 187-198 *passim*
Laymen's Commission, 27, 240, 263-265, 312. *See also* Christianity
Leibniz, Gottfried Wilhelm von, 22, 120, 298
Liberalism, political, 164-170, 191-192
Lippert, Julius, 133
Locke, John, 32, 298
Löwith, Karl, 192
Love: and creativity, 44; and reality, 81-82; and hope, 96; and particularity, 97-98; in medieval philosophy, 118; and immortality, 232-233
Luther, Martin, 245

Machiavelli, Niccolò, 209
MacIver, Robert, 290
Madison, N. H., 37, 201, 264
Malebranche, Nicolas de, 298
Marcel, Gabriel, 35, 36, 96, 117, 199, 216, 311, 312
Marriage, 203
Martin, James A., Jr., 70
Martyn, Henry, 265-266
Marxism, 65, 211, 321. *See also* Determinism
Māyā, 52, 116, 298, 320
Meditation, 176-177
Melville, Herman, 257
Methodism, 1-5, 26, 52, 216, 242
Mill, J. S., 164
Miller, Dickinson, 26

Mind-body problem, 129-138
Mitty, Walter, 98, 138
Modernity, 117, 119-120, 216-217, 221-222, 314; and Christianity, 285. *See also* "Passage beyond modernity"; Secularism
Modernization, Asian, 284; role of religion, 284-285
Monadism, 21-22, 41. *See also* Solipsism
Montague, W. P., 292
Morgan, Augustus de, 17-18
Mott, John R., 263
Munich, University of, 182
Münsterberg, Hugo, 11, 187
Murthi, T. R. V., 38
Mysticism, 24-25, 51, 52, 62, 107, 116, 241-246; James on, 23-25; Asian "lay mystics," 277; "common mysticism" of everyman, 302, 362, 368-369n23. *See also* "Nuclear awareness"
Mythology, Greek, 165

"National premise," 205; of the U.S., 206-208; American versus Russian, 208-211
Nationalism, Asian, 270
Nazism, 181-182, 257-258
"Necessary interests," *see* Instinct
Nehru, Jawaharlal, 287
Neurosis, cultural, 98, 133
New Testament, 271
Nietzsche, Friedrich, 156-157, 159, 185, 251-252
Nirvana, 272
"Nuclear awareness," 225-226, 241-244; and piety toward nature, 302-303. *See also* World faith
Nürnberg Court, 183

Ockham, William of, 76
Olds, C. B., 271
Ontological argument, 108-114
Oriental religions, 238-239, 266, 273, 275; significant characteristics, 276-280. *See also* Buddhism; Christianity; Hinduism; Jainism

Panikkar, Raymond, 260, 275
"Passage beyond modernity," 287-296;
  role of Christianity in, 296-310
Peirce, Charles, 16, 107, 256
Perry, R. B., 292
Plato, 161, 165-166, 173, 189, 209, 291
Positivism, logical, 60, 89
Pragmatism: James's, 27-28; Hock-
  ing's "negative pragmatism," 28;
  "action theory" of, 53; and evil,
  75-77
Prestige (of the state), 204-205
Property, 209-211. *See also* Deter-
  minism; Marxism
Protagoras, 179
Protestant theology, 55-56, 238, 257-
  258, 267
Ptah Hotep, 224
Puritanism, 8-9

Quantum theory, 150-151

Radhakrishnan, S., 52, 116, 123, 259,
  304
Rao, Mark Sunder, 275
Realism: natural, 39, 66-67, 111; in
  art, 223; scientific, 58-60, 89, 122,
  316, 318
Reck, Andrew, 315, 348-349n43
"Re-conception" (of religion), 238,
  261, 271, 296; of Christianity
  though existentialism, 301; and the
  meeting of religions, 305-308
Reflection, 229-231
Reformation, Protestant, 165
Relation: De Morgan on, 17-18;
  Royce on, 18-19. *See also* Community
Relativity, theory of, 147-148
Religion: Hocking's personal, 1-6;
  and "nuclear awareness," 11;
  James's *Varieties of Religious Experience*, 23-28; and commitment,
  50; primitive, 51; and myth, 54-
  55; and subjectivity, 62-64; and
  ultimate assurance, 84-85; and education, 173-174; and modernity,
  221-222, 290; of mystic and proph-

et, 235-255. *See also* Buddhism;
  Christianity; God; Hinduism; Jain-
  ism; Oriental religions
Renaissance science, 118-119
Repression, 132-133; and art, 217-218
Resentment, 62; against economic
  exploitation, 210-211; against God,
  251, *see also* Nietzsche
Richardson, Cyril, 109
Rights, 166-167, 174, 187-198 *passim*;
  for black Americans, 197-198
Robinson, J. A. T., 274
Rockefeller, John D., Jr., 263, 264
Rousseau, Jean Jacques, 163
Royce, Josiah, 15-31 *passim*, 32, 42,
  75, 83, 91, 109
Russell, Bertrand, 94

Sankara, 106. *See also Advaita Ved-
  ānta*
Santayana, George, 69, 187, 256, 302
Sartre, Jean-Paul, 76, 85, 293-294, 313
Schiller, Friedrich, 222
Schleiermacher, Friedrich, 51, 245
Schopenhauer, Arthur, 71, 135-136
Secularism, 69, 236; in education,
  174; and mystery, 245; and salva-
  tion, 251-252; and Christian mis-
  sions, 269, 308; and natural science,
  294-295. *See also* Modernity
Serampore, India, 266
Serf, 166
Sexuality, 153, 154, 178-179, 261
Shady Hill School, 171
Sin, 250-253; and forgiveness, 253-255
Smith, Huston, 317-321
Smith, Wilfred Cantwell, 235, 236-237
Socrates, 179, 291
Solipsism, 22, 32, 86, 91, 93-94, 138,
  316; in art, 219; in existentialism,
  220, 293; and the dilemmas of
  modernity, 292-303
Solitude, 176-177, 221-222, 289, 291,
  310; of the "lost soul," 84-85; and
  sin, 250-252
Soul, 165-166, 250
Soviet Union, 66, 208-211, 219
Space, 144-148

Spencer, Herbert, 4-6, 68
Spinoza, Benedict, 35, 298
Stoicism, 79, 82-83, 253
Subconscious, the, 136-137
Suffering: creative, in Husserl, 8, 10-11; and will to create, 185; of Jesus Christ, 216; as *angst*, 216-217
Suicide, 105
Syncretism, religious, 275, 304. *See also* Synthesis; System
Synthesis, 34, 37-40, 70, 101, 304
System, 33-36, 101; Hegel on, 34; Marcel on, 35; Kierkegaard on, 61; and anti-system, 216; in comparative religious philosophy, 283-284

Tagore, Rabindranath, 176
Technology, 57, 96, 119, 258, 297-298
Temple, William, 318
Tillich, Paul, 105, 123, 302, 360-361n22
Toynbee, Arnold, 25, 192, 259, 304

United States: Hocking and the American character, 8-10; U.S. education program in Germany after World War II, 172-173, 180-186; civil rights movement, 197-198; "Americanism," 204; "national premise" of, 206-209; current aesthetic values, 219
"Unlosable, the," 192, 309
Upanisads, 116

Van Leeuwen, Arend, 280-284
"Vestibule of satisfaction," 161-162
Victorianism, 76, 77, 133
Vietnam, 261

Werner, Frederick, 149-151, 311, 349-350n50
Whitehead, A. N.; on the realism of "here we are," 88, 89-90, 97, 98, 220; on "the bifurcation of nature," 122; on "prehensions," 130, 293; *Science and the Modern World*, 297
Whole-idea, 47-50, 52, 61-62, 78, 80-81, 92, 189. *See also* Absolute
Will-to-power: in Christian missions, 27, 286; against despair, 62; in the individual, 134-137, 156-160; Freudian view of, 136-137; Nietzsche on, 156-157, 159; in education, 175, 177; in German nationalism, 181-182; and natural right, 196; in the state, 201-202; in art, 218; toward a destiny, 226-228, 233; as ambition, 245; as prophetic power, 246-248; and religion, 261-262; and suffering, 310
Woods, James, 264-265, 312, 313
World faith, 247-248. *See also* "Nuclear awareness"
Worship, 24, 26-27, 244-245

Yale University, 12, 187